MW00985524

No
New
Things

Ashlee Piper

No New Things

A Radically Simple 30-Day
Guide to Saving Money,
the Planet, and Your Sanity

CELADON BOOKS
NEW YORK

NO NEW THINGS. Copyright © 2025 by Ashlee Piper.
All rights reserved. Printed in the United States of America.
For information, address Celadon Books, a division of Macmillan
Publishers, 120 Broadway, New York, NY 10271.

www.celadonbooks.com

The Library of Congress Cataloging-in-Publication Data is available
upon request.

ISBN 978-1-250-38216-0 (paper over board)

ISBN 978-1-250-38217-7 (ebook)

Our books may be purchased in bulk for promotional, educational,
or business use. Please contact your local bookseller or the Macmillan
Corporate and Premium Sales Department at 1-800-221-7945, extension
5442, or by email at MacmillanSpecialMarkets@macmillan.com.

First Edition: 2025

10 9 8 7 6 5 4 3 2 1

For Banjo

Contents

Introduction

It wasn't that long ago that I was leading a completely different life. I was a political strategist with a roster of high-profile clients, making a salary that still makes me misty, and living in a bustling city. Life should've felt epic, and I get that this might make me sound like a complete brat, but it didn't. You see, the nature of the business had me working 24-7—I was on call for every emergency or snafu. And when I slept, I did so with my phone tucked under my pillow, ringer on, waiting for the late-night call that some presentation or campaign needed fixing RIGHT FREAKING NOW. I'm not saying these are necessarily bad things, and even though I was feeling stressed and kind of lost, I had so much to be thankful for. Many life situations require us to be at the ready, and those can be really exciting and satisfying, but for me, this pace and preoccupation had run their course. I was burned out, and as a means of coping, I'd numb out and self-soothe by browsing for and buying stuff I didn't need or even really want.

I see you nodding, scanning your brain for the last time you went on a soul-soothing spin around the store or a retailer's website. Perhaps this hits a little close to home? The thing about consumerism is that it feels like a remedy, a quick way to get exactly what we think we need. But had I paused and reflected, I would've realized that what I was really craving was more peace, substance, and intentionality in my life and relationships. But I was so stuck in the work-to-buy swirl that I just didn't know how to get there. Heck, I couldn't even put my wants into words.

I let overconsumption, be it a spree at TJ Maxx or constant food delivery orders from the restaurant literally 0.3 miles from me, be my balm, and soon, I found myself in a never-ending cycle of working constantly just to pay off the debt I was amassing from buying things that I thought would fix my life. I also fell prey to the all-too-common "I just don't have the time" trope. Me, an almost thirtysomething, gainfully employed, child-free human—arguably one of the least burdened groups in society—not having any time? It's laughable, but it was true only because I was either working or shopping my way into the ground. Instead of recognizing and addressing the root of my discontents, I was throwing stuff, lots and lots of stuff, at the problem. Now, I wasn't necessarily in the danger zone of creditors beating down my door, but the situation I'd wedged myself into wasn't comfortable for me. I regularly felt panicked about money, I felt unhealthy, I felt unsteady. And what's more is it never occurred to me to, ya know, stop buying stuff as a means of getting relief. No, no, that's too simple to actually work. Besides, who can go without buying new stuff? I'd never heard of something so outlandish! Instead, I thought I just needed to buy *cheaper* stuff. Sure, that'll work.

Can we have a moment of silence for how freaking wild this is? I was so conditioned by consumerist culture that I actually believed that the solution to my highly uncomfortable, absolutely unsustainable situation was to just buy *less expensive* stuff. And it wasn't like I was eating Tide PODS or pounding Four Lokos every weekend. I had a master's degree from Oxford. My prominent politician clients entrusted my counsel to help them get elected. I was just hooked on a drug I didn't even recognize as a drug, because it's such an ingrained part of our culture. In the Western world especially, consumerism is an addictive practice. And you and I and basically everyone else are unwitting addicts. Now, this may smack as dramatic, but don't worry; I'm not going to start talking about red pills or how birds aren't real (they're real). I'm just saying that when we reach for something over and over again to soothe or celebrate nearly every human condition, and we don't even realize we're doing it, even though we know it's not good for us, or it's making us downright miserable, well, that's the very definition of addiction.

If you'd looked at my apartment, you would've thought I had everything someone could ever want to be happy. But behind the clothes were more clothes, tags still on, sized too small, bought for an aspirational life I wasn't living, because, let's be real, I was barely living. I was working and shopping. Shopping and working. My shelves were lined with functionless tchotchkes that collected dust and books I claimed I never had time to read. Balances were lingering on my credit cards, and my checking account perpetually teetered on overdraft. My living room was littered with decorative throw pillows (how the hell can one relax on a pillow that has freaking sequins?) and workout equipment I'd bought hoping it would change my life, only to eventually realize the truth: *things don't change our lives.* My stuff was stressing me out, my quest for more of it was consuming me and draining my finances, and most sobering of all, this situation was my doing. It was time to get my shit together.

If any of this sounds familiar, I want you to first shake off any shame. This book is designed to take you through the same journey that not only helped me but fundamentally changed me to heal these impulses. So, after we face the uncomfortable bits, I can assure you that there's a ton of freedom and good feels on the other side, okay? Okay. I also want you to take comfort in knowing that you are not alone: 54 percent of Americans report feeling stressed by their stuff, 60 percent say they don't have enough time in the day, and 80 percent are in some form of consumer debt.[1] And yet, despite these realities, we use the term *retail therapy* like it's a genuinely therapeutic process. It's almost comical—and criminal—how consumerism has become such an ingrained part of who we are and how we define our worth.

Thankfully, during this time, I became personally interested in sustainable living and eventually left my corporate gig to make it my life's purpose. And I found that purpose to be an incredible antidote to my mindless, autopilot consumption. This new direction reinvigorated me and sparked a clear-eyed assessment of my life, where it had run aground, and where I wanted it to ultimately go. As I built my career in sustainability, I found that so many of the habits that were great for the planet were also great for my peace and my finances. I simplified my stuff and settled into a lifestyle where nearly 98 percent of my possessions were procured secondhand, with way more discernment and intention. I sold the mountains of stress-bought shit I didn't need, which helped me pay down debt, declutter my physical space, and ease my mind. And through this process, something in me had sneakily shifted—my relationship to shopping.

It used to be that the only times I'd see my friends were to browse stores or to go out to the clubs on the weekend. Shopping was my recreation, and even when most of it moved into the digital, e-commerce arena, browsing on my phone before bed for that next life-changing, influencer-endorsed item became my ambrosia. Today, it's almost the opposite. I still appreciate stuff—I like beautiful things, things with nostalgia and utility, things that help me work more efficiently. But I don't worship at the altar of stuff like I used to. And most importantly, I don't expect the latest thing to heal me or alleviate my stress. Things are just tools, and good tools are useful, but *they* should never use *you*.

In 2013, after gradually moving toward this new reality and feeling the very tangible benefits of a life less smothered by overconsumption, I thought, *Hey, wouldn't it be FUN to see if I could buy nothing new for an entire month?* And, thus, No New Things was born. Now, to most people, this would not be fun. Like, not even in the neighborhood of fun. A trip to an amusement park is fun. A date with Keanu Reeves (I can only imagine, but yes, I do imagine) would be fun. But a month of nothing new? Was this even feasible? Would it be gross and sad? Had I entered cry-for-help territory?

Let's start with the main question I fielded before and during that time (and basically every day since): WHY? If I had to boil it down to a single word, it would be *relief*. But for me, for me, the impetus for No New Things was as multifaceted as the benefits. The Challenge was a straightforward way to ease some of the burden on the planet, cut clutter, save money, and reclaim some precious time by turning off the shopping tap. And, yes, it *is* what it sounds like: I aimed to go a month without buying any new things, with some caveats that I'll get into in a bit. Usually when folks hear this, they're immediately worried I was walking around wearing used underpants and smearing on crusty, secondhand makeup. Let me personally assure you that those things did not and will not happen. Instead, I was sporting clothes I loved, relaxing in a home that felt peaceful, and enjoying a bank balance that no longer scared the hell out of me, all while feeling contentment in my present and excitement for my future.

I gave myself a check-in point at a few weeks in. If I was really struggling, I could make adjustments or jump the proverbial ship. But something happened after I got my sea legs that first week. Strangely, unexpectedly, perhaps maniacally—I actually loved it. Sure, No New Things stretched me. And yes, it meant I had to get better at planning ahead and more creative with how I sourced things. But the benefits were even beyond my hyperbolic and overactive imagination. Most notably, I saw immediate cost savings. Like, who knew when you don't blow your wad on a bunch of crap you don't need that you'll probably save money? I also found myself paying off consumer debt (which is way easier when you're not accruing much at the same time) and having more time to devote to relationships, my goals, and, hell, just plain leisure. Like real, staring-at-a-bird-in-a-tree or reading-a-good-book leisure. Life felt less stressful. And this wasn't just a feeling—life concretely IS less stressful when you've hopped off the hamster wheel covered with stuff, running toward the acquisition of more stuff. Bonus? I became more creative and was able to be resourceful more quickly. Like, if you had asked me at the beginning what I could use instead of buying a new nightstand, I would've taken a solid hour to come up with a formidable response. Now? Oooh, I've already got six ideas for how to upcycle things to be the best damn nightstand you've ever had.

Oh, and I made unexpected friends. It sounds ridiculously homey and almost made-up, but the neighbor who lent me her rolling pin and later taught me how to make biscuits from scratch? Yeah, that's Jean, and she's my friend now. The folks who run the consignment shop down the street? We're almost to the nicknaming stage of our relationship. At a time when loneliness is so pervasive and detrimental that it's been branded by the surgeon general as an epidemic that hastens death as much as smoking fifteen cigarettes a day,[2] forming these types of new connections filled my cup. My existing relationships also expanded and thrived, including, and most importantly, the one with myself. I began to see how much of my self-worth was wrapped up in the acquisition of new things. And the more I freed myself even a little bit from that cycle, the more clearly I saw and appreciated me for who I was—the real me, without all the stuff.

So, I carried on. For nearly two years. Yep, 683 days of shopping my own closet, gifting experiences and thoughtful secondhand finds, outfitting my life with creative upcycles, and thoroughly enjoying an inbox free from constant promotions and receipts. In that time, I saved around $36,000, both from not buying items and from selling stuff I had that I didn't need. I paid off all my credit card debt—and I don't say this from a moral high ground. In a capitalistic society that requires you to have a credit card to build, well, credit, debt is morally neutral in my book—but that doesn't make it any less stressful or detrimental. Having the time to prepare nourishing food and move my body regularly meant that I got healthier than ever before. I invested the time I got back from shopping less into nurturing my relationships and tackling goals I'd long been putting off. On the heels of doing No New Things, I landed my first book deal, got an unexpected promotion at work, and began volunteering—something I said I "just didn't have time" to do before. I felt focused, clear, and unburdened, able to live the life I'd dreamed of without the distractions of consumerism and stuff.

Since that time, I've done No New Things *Lite*—little one- or few-month Challenges every year to keep my habits sharp and get back in touch with that lovely stasis that the Challenge provides. For years, I did No New Things blissfully solo for my own enrichment, not really thinking anyone would care. Until one day, I shared that I was embarking on a new Challenge Lite with my relatively modest Instagram following—and suddenly, everybody (well, almost) wanted in. I felt like Luke Wilson in *Old School* when he goes to the office and he's hounded by dudes wanting to join his all-ages fraternity. My messages were flooded with "Ashlee, I NEED this" or "Hey, this No New Things thing? I want *in*." And then when folks followed along with me during that month, so many asked that the Challenge become a book so they could have more comprehensive guidance whenever they needed. So here I am, giving the people what they want.

In July 2022, I had over twelve thousand people sign up to do No New Things for the month, and only two of those people were related to me. In February 2024, organizational wizard Shira Gill had her nearly one hundred thousand-person community follow along as she chronicled her No New Things journey for the third time. A month might seem short in comparison to my nearly two years, but it's more than enough time to reap the benefits and develop the mindset that makes this Challenge so transformative. Once she made her societal debut, my No New Things debutante proved to be much more impactful than I could've ever expected. We'll get into more specific participant experiences as the book progresses, but holy shit, so many of them are victorious and moving.

People paying off crushing debt and saving their relationships. Folks prioritizing their mental health. Individuals finally getting after the life goals they thought had flown the coop. Even one week in, participants were noting remarkable changes in their mental, emotional, physical, and financial health. They'd share revelations with me like "Ashlee, I shop when I'm sad, especially at night" or "I think I buy stuff online because I'm procrastinating on cleaning out all the keepsakes I shoved in the basement after my husband died." Yeah, this Challenge goes deep. For many of us, these are connections that we rarely have the clarity to make or the time to understand.

Perhaps the best part of No New Things is that it packs this huge payoff while still being so damn simple. Now, mind you, I said No New Things is simple, not necessarily easy. Remember when I mentioned that in the thick of being controlled by over-consumption, I thought the solution was not to buy less stuff, just less expensive stuff—and we all shared a hearty chuckle? Well, you can think of No New Things as an Occam's razor—the age-old theory that the best solution is often the simplest—to overconsumption. Instead of convoluting the issue, we're simply turning off the buying-new-stuff tap while cultivating better-for-you habits along the way.

And despite my reverence for the infomercials of my '80s upbringing, the Challenge is a zero-gimmicks zone. I know, I'm breaking a lot of hearts here, but no, I will not be trying to sell you No New Things–branded merch. Having too many logoed water bottles and tote bags is probably part of why you're here in the first place. The Challenge doesn't require any special supplies or lofty social connections to participate. It just asks that you show up as you are, with an open mind, and move through the daily action items that will revolutionize your life, finances, and feelings in just four little weeks. Sounds pretty great, right? I know I'm biased, but it sounds that way because it is.

Let's address the metaphorical elephant in the room, though. I totally recognize that this book, especially in its physical form, is very much "a new thing." But once you dig into the Challenge, you'll find that we're not anti–new things forever over here, especially if that item has major utility. Dare I say this is a "buy once and then share with everyone you know" purchase that's far from single-use and will actually make your life better? Of course, you may also opt for an audio or ebook version, or borrowing from a friend or your local library, for a less-thingsy approach to getting in on No New Things.

And if you thought this book was just going to help you buy less shit, well, I'm sorry, friend-o, but you're going to get way more than you bargained for. This isn't some flimsy one-and-done tome with little daily to-dos you'll forget after you've turned the page. No, no, that's not how I wanted to do this. Because overconsumption is epidemic to the point of being ingrained in our psyches from birth, I wanted to give you the historical background as to how we even got here. Like, have you ever wondered how we went from our Depression-era grandparents who'd wash and reuse tinfoil and cherish and mend the same shirt for decades, to a population that spends $1.2 trillion each year on nonessentials[3] and owns double the amount of stuff than folks did fifty years ago?[4] The answer is not that our ancestors had more willpower than we do. It's that America radically and fundamentally changed post–World War II, when purchasing became a patriotic mandate, and marketing blossomed into a *Little Shop of Horrors* entity that still permeates every aspect of our lives today.

We've been molded over the decades to conflate our worth with the contents of our homes, instead of the content of our characters, and that message is reinforced via the thousands of advertisements we're assailed with on a daily basis. So yes, while it requires some personal will to hit the Purchase button, it's so important to remember as you go through the Challenge that your doing so, more than you or your bank account would like, is not entirely a monster of your own making. And as both someone who's learned so much from this Challenge and who's spent decades as a researcher, marketer, and professor, I wanted to pull back the curtain and reveal the negative and profound impacts this overconsumption, marketing, and production trine has on our lives. Because we will never change our habits if we don't first unmask and understand their origins.

With that historical foundation, you're then ready to get into the Challenge. We'll cover the multitudinous reasons for giving No New Things a go and how it works, followed by the actual Challenge's prep, execution, and cooldown. Like a good workout, you are given emotional and logistical exercises to set you up for success (consider me your personal hype woman). Then the 30-Day Challenge features daily action items with guidance, situation navigation (a.k.a. "It's my sister's wedding! What do I do about an outfit?"), and examples from real humans who've done No New Things. The Challenge also features four weekly themes and reflections so you can quantify and celebrate your wins, understand challenging moments, and get amped for a great week ahead. There's also a section on extending or winding down from the Challenge, so the No New Things habits and mindset stick. The thirty-day calendar is customizable, like a *Choose Your Own Adventure* book, so you can rearrange action items without missing out on important life events and good times. Because that's what we're doing this for anyway—a life less burdened by stuff, open for way more good times. And as anyone who's been to a karaoke dive with me knows, I like me some good times.

At a time when saving money, saving the planet, and saving our sanity are overcomplicated by SO MUCH INFORMATION AND INFLUENCING EVERYWHERE OMG, No New Things feeds three birds with one scone. And that's my most sincere hope with this book—to reach more people, give them the tools, guidance, and support to shift their mindsets and habits, and in turn, live better lives while also being better to others and the planet. It's the biggest win-win-win since that time they put a Baskin-Robbins and a Claire's right next to my junior high school.

Part 1

Get to Know No New Things

How the Challenge Can Revolutionize Your Feelings, Habits, and Finances in Just 30 Days

Why Do No New Things?

When I first concepted the Challenge, transparently, it kind of scared the crap out of me. Short of going through Navy SEALs training or something else that I'm completely ill-equipped to do, this felt like the mother of all self-imposed experiments. And that's coming from someone who once gave up coffee for a whole six months (sorry for being the worst person ever, by the way). And maybe that's how it feels to you right now—scary. I knew I'd need to dig deep to trade my short-term wants for that long-term satisfaction that annoyingly only seems to come from aligning with our values. And the anticipation of that can feel, well, frightening. But once I took stock of my reasons for embarking on this journey and realized what I stood to gain, I felt calm and excited. I went from expecting that No New Things would deplete and defeat me to being pumped for the experience to positively transform me for the better, forever. So let's explore that a bit. If you're wondering if the Challenge is for you or what it can do for you, ask yourself these questions:

1. *Is my stuff stressing me out?*
2. *Would I like to get a better hold on my spending?*
3. *Have I experienced climate anxiety?*
4. *Do I feel like I never have enough time?*
5. *Do I seek a life with more contentment, creativity, and clarity?*

6. *Am I conflating my worth and purpose with stuff?*

7. *Am I interested in understanding why I make impulse purchases?*

If you answered yes to any of these, No New Things is very much for you. A lot of people think they need to be in major financial straits or tussling with a clinical shopping addiction to embark on the thirty days, but that just ain't true. Because we're all products of consumerist conditioning, No New Things works its magic on almost anyone, no matter how together or not you may think you are.

Reason 1: Your stuff is stressing you out. We're so consumed by consumerism (put it on a shirt) that we often fail to see that for every item we bring into our lives, we become its inventory manager. That's right: from the moment of purchase, you are responsible for the upkeep, repair, and end life of your things—and that, my friend, is more of a full-time job than we often realize. And if the popularity of organizing television shows hasn't hit it home for you: we are also a society buckling under the weight of our shit. And I don't just mean that figuratively or poetically. Americans live in homes nearly triple the size of those of the 1950s,[1] featuring expansive attics, garages, basements, and walk-in closets. And yet, we have so much stuff that the US boasts more self-storage facilities than Starbucks, McDonald's, and Subway restaurants combined.[2] It's been estimated that there are enough garments on the planet right this freaking second to dress the next six generations,[3] and yet we buy sixty-four new clothing items and seven and a half pairs of new shoes each year.[4] That expression "The things we own, own us" isn't wrong—we've just been conditioned to not clearly see how freaking owned we are.

Perhaps most importantly, 54 percent of us genuinely believe our stuff is a root cause of our stress, and 70 percent of us want to buy less.[5] In one study, women who saw their homes as cluttered had much higher levels of the stress hormone cortisol throughout the day.[6] Go ahead—look around your space. Do you feel awash with calm and contentment, or are you annoyed by the mental load that accompanies the piles of items you need to return, put away, clean, or get rid of? For most of us, it's the latter, yet 78 percent of us feel so overwhelmed that we don't even know where to start.[7] It's scientifically proven that we're less stressed when we have and buy fewer items, because we're not saddled with the aforementioned economic and mental demands of ownership, the cleaning, storing, fixing, and off-loading that accompany possessions. And because money tops the list as a primary stressor for 72 percent of us, it probably seems like a big duh that spending less of it, especially impulsively on crud we don't really need, can help alleviate some of that concern.[8]

No New Things slows the influx of new stuff, redirects your focus to your existing possessions, and helps you build the mindset and habits necessary to be more judicious when considering acquiring future things. Perhaps most important, this Challenge anchors you to, once and for all, prioritize your peace over your possessions. And I promise that alone is reason enough to start right now.

Reason 2: You want to better steward your money. Whether your goal is to spend less, aggressively save, or generate more income, No New Things offers support on all fronts. Especially now, when inflation is a-ragin' and the price of groceries has folks weeping in the aisles, money's tight and on most everyone's mind. But has that stress stopped us from impulse-buying useless things? Nah. Here are the sobering facts: 80 percent of us are in some form of consumer debt,[9] and yet we keep buying, with the average adult spending $18,000 per year on nonessentials alone.[10] And that societally conditioned quest for stuff that drives us deeper into debt also comes at the expense of our security and future prosperity; 56 percent of Americans don't have enough savings to cover a $1,000 emergency,[11] and 25 percent have absolutely no retirement savings, including, frighteningly, nearly half of all baby boomers.[12] Yet 28 percent of us prioritize purchasing the latest tech gadget over fulfilling basic financial obligations like paying rent or bills.[13] Now, I know I went hard with the stats there, but what's extra wild is that we don't even enduringly enjoy the stuff we sacrifice so much to buy. Sixty-four percent of us ultimately regret our short-term purchases like clothes, cars, and electronics, but that feeling of regret is not potent enough to keep us from continuing to buy unnecessary crap at the expense of our long-term goals.[14] If you're like most people, you read this with half of you thinking, *That's madness*, and your other half nodding along—because, no matter how logical and bright you are, you're probably mirroring this behavior in some way. This is not because we're not aware or not smart but because we've been practically coerced to spend, spend, spend, regardless of how healthy or wise a decision that may be for us.

If you're in any of the above statistical groups, rest assured, you're not stuck there forever, and No New Things might be the nudge that helps you get unstuck. Sure, there are circumstances that can make getting to a more confident financial situation difficult, and you may currently be there. But I promise that learning to curb overconsumption, to delineate between items you actually need versus what sophisticated marketing influences you to want, will set you up for a stabler financial future, no matter how much debt you have or savings or earning potential you feel you don't. And while No New Things is not intended to be a replacement for financial advisors and debt counseling, I think most professionals in those fields will agree that buying less crap is a fantastic complement to getting you to your goals that much faster. And, hey, if your finances are rock solid and none of the above resonates, No New Things is still for you. Because overconsumption is in the very fabric of how we operate: no one, even the financially flush, is immune. Understanding and managing shopping impulses creates ripples in other areas of your life. Participants who were otherwise financially fit noted newfound levels of discipline and satisfaction across all areas of their lives. So yeah, the Challenge is for anyone, no matter how much your mind is on your money or your money's on your mind.

Reason 3: Overconsumption is killing the planet, and you want to help. Maybe you're someone who doesn't think about (or even believe in, which is okay, but stick with me here) climate change. Or perhaps you're among the 62 percent of people who experience climate anxiety on the regular.[15] No matter what camp you're in, I'd urge you to be open to the causal link between our consumerist behaviors and the degradation of our planet. And if you have children or grandchildren, or you're a human being who wishes to leave a livable legacy for the many generations of people, plants, and animals to come, it's time to start giving a damn.

Production and consumption of goods, also known as *supply and demand*, is a symbiotic system that relies largely on us to drive—you guessed it—demand. And while there are some industries and companies that intentionally overproduce even when there isn't much demand, this exchange is a strong driver of climate change. Since 1945, industrial productivity has soared by 96 percent in almost every area—goods, agriculture, services, and fuel—to keep pace with our consumerism.[16] And this rise in production has spiked harmful global emissions. For instance, the atmospheric concentration of CO_2 alone, just one of the many gases that hastens climate change, has increased by a whopping 43 percent since World War II.[17] And this tracks because as our purchasing habits have shifted from moderation to overconsumption, industry has kept pace, producing an abundance of items, thus requiring significantly more resources and generating more waste than ever. In fact, at our current consumption levels, we will need nearly two Earths to provide the necessary resources and absorb all that waste.[18] Our consumerist demands are so powerful that it's even estimated that by 2050, the ocean will contain more plastic than fish.[19] If you're reading that and going, "No way," I want you to look around your home and in your trash cans right now and play I Spy with plastic. Yeah, I'm serious. I'll wait. You see the soft shopping and food bags, the bottles of soda and tubs of yogurt, the mailers, the Bubble Wrap, the cling film, the Styrofoam, the tape, the containers, the pens, the kitchen tools, the clothing made from synthetic fibers, the phone cases, your shower curtain liner, the cheaply made must-have crap you were influenced to buy on Temu? Phew, lemme take a breath. I don't want this to devolve into a diatribe on plastic (believe me, I could, and yeah, that makes me super fun at parties). But for a relatively young material that's only been on the consumer scene for about seventy years,[20] we've certainly created the demand that's led industry to supply us with gobs of it. And by gobs, I mean nine billion tons since 1950, none of which ever fully biodegrades.

I know. It's heavy. Climate change is not a tiny issue, so it's natural to think that refraining from buying new things seems too inconsequential to make a dent, right? I get it, because I used to think that, too. But remember Occam's razor, baby—simplicity is often the best way forward. Not buying new stuff in favor of using what you already have or that already exists 1) relieves the resources used and pollution caused from production of new items; 2) extends the utility of existing things, diverting them from the landfill; and, perhaps most importantly, 3) lends valuable intel to retailers about the kind of future you want by voting with your dollar. And sure, if you were the only person in the world doing or ever to do the Challenge, I could see how that could feel a little meh. But you're not. Thousands of people have done No New Things before this book was even a thought. Now think of how many people are doing it today, right now, alongside you. Imagine the impact that many individuals not buying new things for thirty days can have at scale. Forgive me if I sound delulu, but I'd wager it's enough to at least upset and potentially even begin to dismantle a late-stage capitalistic system that's crushing the planet and our futures.

And if you still think you're just one little person, well, to that I say, "Hell yeah," because individuals are extremely powerful. We've literally course corrected huge ecological disasters like the ozone layer and acid rain because individuals began to care and inspired collective activism, which then influenced governments to create policies and regulations. If you think your personal choices and habits don't matter, tell that to the board members at large companies who throw billions of dollars at determining whether you're going to buy almond milk instead of oat, or a hybrid vehicle over one that's electric. Heck, we didn't even have many of those options a decade ago, but consumer sentiment and purchasing drove the market to meet our desires. This is the very essence of power, and we can wield it in a way that hurts or helps the planet. And surprise, surprise! This Challenge will guide you toward habits that not only benefit your life but also empower you to more naturally make the kinds of decisions that take care of this precious, spinning orb we call home.

Reason 4: You want to reclaim your time. Perhaps one of the most unexpected reasons for giving No New Things a shot is the most personally important: the time wasted on consuming and overconsuming. You've likely heard that time is our most precious nonrenewable resource. You've probably also heard that the average American wastes nearly two and a half hours a day on social media and another three hours zoning out in front of the tube (both of which are monetized to the max to sell us products, by the way).[21] But did you know that we spend nearly one and a half hours each day shopping,[22] and fifty-five minutes a day just looking for things?[23] That's right; we have so much stuff that we are sifting through other stuff to find specific stuff to the tune of nearly fourteen days a year wasted. And when we get into gendered data, it's estimated that the average woman spends about four hundred hours per year shopping.[24] That's nearly eight and a half YEARS in a lifetime.

It may seem melodramatic to ascribe such detriment to something as supposedly harmless as shopping, but it's worth asking yourself what you would do with a few extra hours every day, or better yet, extra years in your life. Would you spend more time with your kids? What about that novel you wanted to write or that race you were going to train for? Maybe you'd go back to school or start a new career that excites you? Heck, you could finally travel to Costa Rica and volunteer at that sloth sanctuary you've been stalking on Instagram. Or maybe you'd just get more sleep. I highly doubt many of us would use that extra time to shop. If you've ever lost a loved one, you know the cruelty of the currency of time and how you'd do literally anything to get more of it, and yet many of us fritter away valuable years acquiring stuff. If you're among the 80 percent of Americans who feel that there are never enough hours in the day,[25] it's worth removing the rose-colored "Shopping is fun!" glasses to see how consumerism has siphoned time away from the pursuits and moments that actually make your life worth living.

Reason 5: You want more contentment, creativity, and clarity. Do you feel like most days, you're operating on hard mode? Like you're just going through the motions, not really feeling inspired or fulfilled? Perhaps you feel so overwhelmed by the everyday hustles that you simply long for more clarity? Or maybe you struggle to access your creativity or contentment. No New Things creates the conditions that can bring about the epiphanies needed to redirect your life—namely, the limits necessary for cultivating creativity, the perspective to see how much abundance you have, the silenced promotions that cut the compare-and-despair trap that threatens true fulfillment, and the time back that allows you to explore your purpose. You need constraints to tap into creativity and freedom. You need perspective to recognize your abundance and cultivate contentment. You need relief from constant marketing and social media to gain clarity and ease.

We often misconstrue the unlimited choices of capitalism with freedom, but too much choice leads to decision fatigue and apathy. Individuals make upward of thirty-five thousand decisions a day.[26] Yes, you're an individual, so that means you devote brainpower to making thousands of decisions every day. If that sounds staggering, that's because it is—what to eat, when to make a phone call, which route to take, what color shirt to wear, and on and on—decisions dictate our lives. And those seemingly little choices add up and max us out, resulting in palpable overwhelm. This "paradox of choice" is not great for us. It requires our brains to work harder, causing stress and indecision, and is even shown to make it more difficult to exercise self-control.[27] Anecdotally, we know this to be true. We've all had hellish days where the kids are screaming, your boss is being a total dick, your hair is not cooperating, and basically, nothing seems to be going right. Suddenly, there's a Twix double pack right by the gas station register or an ad for that skin care system you saw on Instagram pops up on your phone, and you think, *Oh, screw it*, and buy the dang things.

When we're overwhelmed by choices, we aren't thinking clearly. So it should come as little surprise that shopping less, especially online where we're bombarded by constant suggestions and endless options, can markedly reduce the clouded thinking that accompanies daily decision burden. Through the Challenge, you will significantly reduce your exposure to consumerist influences that exhaust your spirit and overcomplicate your life. And in return, you'll create the space and restrictions necessary to enjoy more clarity, creativity, and contentment.

Reason 6: You want to stop conflating your worth with stuff. While it's virtually impossible to not place any value on things, our consumer culture requires that we use material items as benchmarks of our identity, sense of belonging, and social status. Under this arrangement, we never have enough stuff, or the right stuff, and thus are stuck in a toxic compare-and-consume trap that creates significant distress and undermines our sense of self. Whether we want to admit it or not, modern marketing has turned us into creatures who shop our insecurities and fears. For instance, folks who feel uncertain about their socioeconomic position tend to buy items they feel will elevate their status (at least in the eyes of others),[28] with more than half of luxury items being purchased by people in low- or middle-income brackets.[29] If we're self-conscious about our skin or weight, we're more likely to buy hoards of products geared toward "fixing" those issues. Instead of addressing our fears or feelings through legitimate therapy, 96 percent of us engage in "retail therapy" as a way of momentarily silencing our emotions.[30] And yet this supposed cure is also the cause. Stuff-related mental illnesses like compulsive shopping and hoarding, a *DSM*-recognized clinical disorder, have increased exponentially in just the past few years.[31]

We're so consumed by consumerism that we see it as the antidote to everything. Depending on how we're feeling and what we need, buying stuff can be conflated with security, entertainment, and enrichment. Nearly half of us list shopping as one of our hobbies (remember the SHOPPING IS MY CARDIO shirts?).[32] Read that again. An activity that causes so much emotional distress, financial tension, and environmental ruin is a fucking hobby? And some of y'all have the nerve to knock folks who play Dungeons & Dragons for fun. We also lionize consumerism as a modicum of our intrinsic worth and personal development. From L'Oréal's iconic 1971 tagline "Because you're worth it" to Gillette's "The best a man can get," we're fooled into thinking that our value or social status can be bolstered by something as artless as selecting the right shaving cream.

How often have we heard someone justify a big-ticket or luxury splurge by saying, "I'm investing in myself"? No, man, learning a skill, mastering a craft, honing the qualities that make you a person of good character—those qualify as advancing yourself. Things can be fun and exciting, but don't get it twisted; stuff is never an investment toward you becoming more of who you're meant to be. These warped rationales cause us serious distress, with 71 percent of buyers reporting they actually feel worse shortly after buying things.[33] Under a system that benefits from us never feeling like we have or are enough, using stuff as a goal-post of our worth and growth is a fool's errand. Shopping gives the illusion of being a solution to our insecurities and fears, but it never works, because what we're really seeking isn't sold in a store.

Reason 7: You want to regain control over your impulses. Or at least better understand them and, moreover, understand how we became a society of rampant consumers in the first place. When I hear from Challenge participants, they'll sometimes defeatedly say, "Ugh, I have no willpower." Nope, you're just a perfect product of conditioned consumerism. And that is by design. Since the boom of postwar industrialization and the attendant rise of modern-day advertising, we've become creatures habituated to what I call *conditioned consumerism* (and when I'm feeling extra spicy, *coerced consumerism*). Shopping replaced baseball as the great American pastime, and having bigger, better, more luxurious and futuristic things supplanted the "make do and mend" ethos that got us through the Great Depression and global conflict. The result is a manufacturing system that stopped repairing items and a populous of consumers hungry for newness in the form of convenient, off-the-rack, cheaply overproduced, on-demand crap.

And marketing has kept pace, with many companies today aiming to hit you with dozens of impressions (on social media, on TV, on the internet, on billboards, on your phone, in the middle of your favorite podcast or show) to get you to buy even more stuff. They know you, they know your feelings, and they weaponize that intel to make you feel less than so you'll buy more.

Because the lower you feel, the higher you'll buy. Brands aim to know you so well that they can then use your feelings, fears, and even seemingly innocuous data points like weather conditions to drive you to buy—and to keep buying.[34] Doesn't that piss you off? Like, yes, the investment in getting to know you is a little flattering, but using all that personal data to manipulate and make you feel crummy? That sucks. And it happens all day, every day, so deftly, so artfully, so strategically, you don't even know it. All you know is that you really, really want to buy that supplement you just saw on TikTok. Wouldn't you like to be so wise to this game that you can stop the bad feelings and spendy impulses before they start? Think of how freeing it would be to see an advertisement for the twentieth time and it have zero bearing on your sense of self-worth or actions. You can absolutely get there, and No New Things can help.

Getting all this time, energy, and control back was and continues to be the most attractive part of No New Things for me and for the tens of thousands of people around the world who've participated in the Challenge. I promise I'm not trying to be an anti-capitalist Chicken Little, but if you were out here believing that shopping is a harmless little activity that bears no consequence in your life, I urge you to reread this chapter. Imagine your life with more of what you want and less of what you don't. Maybe that's more time, more peace, more stability. Perhaps it's fewer promos crowding your email inbox, reduced clutter, and eased money woes. Maybe these scenarios don't feel attainable or you just don't know where to begin, but you'd certainly like to try? Well, the great news is that you're here, and if you're yearning to exert control over coerced consumerism and reap many or all of these ancillary benefits, you are in the right place.

What Is No New Things?

Now that you've identified your reasons for giving No New Things a whirl, let's get into the mechanics of the Challenge. You might be wondering how far we're taking this "nothing new" directive, worried that you'll be dumpster diving for your next meal or holiday gifts. Listen, I'm bold, but I'm not bananas, so when I created the Challenge, I gave myself a few caveats to make it both plausible *and* enjoyable. For instance, I could buy groceries and certain personal items (ahem, toothbrushes) new that probably are best procured, well, new. I could pay bills, get repairs done on my car, my dwelling, my pets, and myself. And because I wanted this to be a habit-shifting experience, rather than one of deprivation, I was absolutely permitted to engage in enjoyable activities and personal upkeep, like getting my hair and nails done, hitting up a fun workout class, going out to eat, or splashing out on a vacation. No New Things also preserves your ability to be generous and supportive of your network and causes that you care about. So I could donate or give money, use gift card balances, and even buy new-with-tags items secondhand.

In summation, you may spend money on or acquire in the following categories for yourself and every member of your household. Note that the parentheticals are just suggestions, but they're not exhaustive (I'm not telling you to start getting

Botox or buy probiotics if you don't already do or use those things). You'll likely have plenty of other areas and activities that fit these categories that are not explicitly mentioned. So just use common sense and discretion as to what feels like a fit under this rubric:

Bills & Investments	• Bills and financial imperatives (credit cards, loans, utilities, rent, mortgage, car payments, tuition, insurance [health, life, car, pet, home], legal fees, court-mandated payments, transportation passes) • Investments (401(k)s, IRAs, stocks, retirement, financial planning, tax preparation, accounting software, apps, and services) • Repayment programs (bankruptcy payments, debt counseling, financial advising)
Entertainment & Experiences	• Excursions (amusement parks, roller-skating, karaoke) • Experiences (shows, concerts, theater, ballet, opera, museums) • Restaurants (eating out, booze) • Transportation (rideshares, rentals, public transit, trains, bus, airfare) • Vacations (airfare, hotels, travel costs)
Essential Items	• Groceries • Items best procured new for hygiene reasons (toothbrushes, undies)
Generosity	• Experience gifts • Monetary gifts (including gift cards and vouchers for others) • Monetary or in-kind donations to organizations

Health & Personal Development	• Fitness and wellness (gym memberships, workout classes, sports leagues, dance and other lessons, physical therapy, massages, acupuncture)
	• Health care (medical, dental, mental health, health spending accounts)
	• Medications, supplements, and devices
	• Personal and professional development (coaching, mentoring, lessons, classes, personal and professional development, certifications, licenses, memberships)
	• Veterinary care and pet insurance
Repairs & Upkeep	• Home repairs (parts, appliances, services, supplies)
	• Personal upkeep (hair, nails, tanning, facials, massages, acupuncture, lashes, cosmetic enhancements)
	• Possession upkeep (dry cleaning, tailor, cobbler, housekeeping, rug and furniture cleaning, appraising, restoration, painting)
	• Vehicle upkeep (parts, services, car wash and detailing, oil changes)

These exceptions aside, the Challenge gently nudges you to identify ways other than buying new to get items you may want or need. For me, this meant that I'd bid Bezos and his ever-convenient Amazon.com adieu, that I'd have to do a bit more planning and get better connected to the sharing economy and free resources in my world (there are daily action items that will shepherd you through doing these, FYI), that I wouldn't sashay out of a store with my bevy of new goodies, but most of all, it meant that I would have to part ways with that hit of cheap dopamine that comes from browsing my phone late at night and hitting the pulsating Buy Now button. All of that may sound freaking difficult, but don't worry; this book will take you through every moment with guidance and strategies that have faithfully shepherded thousands of folks through the Challenge.

For everything else you may want or need during No New Things, you'll use what I call the SUPER System, because it's super and you're super, and acronyms help everyone remember stuff more easily:

S	Shopping secondhand (thrifting, consignment, online resale)
U	Using, upcycling, or reimagining stuff you already have
P	Paying nothing (using store credit or memberships you already have, items you get for free via free groups, finding them, like in the alley or on a stoop, or from your networks)
E	Experience, donation, and monetary, non-thing gifts (used mostly for gifts for others)
R	Renting, borrowing, or sharing

The SUPER System is a series of consumerist-alternative actions rooted in the principles of circularity. While capitalism operates within a wasteful produce-purchase-pitch model, circularity offers ethical alternatives for meeting our needs. Capitalism focuses on the egoic needs of the individual, while circularity nurtures the collective. Consumerism depletes resources, while circularity repairs and regenerates. In other words, a circular approach is the antidote to overconsumption, as well as the collateral damage that accompanies it.

The SUPER System also urges you to get a little creative; to scan your brain for ideas on how you can make do with what you've got or who in your network might be a borrowing buddy. We're so conditioned to just fire up the internet anytime we need something, and I would argue that this on-demand conditioning has not only made us wasteful but has laid waste to our creativity. Using this system creates the parameters necessary for your brain to get resourceful, and it can be incredible for stoking your ingenuity.

As psychology would have it, the above guidelines also cause *friction*, or intentional difficulty in the purchasing process (more on the science and importance of that a little later), which allows us to take a pause to determine whether we just want something for a hot second or we actually really need it. This is important because the normalization of consumerism and proliferation of marketing have warped how we determine wants versus needs. How many times have you heard a product called "essential" or a "must-have"? Yeah, when you hear that for decades about a freaking bikini or hair pomade, your brain starts to think, *Hey, this is a need*, when it's not. Folks who've done the Challenge often describe using this system as "a breath" or "a pause" that allows you to unpack that conditioning and determine what's essential for you. And it's in that pause that we can cut through the marketing noise, gain immense clarity, and reclaim our buried resourcefulness.

Because mindset is a huge part of this transformative journey, I tracked my feelings and impulses in a journal. And without giving away too much, lemme just say WHOA and WOW with a hearty side of cringe. What a juicy-ass journal that became. I had no idea how internalized my consumer habits were or how much my shopping impulses were governed by simple things like time of day, temperature, my mood, and even baby-feels like if I'd skipped lunch or was wearing pants that cut into my tummy. These were base-level impulses and triggers that I had playing in the background all the time, like a wacky computer program, and yet, I had never paused long enough to understand them for what they were and learn how to manage them.

And that's really what No New Things is—it's a pause, *not* a prohibition. We're not anti-things or even anti–new things over here. This isn't No New Experiences or No New Friends (you can have and enjoy both during the Challenge—in fact, I insist!). We're just taking a sec, a nice long exhale before we jump back into the simulation that maxes out our minds, our finances, and the planet, hopefully armed with the cheat codes that can help us beat the level and find some peace in a system that thrives on our discontent.

Part 2

How Did We Get Here?

How History, Marketing, and
Psychology Converged to
Make Us the Perfect Consumers

From Citizens to Consumers

Every time I wonder how we became these conditioned creatures in a consumerist cyclone (say that three times fast), I hear David Byrne's exaggerated voice in the song "Once in a Lifetime," saying, "Hooo-ooow did I get here?" To properly answer the question, we must hop in the way-back machine and bear witness to the social phenomena that morphed us from community-centric, moderate consumers to individually minded, practically certified shopaholics.

The year is 1945. The place? Well, let's go with the United States. World War II has been won; the Allied forces have defeated the Nazis and were promising to bring troops home by February 1946. It was a time of triumph where the general vibe was relief and freedom on the most braggadocious of levels. You're probably wondering what the heck this historical walk down memory lane has to do with consumerism and your embarkation on the No New Things ship? Stick with me—it'll all make sense in a sec.

To understand why this time period is so important, we have to go back even further, to 1942, shortly after the attack on Pearl Harbor, when America formally entered World War II and then president Franklin D. Roosevelt ordered the establishment of the War Production Board. This board allocated scarce resources like rubber, sugar, gasoline, and soap, and oversaw the conversion of factories that were making toys, automobiles, and small appliances to start making military equipment like tanks, rifles, ammunition, airplanes, and ships. At the peak of its war effort, in late 1943 and early 1944, the United States was manufacturing almost as many munitions as all of its allies and enemies combined, marking one of the largest industrial booms in history.

While millions of people, mostly men, were deployed overseas to fight, an estimated eighteen million Americans, many being women and people of color, worked to support this incredible industrialized boom. With everything from food and textiles and metals going to the fight, resources for the home front were scarce. I remember my 109-year-old nonna, who was an Italian translator for the US military at the time (one of the two hundred thousand women who were in the service), telling me about how she'd use eyeliner to draw lines up the back of her legs to resemble the seams of silk stockings because silk was so scarce.[1] Americans were urged—nay, practically bullied—to invest any spare income into war bonds (to the tune of $185 billion by the end of the war) and were encouraged to ration food, create self-sustaining gardens (hence the term *victory gardens*, of which an estimated twenty million were planted), repair everything they could instead of buying new ("Make do and mend" was a popular tagline), and generally live with moderation and restraint.[2] It was a difficult time, but also a strengthening one, as Americans banded together against a common enemy and with a deep collectivist purpose.

Quality to Crap: The Rise of Planned Obsolescence

While we're on the subject of manufacturing, have you ever wondered why so many modern-day products feel shoddy, while older items seem to withstand the test of time? Or maybe you've noticed that we've gone from having four fashion seasons to fifty-two micro-seasons, with new collections being released every week?[3] And why can't you seem to find repair options for, like, anything you buy these days? Well, darling, we have planned obsolescence to thank. And if you're wondering to whom you should send a nastygram for this ultimately terrible development, look no further than the guy some have called "the greatest businessman in history," Alfred P. Sloan. A few decades prior to World War II, Sloan was racking his brain, trying to figure out how to make Americans buy more cars. Why cars? you might ask. Well, Sloan was the then CEO of General Motors, so that tracks. You see, though the Roaring Twenties was painted as a time of decadence, most people still looked at the stuff they bought as lifetime investments, and thus the folks who were going to buy a car had, well, already bought one. As you can imagine, this consumer standstill wasn't so great for GM's bottom line. And Sloan, who's most famously quoted as saying that GM existed "not . . . to make motor cars" but "to make money," knew he had to find a way to drive Americans to buy more stuff.[4] Enter his strategy of *dynamic obsolescence*, or the deliberate shortening of the lifespan or attractiveness of a product to force consumers to purchase functional replacements. To stoke desire, GM began doing something that up until that point was unheard of—releasing new automobile models every year. Each new version featured slight stylistic or functional tweaks, entreating folks to upgrade because, under Sloan's obsolescence, owning the latest model was a sign of status.

Competitor Henry Ford absolutely hated this concept. Like, for real, he's on historical record talking shit on obsolescence in favor of durability and ethics. The guy just couldn't stomach building something with the intention of it rapidly becoming outdated. So he continued to offer Ford's only model, the Model T, in a single color at an affordable price. Sounds pretty shrewd and commendable, right? No, at least not in the eyes of consumers who took Sloan's bait and started buying GM cars like crazy, not because their existing ones were toast but because trading older for newer was now fashionable.[5] Word of GM's successful stunt began to get around, and other areas of manufacturing soon quietly, but enthusiastically, got on board.

Why did I just describe this spitting contest between two captains of industry? Because this strategy of creating goods with intentionally short lifespans didn't just change how things are made, it transformed how we buy. Planned obsolescence took us from people who made the occasional, practical purchase to full-time consumers who bought new stuff just for fun. And it drove industry to make multiple versions of items more frequently that weren't substantively different from their predecessors. It's why the market today is saturated with constant new releases and poorly made, usually inexpensive goods that can never be repaired, with parts that can never be replaced, locking us in a cycle of perpetually trading up and buying more. Fun.

Marketing Gets Its Moment

Okay, back to 1942. Just as industry was ramping up with our involvement in the war, so was the field of marketing when the Advertising Council was formed as a way of combating foreign "anti-American" sentiment. In conjunction with the Office of War Information, the Council churned out dozens of campaigns promoting behaviors that benefited the collective, like the carpooling, victory gardens, and rationing, which we touched on a little bit ago. And these ads didn't mince words either, with messaging that asserted that if you're "not carpooling, you're riding with Hitler" or that "wasting food helps the Nazis."

For a period of time, manufacturing was devoted primarily to wartime efforts (even the production of Sloan's and Ford's automobiles were suspended for a few years), and people were belt tightening, not recreationally buying things. You'd think companies would've downshifted on their advertising spending, then, right? Wrong. From 1941 to 1945, advertising expenditures *grew* from $2.2 billion to $2.9 billion, because while companies couldn't pimp products without seeming like they couldn't read the room, they wanted to take advantage of this tremulous time to lock in consumer loyalty.[6] This pre-victory period in the United States and the allied West was kind of like the modern-day dating phenomena of *breadcrumbing* or *parking*—companies were keeping consumers warm, waiting for the right time to strike. As advertising historian John McDonough says, "Ads emphasized two constant themes: what the advertiser was doing to help the war effort now and how today's sacrifices would pay off in a dazzling array of new products consumers would enjoy after the war."[7] For instance, a Westinghouse ad from 1944 promised consumers they "can look forward to the day when your home can launder shirts." Anyone else still waiting for that day? But you can see what companies were doing here—they were stoking the dopamine by getting Americans excited to buy once the war was won.

Creating Captive Customers

Upon declaration of victory for the Allied forces in 1945, plans were made for troops to begin coming home. And those troops, mostly men, needed jobs. So all those folks who'd been holding it down on the industrial front for years, many of whom were women, were given the unceremonious boot back home so men could take their places. Yeah, that sucks for many reasons, especially because 80 percent of women wanted to keep working after the war.[8] This wasn't a voluntary exodus from the workforce; it was forced by design. Think about it: women being back home created a largely confined consumer population—an audience, if you will—ripe for the advertising explosion that was about to take place.

And what about all those factories? We didn't need propellers or parachutes anymore, really, so manufacturing needed to pivot yet again. But to what? Oh! How about that "dazzling array of new products" McDonough referenced? You know, the stuff folks living modestly for the past decades, slogging through wars and rationing, could scarcely dream of? So factories nimbly altered their assembly lines to start making luxe convenience items like dishwashers and flashy cars because, well, they could (and they had to, to make their infrastructure worth it and keep returning soldiers employed). And while you might think that the average American who'd been scraping and scrapping for years wouldn't want that newfangled, fancy-pants shit, you're wrong. The long-fought victory from a global war only exacerbated feelings of fatigue around moderation, and the people wanted a prosperity that went beyond peace. They craved a new definition of the American dream, one steeped in being the best, where things, especially new, shiny things, defined who you were and where you fit in a victorious society. And this, friends, is the part of the tour where I welcome you to late-stage capitalism.

Moreover, Americans, especially white Americans, were actually pretty flush with cash at this time, thanks largely to that $185 billion in war bonds and another unsung element. Though most barely made even half of men's wages for the same job, and many had been brusquely booted from the factories they had kept afloat for years, women saved much of their wartime income, which they then contributed to down payments on starter homes.[9] By 1945, Americans were saving an average of 21 percent of their personal disposable income, compared to just 3 percent in the 1920s.[10] And while all this cultural and industrial confluence was happening, those advertising agencies who'd been so darn clever with their motivational wartime messaging were taking note and becoming more formalized. The 1950s became the "advertiser's dream decade," with agencies à la *Mad Men* popping up all over Madison Avenue. After all, somebody's gotta market these flashy new goods to the people—and by "the people," I mostly mean white women who were now home, flipping through *Ladies' Home Journal*, directed to lust after and beg their husbands for the newest frock or kitchen gadget. And message they did. The extreme contrast between pre– and post–World War II messaging mirrors the convergence of industry and consumerism—purchasing had become patriotic, and after years of restraint, the people were literally and figuratively here for it.

Purchasing Becomes Patriotic, at All Costs

So, we see a seismic shift from measured consumption to folks splashing out on new, never-before-seen items. This ramp-up also marked the proliferation of materials wrongly deemed *single-use* or *disposable* like plastic. The plastics industry experienced over 15 percent growth between 1946 and 1960, and by 1960, plastic had surpassed aluminum in production.[11] And this rapid acceleration is especially scary when you realize that every piece of plastic ever produced still exists. Sure, some of it breaks down a bit, but that's not real biodegradation. It becomes tiny microplastics, which have been found to be in everything from testicles to breast milk, and account for each of us unintentionally consuming an estimated credit card's worth of plastic every week.[12] Good times.

Moreover, the development of subdivisions and homebuyer initiatives, like the GI Bill of Rights, and women saving so much of their income made owning starter houses a breeze for returning soldiers who wasted no time getting hitched and starting families. The concept of suburbs flourished at this time, giving white families an escape from the supposed horrors (see: cohabitating with non-whites) of urban living. For women, especially, the suburbs were communities of constant surveillance that offered two modes of conformity: wife and mother. And while we're fed these Norman Rockwell images of happy housewives, many women struggled with the dramatic loss of financial and professional independence, missing their families (the suburbs decimated multigenerational living situations), and feeling like their husbands, who'd been gone for years prior, were strangers. Though they couldn't outrightly say so, many women felt lonely, disconnected, and bored.[13] Not quite the picture we're shown in *I Love Lucy* or the history books but exactly the emotional state marketers know will drive people to overconsumption.

And because it just wouldn't be a patriotic party without further disenfranchising the historically disenfranchised, the suburbs also left people of color and the poor, who were barred from living in and sometimes even entering suburbs, to pick up the pieces in inner-city neighborhoods that became more segregated and under-resourced than ever before. So, when Uncle Gene starts waxing poetic about how the greatest generation "actually revered people who fought for our freedoms," be sure to add an asterisk by the word *people* to denote that the reverence was really just reserved for white men.

And along with the oppression came the zeitgeist: *Purchasing is patriotic.* Anything worth having was billed as bigger, newer, flashier, and more convenient. Off-the-rack "fast fashion" became more widely available, replacing homemade and limited-run, made-to-measure garments. Meat at every meal rose to be symbolic of someone really making it. And let's not forget the meteoric expansion of television ownership, and in turn, commercials. In 1946, the entire country had fewer than 17,000 television sets. Just three years later, consumers were buying 250,000 sets *a month*, and by 1960, three-quarters of all families owned at least one set and watched television four to five hours a day.[14] You know what that means? Yep, a LOT of captive ears and eyeballs for advertisers to dazzle.

Maybe you're thinking that I'm getting far afield from what's supposed to be a challenge to not buy new things with this, but it bears repeating that absolutely no system or situation exists without intersectionality. We have to first see how it's all woven together to get the full picture of how oppressive the origins and modern-day manifestations of marketing and consumerism have become. So the next time you wonder how we got to the metaphorical "here" of Western overconsumption culture, you can pinpoint almost down to the year when things began to shift.

And the cycle continues today—marketers market, advertisers advertise, consumers consume, and industry continues to meet and expand the demand. These aren't strange bedfellows; they're an intentionally symbiotic fit, a product of late-stage capitalism in its most perfect application. To be a good citizen, one must consume. And through it all, our attitude toward consumption was being reprogrammed from meeting needs to manufacturing mythic wants. As time goes on, this production-consumption loop continues to wield devastating impacts not only on our health, our wallets, and the perpetuation of inequities, but on our planet.

Marketing Made Me Do It

I t's impossible to talk about overconsumption, or even general consumerism, without exploring how marketing and advertising permeate so many aspects of our lives today. And for clarity, marketing is the pursuit of identifying and strategizing how to meet customer needs, while advertising is an active element of marketing, the application of that strategy. We touched a bit on the humbler, more philanthropic origins of advertising during World War II, and then traced its explosion from the 1950s on. But what's happened since then? Allow me to pull back the curtain on the great and powerful Oz that is modern-day marketing, because it is indeed mightier and more omniscient than we think.

To establish my street cred here, I've been a professor of marketing, a high-level political strategist (which is kind of like a marketing director for candidates and campaigns), and a marketeer, a term for folks who work in the field (which, no, is not as fun as being a Mouseketeer). I was also a creative director for a prominent start-up and a director of copy for a Fortune 500's digital marketing arm. I've probably written slogans and subject lines you've seen and interacted with, and created messaging for everything from government referendums designed to protect wetlands to promos for whitening toothpaste. And all these gigs didn't happen because I'm some corporate shill just trying to make a buck. It's because I know that marketing has tremendous power, and when done ethically, it can change hearts and minds in big, important, movement-creating ways. But I've also seen how the proverbial sausage is made, and here's my take on the 99.9 percent of the marketing you're exposed to on the daily: *it's designed to keep you feeling like you'll never have or be enough.*

Making You Feel Less So You'll Buy More

In the 1920s, propaganda, the official old-timey name for what we'd now consider public relations, was undergoing an extreme makeover, largely thanks to an Austrian man named Edward Bernays. The nephew of Sigmund Freud (yes, the founder of psychoanalysis), Bernays was hard at work using, perhaps for the first time, mass psychology to design public persuasion campaigns for American clients like Procter & Gamble and CBS. By leveraging social sciences data and pulling from history and current events, Bernays believed he could manipulate public opinion and, in turn, consumers. The dude produced a lot of bangers, but he's probably best known for his campaigns for American Tobacco Company, which manufactured Lucky Strike cigarettes.

At the time, women smoking was considered immoral and unladylike. This taboo was Bad News Bears for tobacco companies because it blocked them from making customers out of, like, half the population. So Bernays had to bring out the big guns and used psychoanalysis to determine what women of the time wanted to feel and be. The verdict? Thin. Shocking, I know, that during the decade of waifish flappers, women overwhelmingly wanted to be slim. So early marketing focused on standing cigarettes up as the solution to keeping trim. Want a snack? Have a smoke instead. Even medical professionals got in on the action and were recommending cigs as a replacement for sweets, even to pregnant women. But this wasn't enough progress for Big Tobacco. Women were smoking at home in secret as a way to lose weight, sure, but they weren't screaming it from the rooftops, ya know?

So, a few years later, Bernays found something with more gravitas that he could capitalize on: women's desire for equality. The feminist movement was gaining momentum, and Bernays, in consultation with psychoanalysts, determined that calling cigarettes "Torches of Freedom" would be a clever way to take advantage of the zeitgeist. By doing this, he set smoking up as the ultimate feminist rebellion. When gals partake in something traditionally deemed only acceptable for men, it's an act of emancipation, a big middle finger to the patriarchy. Like, literally, during feminist marches, iconic activists would holler, "Women! Light another torch of freedom!" and everyone would start busting out the cigs. Bonkers as it may sound, these tactics worked, and women's smoking increased 560 percent well into the 1970s.[1] And marketing, armed for the first time with the addition of psychological insights, began morphing into the emotion-manipulating industry it is today.

There's a saying about the American health care system, that there's no money in people being healthy or dead, but there's loads of money to be made on sick folks who are in the in-between. The same goes for marketing. It's tough to advertise useless crap to secure, promotion-immune people, just as it's, well, not effective to pimp stuff to the deceased. But the folks who are in emotional limbo, those struggling with fear of what they see on the news, or financial issues, or, hmm, loneliness because they got cut from the workforce and now have to play housewife in the suburbs? Oh, they're ripe for the picking. Companies are extremely interested in our aspirations and insecurities, as well as the situations and conditions that exacerbate those feelings. Why? Because every fluctuation in our emotions, environment, and social phenomena has some bearing on our consumer behavior.

For instance, when people are sad or scared, they tend to make more impulse purchases of comfort items. When we feel out of control, we gravitate to buying practical things that will help us problem solve or regain agency.[2] This all tracks when we look at shopping trends during the pandemic, a time when many of us felt a crummy mix of sad, scared, and out of control. On one hand, sales of weighted blankets, cozy athleisure, alcohol, luxe skin care, and frozen pizzas soared. On the other, so did buying seeds, bread flour and yeast, and household cleaners.[3] Heck, one-third of Gen Z and millennials credit the combo of pandemic confinement and social media salesmanship to their development of full-blown shopping addictions.[4] If you feel insecure about your body or looks, you're more likely to impulsively buy beauty products and clothes.[5] Even temperature and weather conditions impact our spending. When we're uncomfortably cold, our decisions become emotions-based, as opposed to rational, and we're willing to spend more on something.[6] And remember malls? If you were like me, you were probably too focused on your high school crush to notice, but most of them had little to no windows. And that was intentional, a way to starve shoppers of sunlight, so they'd lose track of time and be drawn instead to the artificially bright lights that illuminated merchandise.[7]

We're also more prone to overconsumption when we're experiencing an emotional or logistical extreme, like feeling really excited about a promotion, nervous about money, or heartbroken from a breakup. This is because human beings are constantly endeavoring toward a stasis of comfort, belonging, and stability. Marketers know this, so they pull different levers, like time of day, fear of missing out, and scarcity messaging, to prey on our base desire for security. It's no coincidence that you receive too-good-to-be-true promotions on payday or after you pocket your tax refund. It's not a coinkydink that the threat of an item "going fast!" can make you forget all about your anguishing bank balance. Or that the fear of missing out on a limited-edition thing really hits when you're feeling crummy about your social status. How many times have you been swayed to make a purchase because the ads say it looks or smells "expensive"? Yeah, for someone who desperately wants to be seen as wealthy by anyone and everyone, those are magic words.

This emotional puppeteering has a lasting impact on our definition of normal consumption by blurring the lines between actual needs and wants. Think about it: retailers deem things "must-haves," and influencers tell us the stuff they're hawking is "essential," when I'm pretty sure Maslow never had an in-shower speaker or inflatable airplane bed at the top of his hierarchy of needs. The reality is you're never just being sold a product; you're being sold a dream—and that dream is usually whatever you wish you were or had more or less of. And of course, you're led to believe that you can only arrive at that ideal state by clicking the Buy button.

The Impression That You Get

Well into the 2000s, when ads were mostly limited to TV, radio, and paper, marketers generally abided by the "Rule of 7," or that it would take about seven brand impressions for a potential customer to purchase a certain thing. This rule originated from 1930s research that found that a person needed to see a movie poster at least seven times before they would go to see the film. Nowadays, with our ever-on technology and apps, marketing strategy aims to reach you on every possible platform, from social media, text messages, and push notifications on your phone, to commercials during your favorite podcast, playlist, movie, or show, to pop-ups in the middle of a mobile game or article, to strangely intuitive advertisements in the sidebar of your favorite search engine. Phew! That's . . . a lot. Advertising's omnipresence has become such an automatically accepted part of how we live that we have to *pay* to remove commercials from our streaming services. And though few studies exist that pinpoint the ideal impression amount, short consumer attention spans and fierce competition have driven many Fortune 500 companies to aim for twenty-six-plus exposures to clinch the sale. That's four times more impressions than just a few decades ago. This means you're getting attacked from all sides, all the time, everywhere you seek entertainment, relaxation, or information.

Getting to Know You

Marketing is not like the old days. Ponytailed Peggy Olson and some half-drunk guy with a loosened tie and undone gut button are no longer the lone employees sketching out a logo and tagline late into the evening. Nah. Today, companies collectively spend nearly $515 billion annually on marketing in the US,[8] much of which is devoted to consumer insights, data, and research. Do you ever feel like no one really takes the time to get to know the real you? Think again. Companies do. Boy, they do. There are entire departments dedicated to consumer insights that track how you buy, when you buy, what you buy, as well as your demographics like income, gender identification, marital status, and more. I don't want to sound like I'm wearing a tinfoil hat, but this shit is very real. Are you a member of a loyalty program or have a brand credit card? Companies love that because they can track everything you've ever bought and create targeted ads and deals based on your interests to get you to buy more.

And we see this so much more intensely toward women. While sure, dudes buy stuff, in the United States, women control 85 percent of all consumer spending, to the tune of $11 trillion.[9] More than three-quarters of American women identify as the primary buyer for their households.[10] Ninety-three percent of food purchases? Made by women. Ninety-two percent of vacations? Booked by women. Heck, half the products typically marketed to and for men (looking at you, Axe body spray) are purchased by women.[11] And that's just the beginning. By 2028, women are expected to own three-quarters of global discretionary spending, making them arguably the most powerful influencers in the world.[12]

So, yeah, companies could put a professional pickup artist

to shame with how much time and money they devote to under-standing what women want. Using a complex and surprisingly legal cocktail of loyalty program and store card data, internet cookies, and demographic and location information, predictive analytics can often formulate some freakily good guesses as to what you're going to buy when. For example, if you get a sixty-day supply of multivitamins using your loyalty card, the store can remind you to restock in fifty or so days. Maybe you purchased a box of tampons online. Excellent. Now the store will know to email you a coupon for another in about twenty-eight days. Or maybe you're in the fun gray-area age range where one day you're receiving promos for ovulation tests and the next you're getting ads for walkers (points to self).

Of course, as with all tactics, this can and does backfire reg-ularly. There's the urban legend of Target's predictive analytics gone awry when an angry father came into the store wondering why his teen daughter was getting maternity coupons, only to find that the retailer, armed only with the data points that she'd bought zinc and unscented lotion, determined his daughter was knocked up before he did. More substantiated and widespread, however, is the barrage of baby product promos retailers will lob at someone the moment they purchase a pregnancy test.[13] To the algorithm, this is a simple chain of events that makes sense. But to the people struggling with infertility or pregnancy loss, for instance, those ads are cruel, insensitive reminders of traumatic situations.

The Same Old Stereotypes

And when we dig into advertising that uses indicators like location and race, well, things get even more disconcerting. For instance, if you live in a certain zip code, that factor alone can determine what kinds of ads you see and where and how you see them. At first blush, this seems like a good strategy because local businesses can reach nearby customers. However, like many well-intentioned

marketing strategies, it's been misused to create ads and deals cal-
ibrated based on income, race, and socioeconomic status. For
instance, companies have been found targeting communities of
color with sham products and scams, high-interest credit cards
and payday loans, and promotions on junk food, while predomi-
nantly white areas receive entirely different ads for healthy food,
quality health care, and secure investment opportunities. This difference further perpetuates harmful inequities that plague under-
resourced communities. Zip code marketing doesn't stop at race
and economics. It can also utilize age and disability information
to turn your nana's sweet little senior community into an absolute
playground for scammers looking to take advantage of a vulnera-
ble, less tech-savvy population. Is it always like this? No. But in the
wrong hands with the wrong motivations, any marketing tactic
that leverages your data can be harmful.

Marketing is a reflection of society, so it often upholds and
reinforces stereotypes and norms, no matter how dangerous or
seemingly outdated they may be. And while society seems to
have evolved a bit toward gender equality, a lot of promotions
still parrot reductive typecasts. For instance, men speak about
seven times more than women in ads and are featured as the primary decision-makers 78 percent of the time.[14] Which is bananas
because, hi, didn't we just cover how much consumer spending women control? A survey of advertisements across fourteen
countries found that only 3 percent showed women as "funny or
doing something that required any form of intellect."[15] Which is
also wild, given that in the US, more women than men hold college degrees.[16] This is just old-guard sexism trying to masquer-
ade as art imitating life. And it goes beyond gender to exacerbate
racial inequities and uphold unrealistic beauty standards. Like
how ads for unhealthy products reinforce systemic food depression by not only disproportionately targeting Black and Hispanic
communities but by featuring more actors of color partaking in
the products.[17] The negative impact of advertising on body image

and self-worth, especially for women, has also been well doc-
umented for years. A majority of ads still feature "traditionally
thin" actresses, and this constant visual reinforcement creates
major problems. Sure, you're probably aware that many women
generally feel like crap after seeing said advertisements, but did
you know that 50 percent of three- to six-year-old girls worry
that they're too fat?[18] You heard me correctly: literal children are
so exposed to skinny TV ladies as the standard that they're con-
cerned their still-growing bodies are too big. And with the average American being exposed to (*assailed by* is a better term for it)
anywhere from three thousand to ten thousand advertisements
per day, the cycle is inescapable.[19]

I know, I know. I just dragged modern-day marketing there.
However, consider that our subconscious processes 92 percent of
these out-of-step biases and standards.[20] I don't think I need to
spell out the badness that can happen when we're bombarded by
messaging but lack the consciousness needed to discern what's
true and what's just old thinking cosplaying as truth. This situation force-feeds limiting beliefs, especially to the most vulner-
able, like women and minorities, and most impressionable, like
children, that set us up to feel like we're inherently worth less so
we buy more. Marketing is a tool and, in the right hands, can
be helpful in communicating the virtues of an item or service
someone might genuinely need. But you have to dissociate from
it for a bit to see it for what it is, or it will drive your self-esteem,
finances, and our planet to places we cannot sustainably survive.

Consumerism Is Contagious

Okay, so that marketing portion was kinda heavy, I'll admit. Maybe take a moment to kick back a ginger shot or take a cold shower as a palate cleanser? Why? Well, because now we're going to explore how once marketing lures you in to the shopping trap, it's very difficult to escape. Consumption is a dangerous combination of highly addictive and implicitly cumulative, meaning it builds upon itself. Just as bingeing on gas station hot-roller food and an entire bag of sour candies doesn't make you feel great, and yet you crave it only hours after your guts are bubbling, the drive to consume keeps us coming back to buy in perpetuity. Even when we're exhausted from making endless returns or stressed by our spending, none of those metaphorical bellyaches are enough to keep us abstinent from shopping for too long. And once we buy something, it sets off a chain reaction of us suddenly needing to buy more stuff for our stuff, where consumerism quickly conglomerates into overconsumption. In the words of sociology professor Juliet Schor, "The pressure to upgrade our stock of stuff is relentlessly unidirectional, always ascending."[1] Okay, so consumerist urges build, but if we know it's not good for us to answer the call, why the heck do we keep indulging in this cycle?

This Is Your Brain on Shopping

To better answer that question, we need to understand what shopping does to our brains. And boy, do I wish I had a projector behind me looping those totally awesome '80s "This is your brain on drugs" egg-frying-in-a-skillet public-service ads, but alas, I'll have to proceed with science. When you enter a store, just the act of browsing initiates the release of dopamine, which pop psychology often refers to as "the happiness hormone." But that's not the most complete characterization of our neurotransmitter friend. What dopamine actually does is make us want stuff.[2] So what you sometimes conflate with a feeling of pleasure is really you being flooded by desire—which I totally get, because I too have watched Jon Hamm play Don Draper. Anyway.

Now, let's say you're a little stressed out or excited going into your shopping trip—adrenaline then enters the equation, heightening your senses and making you more impulsive. These two hormones then start to get after it like feral teenagers at a house party, mixing desire and impulsivity, which gives you this all-consuming, hungry-like-the-wolf, thrill-of-the-hunt feeling. You're essentially high, teetering between feeling in control and out of control, which ratchets up the dopamine release even more.

But here's the thing about dopamine—it's released in *anticipation* of a reward, not upon receipt of it. This is why online shopping can feel more satisfying than in-person—because anticipation builds as shoppers wait to receive their orders.[3] So by the time your prefrontal cortex, the brain's decision-making center, determines that something is worth buying, that gorgeous dopamine rush has already started its Irish goodbye. This is why both "the shopping high" and our love for the stuff we've just purchased barely last 'til the water gets hot.

So why then do you keep going back and back, repeating the cycle, if it's such a letdown? Well, that fleeting high is so hypnotic to your brain's reward center that it will return to the source to replicate the rush, even when you didn't like or feel good from the activity. Dopamine's savage like that; it doesn't need you to enduringly enjoy something to make you crave it again and again. That's why you feel compelled to shop, even if you don't need anything. And if you repeat the process regularly or routinely (like shopping at the same place at the same time), dopamine interacts with the basal ganglia, the part of the brain responsible for habit formation, to recognize your behavior as a pattern and eventually automate it into habit.[4]

Gosh, is it just me, or does this scenario sound really familiar? Like, I feel like I've heard about this somewhere before? That's right, it's because this is biochemically similar to what happens when someone is addicted to drugs or alcohol, or anything, really. So when you feel powerless over your shopping impulses, I want you to remember you're wired to chase your next fix. You might know it's not good for you or it makes you feel downright awful, but something strong as hell, something automatic, has commandeered your vessel and is moving you toward the Add to Cart button. It's not completely hopeless, though. Just as your dopamine level fluctuates like a roller coaster the more you shop, it begins to stabilize when you slow your consumerist roll.[5] And by replacing shopping with healthier habits that deliver dopamine, along with longer-lasting hormones like serotonin, your brain's reward center steadies.[6] You already know what I'm gonna say next, don't you? Yeah, No New Things is going to teach you the tools and put you through the paces that help you move into that serener space.

Consumption Is Cumulative

In addition to being addicting, shopping for new things sets off a chain reaction known as the Diderot effect, whereby one new thing initiates a spiral of consumption, which leads you to buy more new things, and so on.[7] In layperson's terms, buying stuff begets buying more stuff. Allow me to illustrate the point via this completely hypothetical situation that absolutely did not happen to me: After a late night of social media scrolling, you've decided you're way too sophisticated for your ten-year-old, built-Ford-tough programmable drip coffee maker, so you impulse-purchase an espresso machine (from a cheapie retailer that shall not be named). As you wait for it to arrive, the anticipatory dopamine builds and you're feeling pretty good about your life choices. When it's delivered, you unpack it and get it all cleaned and set up. You do this excitedly, not realizing that setup alone took you about an hour. Then you use the thing religiously for about a week, until it starts acting wonky and then stops working altogether because, what the hell? Did a part just fall off? Yeah, a piece cracked off. Crap. You contact customer service, but instead of sending a replacement part (not an option), they say they can send you another machine. Fine, that's nice of them, you guess? You hide the broken machine in the closet, alongside your old-faithful drip coffee maker, to clear counterspace for the new one.

For a bit, you're enjoying spending eight hands-on minutes a day making your Italian roast again. Then upon watching some coffee-related TikToks, you're convinced that what you actually need to stay consistent in this espresso journey are those little demitasse cups because they're SO much more authentic, so you buy those and unpack them. Welp, you can't just have them sitting in the cabinet, so you need a holder for those, too. Add to cart, unpack, and set up. Now you've got a beverage-making spread that would make a barista blush, including a newly purchased "aesthetic" canister for storing your espresso and the most precious little scooping spoon, because are you really even enjoying coffee if you're not completely bought into outfitting the experience? Oh, and you need a variety of bespoke bean blends, a grinder, some syrups, and fancy milks, because duh. All of this transpires in a way that feels like a natural progression, without you realizing that the pull of consumerism is contagious and cumulative.

But uh-oh, a spate of busy mornings has you not finding the time to make your beloved espresso, and you can't program this machine like your old one. Then those mornings turn into many, and your machine lies dormant for months, collecting cooking splatters on your countertop. When you finally do reignite your ritual, you find the water tank has gotten moldy and the whole thing needs to be flushed out with vinegar. So you begrudgingly do that. Then you see how much cat hair and cornflake dust has collected on the machine, so you give it a good wipe-down. And forty minutes later, you're finally, finally ready to brew again. But by the next morning, you're rushing out the door and don't use it. *Tomorrow!* you say. After a few weeks of this, your partner insists it's time to bring the old, low-maintenance coffee maker back into rotation because this is uncaffeinated madness. So you break it out of closet purgatory and set it up next to the espresso machine.

Now you're back in the old groove of using the set-and-forget coffee maker and have decided that, despite the hundreds of dollars and many hours of maintenance you've devoted, you're just not made for that espresso life. So you opt to sell the working machine. You clean it, snap and post pictures, write a description, haggle with infuriating people over price, and eventually sell it. Victory! You then spend time boxing it up, bringing it to the post office, and bidding it adieu. But what about the broken one? Well, you can't really sell it, can you? You spend some time researching recycling options only to find that none exist in your area (and the retailer isn't going to take it back and recycle it), so it ends up in the trash and later the landfill. Oh, and the canister, cups, spoon, and various other accoutrements you bought? Maybe you'll sell those, too. You're just too over interacting with the public to post them on Marketplace or in your local free group. Eventually, you end up dropping it all off at the big-box donation center, where maybe the items will be in the lucky 16 percent of all donations that actually get resold.[8] Or not. Most likely not.

Man, just writing all that has me feeling tired. Now imagine the actual tiredness, hassle, and wasted time that scenario would create in your life. We need to remember that *stuff is inventory*, and you, whether you like it or not, are the inventory manager. You may say, "Well, I don't drink coffee, so this doesn't apply to me." Okay, fine, but this journey can be ascribed to almost anything— clothes, toys, appliances, cars, furniture, gadgets influencers swear will change our lives—any *thing*. Again, despite this book's title, I'm not anti-things or anti–new things, but when we take a moment to see the cumulative nature of stuff, we become far more discriminating about the things we allow into our lives.

Buying Begets More Buying

Have you ever started a hobby and suddenly you're awash with all these *needs* before you've even engaged with said hobby enough to know if it's going to stick? Maybe you complete two HIIT workout classes and now you somehow urgently need sweat-wicking ensembles for every day of the week, fancy athletic shoes, upgraded earbuds, and maybe a cool gym bag because there's now too much stuff to fit into your regular workbag? Do you need a mat? You need a mat. Weights at home for when it's blizzarding and you don't want to go to the gym? Yeah, add to cart. What about a fitness tracker? Ooh, great idea. Add to cart. What about pre-workout powder and post-workout shakes? Yes, definitely. A special scale that tells you your BMI? Oh yeah, add that too. Like, we wanna do this right, right? So you buy a lot of this stuff, but like so many phases in life, you don't necessarily stick with the workout routine, because stuff alone doesn't build consistency. Now you've got enough fitness supplies clogging up your living room to support the whole dang US Olympic team, but barely find yourself making it outside for a jog or to your expensive gym. This phenomenon is so common that retailers call it "front loading" or the "January 1 trend," whereby people stock up on stuff to support their hobbies before they've galvanized those hobbies into habits.

The buildable nature of consumerism isn't a bug; it's a design feature. This is pretty obvious when you purchase an item online, and the retailer then suggests other things for you to buy before you even complete the transaction. You know, items "we think you might like" or that are "frequently bought together." And you're lured by that collectivism of suggestion. You're no fool; you know what's happening here. But it feels lusciously curated, like those little AI bots and algorithms are thinking of YOU and your needs. And as humans, we dig that dupe so much that we affectionately call it *personalization*. Like, how thoughtful of y'all to think of little old me! What we don't realize is how much of our behavioral, demographic, and other sensitive data is used by retailers to continually generate and test suggestions that drive us to buy more. So much delicate data, in fact, that recommendation systems are often accused of upholding harmful biases and stereotypes, violating privacy, and hurting smaller businesses.[9] Despite all these concerns, this personalization is incredibly effective, with recommended products accounting for 31 percent of e-commerce revenues.[10] Now just imagine if you hadn't been shown those tailored suggestions—how much money would you have saved? Perhaps you're like 49 percent of us who bought stuff we never intended to simply because we received these kinds of recommendations.[11]

Stuff for Your Stuff

We also see this cumulative consumerism via something the industry calls "the custom complement trap," as in that stuff you just bought suddenly needs other bespoke stuff. If you look closely, you'll see this everywhere. Devices that have proprietary charging ports, programs, and components; furniture with exclusive modular options and special cleaners; hair dryers that come with custom attachments and attendant hair care lines, and on and on.

Just look at the frenzy around Stanley cups, which, by the time of this book's publication, may have given way to another of-the-moment, must-have trend. These insulated chalices are so coveted that people literally wild out to get the latest styles and colors. I mean, sure, the world is on fire, but let's beat one another up over a fucking cup. And you don't just drink from these—no, no, you *collect* them. Like it's somehow positively plebeian to have just one reusable cup. Isn't that bananas? An item that's supposed to help stem waste through reuse has become something we over-consume. But check it out, because marketing wins when we believe we need stuff for our stuff, there's an entire cottage industry dedicated to making accessories for Stanley cups. Not even joking here. These Stanleys are better outfitted than your toddler on the first day of preschool. They have mini backpacks, lip gloss fobs, clip-on fans, and slide-on charcuterie boards—yes, for the cups. And because this madness is so normalized in consumer culture, we never know when we've achieved a level of stuff that's enough, because the limit doesn't exist.

But, in my opinion, nowhere do you see this runaway train more ridiculously than in the realm of home organization. Per the internet, if you want to achieve some order in your space, many influencers and even in-the-flesh, accredited professional organizers will espouse that you really, really, really need to get special containers to organize your things. When in reality, the shoeboxes you already have will probably work just fine. But as we learned from our earlier walk down consumerist memory lane, making do with what you have doesn't make companies rich, so you're going to be shown what a slovenly clown you are for repurposing. Don't believe me? The Container Store, a veritable mecca for the aspirationally and actually organized, boasted revenues of $1.09 billion in 2022.[12] To put that into perspective, that's more than the entire GDP of my resident state of Illinois. I don't say all this to vilify the Container Store or organizing but rather to show how lucrative it is for companies to reinforce the narrative that our stuff needs stuff.

So you're told you need glossy plastic thingies to hold coffee pods. And drawer dividers for your dresser so, God forbid, your socks don't touch your underpants. Oh, and you'll definitely require a few seventy-six-dollar bins to hold your holiday décor and different "aesthetic" boxes for your keepsakes, even though aesthetics has nothing to do with an item's utility. You probably need a label-maker too, unless you want everyone to see your grody, childish handwriting. Your groceries that already come in packages? Well, forget those. If you don't want to be a disgustingly average trash person who has no friends, you'll need to decant everything into beautiful pitchers, jars, and holders so your fridge and pantry look like freaking museums. Let the landfill worry about all the totally suitable packaging you just trashed. And naturally, you're now gonna need more organizers for those organizers. Oooh, like acrylic tiered shelves for your sodas and string cheese so your fridge looks like a heavenly crystal stadium. And on and on, conjuring problems that don't really exist, only to sell us solutions we don't really need.

Like, something's wrong with our society when we're told we HAVE TO HAVE special containers and pouches for every blessed thing. *No, you fucking don't.* Merchants create a frenzy around stuff and then upsell us on more stuff designed expressly for that stuff we just bought. This is called a *trap* because it is. Once you've bought something, you're up to 70 percent more likely to buy a complementary item for it.[13] Stop being hoodwinked by this insanity. I promise you can find your pen when it's floating in your bag without a dedicated pouch that says PENS. And in my twenty-plus years of wearing makeup, I can confirm that yes, you can in fact put your face on just fine in the morning without a behemoth three-tiered, lazy Susan–style display case cluttering up your bathroom counter.

The Intoxication of Influence

If I sound pissed off, it's because I am. This cumulative consumption is encouraged by algorithms, sure, but also via the nearly $22 billion world of influencer marketing.[14] Because brand-driven advertising is old hat, *user-generated content* (UGC), or *influencer marketing*, is seen as more appealing and genuine. Marketers know that repeated exposure to a product from different places and people will drive you to buy the item, even if you weren't all that interested to begin with. And what better place to subject folks to said repeated exposure than the social media channels each of us wastes nearly two and a half hours on each day?

Social media personalities, who in their quest to just make a buck (and sure, sometimes gain clout and virality), are used as Trojan horses to make you feel like your stuff is inadequate, and thus, you need a steady influx of new things to keep up. And we fall for it because it kind of feels like word of mouth or a recommendation from a friend. Except when was the last time you complimented a stranger out in the real world and they replied with an affiliate link? Right, that doesn't happen. And we seem to also forget that influencers aren't our friends. These are parasocial arrangements, or one-sided relationships, and we know nothing about these people aside from the highlight reels they allow us to see.

Moreover, we have no idea if what we're seeing is even true. Those business coaches who *seem* so rich and successful may actually be up to their Maseratis in collections. The couple that *seems* to have it all together might actually have a really toxic relationship. That fitness guru who *seems* to be beaming with confidence might be duping you with filters or struggling with crippling body dysmorphia. Heck, even some "sustainability influencers" (a trend I absolutely abhor for many professional reasons) engage in stealthy partnerships (sometimes with the same fossil fuel companies they rail against) to pimp the hottest eco must-haves, which is all just overconsumption with a green tint. And don't get me started on how many times a makeup influencer, for instance, swears to millions of her followers that a certain mascara is "life-changing," only to be seen returning it to Sephora a week later.

I'm not saying everyone online is a big old fibber who's out to dupe you, but I'm not *not* saying that.

The median age range for influencers is fifteen to twenty-five years old, so Generations Alpha and Z, give or take.[15] Now, remember when we talked about the prefrontal cortex, the part of the brain responsible for good decision-making? Well, it doesn't even fully mature until our midtwenties.[16] Are you picking up what I'm putting down here? Look, I'm not saying that age always dictates wisdom, but I'll be damned if I take financial cues from someone who doesn't yet have the fully formed capacity for good judgment. Sorry, but something just doesn't sit right in my spirit when a nineteen-year-old influencer says they "can't live without" an antiaging cream they're promoting—like, what facial age are we mitigating here? Not all of us have teenagers, but all of us were teenagers, and if you need some perspective, just think back to that time and you'll sober up real quick. Like when my friends and I drank an entire case of spoiled wine we found in a dumpster. Or how I spent my early twenties braving Boston blizzards wearing peep-toed pumps and no coat. Yeah, I'm not going to that version of me for life advice. No hate to my young influencers out there, but I will not be following those shopping hauls down the spiral staircase of overconsumption—and neither should you.

At the very least, can we all agree that there is no such thing as an unbiased review if someone is being paid for that review? Impartiality cannot exist when social media personalities make a commission from you buying something. And today, influencers of all sizes sell their own merch, have storefronts, and engage with social-based shopping services that automatically drive you to sales pages for everything they promote. Instead of seeing these people as our friends, we should see them for what they are: pseudo-entrepreneurial ecosystems at best, and online used car salesmen at worst, incentivized to play our consumerist impulses like a freaking fiddle.

Despite all the common sense I just dropped, 69 percent of Americans say they trust these famous internet strangers[17] and spend accordingly: it's estimated that for every dollar a company invests to have an influencer pimp their product, they enjoy a nearly six-dollar return.[18] If we were playing the stock market and heard about a 500 percent ROI, we'd be starting an Only-Fans to buy shares. Never doubt how much your suspension of disbelief means big money for companies. And because we compare ourselves to these aspirational personalities, we will often spend money we don't have just to keep up, which can result in anxiety and depression.[19] And why be just broke when you can be depressed and broke, am I right? I'm sure I sound jaded by what some might consider the enchanting world of social media influencing, but if trends are any indication of the future, this area of marketing (which is what it is—marketing) will continue to grow as a primary driver of overconsumption, and in turn, overproduction, environmental degradation, consumer debt, and emotional distress. Yeah, it's all interconnected and actually pretty deep.

Take Back Control

Look, the system is entrenched, the marketing is omnipresent, and it's all designed to keep us buying until we die. And yes, that feels pretty heavy, like there's no way out. But while it's not a full escape (such a thing is pretty impossible unless you're totally off the grid), No New Things offers a reprieve from the vicious cycle of that conditioned consumerism that's probably got a hold on you—or you wouldn't have picked up this book. It puts you in a reflection period where you regain control of what you see, what you entertain, and your feelings around that stimuli. It's simple and empowering, and as illustrated above, nobody is coming to save you from your relationship to consumption. I often say, "The quest for more stuff comes from feeling not enough" (we love a good rhyme), and it's not just pithy, it's true. Companies have a vested interest in keeping you feeling inadequate so you'll buy more. So the bad news is that shifting this situation lies with you. But also, the good news is that shifting this situation is up to you. And you're most definitely up to the task, and you're not alone. I've done it. Thousands of others have done it (and are currently doing it!). It's possible. It's rewarding. It'll change your fucking life. And I'm here to help.

Part 3

The 30-Day Challenge

Get to Know the Flow
and Jump on In

How No New Things Works

Now that you know the origins and trappings of coerced consumerism, you're ready to embark on the Challenge. In the coming chapters, I'll lay out everything you need to do, by week and by day, so you feel fully supported as you move through No New Things. And while there's strategy to the order of the action items, the point is ultimately for you to regain and exert control over consumerist impulses, so make modifications as you see fit. Need to rearrange action items because you'll be out of town? It's your life, pal; do you. That said, following the Challenge as it's structured has been proven to yield the most successful results, according to a poll of thousands of folks who've done it. Now, here's how your next thirty days will look:

Your Weeks

There are thirty days total in the Challenge, broken up over the course of four weeks, with two weeks boasting seven days and two featuring eight days. And because tracking feelings is so vital to the Challenge, there are short reflection prompts at the end of each week to help you link emotion to action. How did taking the actions feel? Were there issues? I know you're busy, so these needn't be arduous or long reflections, but rather they're meant to help you check in with yourself. It may sound mushy, but you're likely going to find that the Challenge drums up a lot of interesting, sometimes uncomfortable feelings and attitudes. This is not some touchy-feely new-age crud either; understanding how feelings drive impulses is a major catalyst for positive change as you move through the process. If you're like many of the participants, you might even be shocked by the emotions that come up during certain action items and weeks. This is perhaps the most important part of the Challenge because it's in the discomfort that we begin to transform our relationship with spending and self-worth.

There's also a weekly tally of money saved (from purchases you didn't make) and made (from things you sold), which you might consider an ancillary reward because holy crap does that add up. Many participants say the monetary accounting is one of the most motivating and mind-blowing parts of the Challenge.

Your Days

Each day of the week has a dedicated action item and complementary guidance so you feel fully supported doing the damn thing. Think of these daily actions as priming a new habit because they're cumulative, in that you'll continue to do them and carry the ethos throughout the rest of the Challenge as you see fit. For instance, you may shop your closet as prescribed on Day 18 and then decide you want to do it again later in the thirty days—totally awesome! We're building strong neural pathways that lead to habits here, so repetition as it works with your lifestyle is the name of the game.

And if you were the kid in school who was like, "Hey, I don't know why we're doing this—I don't think I'll ever actually use trigonometry"? Oh wait, that was me (and that's why this isn't a math book, clearly)—well, you're gonna love this next part. Because I never want you to be in the dark about why or how we're doing something, each day you get a juicy educational bit before we jump into the action item, where I doff my professor cap and tell you why what you're doing will help you link action with impact.

Week 1: The Foundations (Days 1–7)

This week focuses on the backbone actions of No New Things. The first three days, 1: Visualize Victory, 2: List Your Loves, and 3: Note Your Needs, are intended to help you get and stay in the right mindset, put alternative activities in place to supplant shopping urges, and have the foresight to know what items you might need to acquire during the Challenge and in what No New Things–approved ways you're going to get 'em. The remaining days are 4: Connect with Community, 5: Track Your Triggers, 6: Wrangle Returns, and 7: Gather Gift Cards. These action items will have you returning eligible purchases and digging up unused cash in the form of forgotten gift cards, corralling your existing peeps and getting connected to sharing economies, and engaging with other practices that ensure you have the logistics and support in place to stay the course. Most importantly is probably Day 5, where you learn to log your emotional and situational states as they relate to spending urges. You'll not only do this every day of the Challenge, but as mentioned above, you'll also keep a running tally of the money you didn't spend, which is incredibly gratifying.

Week 2: Your Habits (Days 8–14)

The first part of Week 2 focuses on habits you'll flex throughout the Challenge that cut down on promotional messaging, like 8: Silence Spending, 9: Block the Shop, 10: Slash Subscriptions, and 11: Delete On-Demand Drains. From muting and unsubscribing from the constant onslaught of retailer or influencer marketing to implementing ways to outsmart yourself from shopping, these action items are like the sentinels who stand watch over your devices and mind. The end of the week gets into practices that are germane to the SUPER System, like 12: Understand Upcycling,

13: Slay Secondhand, and 14: Ethically Off-Load. These will have you getting comfortable and partaking in repurposing, shopping secondhand, and responsibly rehoming items you no longer want or need.

Week 3: Your Space and Stuff (Days 15–22)

Ah, your first eight-day week; now we're cooking. While—boiled down to its simplest form—the Challenge is focused on not buying a bunch of new crap you don't actually need, a huge part of this is cultivating gratitude for and contentment with the many wonderful items you already have. Week 3 focuses on things you can do within your living space to maximize the utility and appreciation of your stuff. And yes, every day features another adorably alliterative task (because joy is essential), so get ready to 15: Unstuff Your Space, 16: Polish Your Possessions, 17: Care for Your Clothes, 18: Shop Your Stuff, 19: Groom Your Grooming, 20: Tune Up Your Tech, 21: Rearrange an Area, and 22: Focus on Food. So whether you're in a tiny house, a digital nomad crossing the country in a Toyota Prius, or living large in a sprawling mansion, you'll be cutting clutter (especially the low-hanging-fruit type you've been staring at and getting annoyed by for months), repairing and spiffing your possessions so they have expanded utility and longevity, and enjoying the glorious space created in the process.

Week 4: Getting Out There (Days 23–30)

In Week 1, you ensure the conditions you are working with set you up for success. Week 2 will have you cultivating habits that serve rather than sabotage you. Week 3 cheers you on as you get your space streamlined, organized, and full of items that bring you joy and utility. By Week 4, you're in the home stretch. You've honed the No New Things mindset and habits in the safe space of your home and within the networks you've established, so let's take them out into the wild and extend them to other areas of your public life. This second eight-day week will show you how to 23: Borrow Before Buying, 24: Get Good at Gifting, 25: Pay It Forward, 26: Socialize Sans Shopping, 27: Travel Thoughtfully, 28: Self-Care Sustainably, 29: Set Goals Without Stuff, and 30: Calculate and Celebrate. This is also the week I totally encourage you to go buck wild because, darling, you'll have made it so far, and you deserve to celebrate in whatever way feels great to you. And just a hunch, but chances are your old way of celebrating by splashing out on an impulse shopping binge is going to feel very different and maybe less appealing now.

Timing

The Challenge is designed to go for thirty days, or about a month, give or take. Why thirty days? you might ask. Well, habit creation, science and I say. While the exact timing varies on how long it takes to forge a habit (estimates range from 18–254 days, which is quite a, well, range), past participants noted that thirty days was a tidy fit into their lives because, as one respondent said, "Sometimes it's easier to have an elevator pitch that says, 'I'm doing this for the month of July,' and be done with the explanation."[1] Moreover, since consumerism is present in basically every aspect of our lives, engaging with No New Things for a solid month starts to build strong neural pathways that divert you away from shopping and toward healthier, more enduringly satisfying behaviors.

That said, you don't have to begin at the first of the month or at any particular time. Start when you feel compelled to, or if you're someone prone to procrastination or you need the "timing to be perfect" like I do, start right freaking now. And while it's designed to go for a whole month, there's no edict here. You can go for a week and then take a break. Folks who've done even just a few days have said they noticed serious positive developments in their savings, creativity, clutter, and available time. So, go in little spurts or do the whole thing as scientifically laid out in the book—while this is not a Burger King, you absolutely can and should have it your way.

Other Things to Keep in Mind

As with all good challenges, there are intense purists and there are flexitarians. You can be either. As mentioned, folks have seen the most success when they follow the structure of the book, but No New Things needs to work for you and your life. So if you absolutely must buy new cosmetics because you're a makeup artist, or you need to acquire last-minute teacher gifts because your knucklehead kids thoughtfully notified you that Teacher Appreciation Day is tomorrow, that's totally okay. Think of me as the Leslie Knope of No New Things Town (great food, attractions, and nightlife, but not a lot of shopping malls here). I am not the sheriff (there is no sheriff), so no one is going to tut-tut you for bending some guidelines to fit your life and needs, especially if doing so in a few one-off instances means you're going to stay the course for the rest of the Challenge.

Life's chaotic, and things don't always (or ever, really) go according to plan. Shit happens, you have to shift, and sometimes we can be ridiculously hard on ourselves for that. I'm not a big fan of calling things *failures*, because I don't believe many happenings are failures. You either succeed as intended or you learn from the unexpected. So we're gonna call what would otherwise be deemed failures by others (or maybe yourself) *not-quites*. And you'll definitely encounter these, so just count on them to crop up. Maybe you needed an item urgently and had zero notice, so you placed an Amazon order with a bit of a heavy heart. Or you couldn't find a gift secondhand and resorted to hitting up the toy store and just buying the damn thing from the registry. It's all okay. Just dust yourself off, note the not-quite and what you learned from the day (or log it more formally, if you'd like), and keep it moving. It's all information that will make every day of the Challenge that much wiser.

This book is meant to be a tool to help you, not bog you down or become yet another arduous part of your day. It's your partner as you move through a deeply transformational process. And because I completely recognize the irony of creating a thing that boldly espouses no *new* things, I hope you'll share this journey with others. In fact, I'd encourage it. If possible, welcome your partners, friends, and family on board with the Challenge (see Day 4 for more guidance on that). Having compadres to share wins and whines with is extra affirming as you dismantle old habits and attitudes and explore and cement new ones. Sharing is caring, and I truly believe the No New Things concept is so helpful and simple that everyone who's able should give it a whirl. And if you're the Lone Ranger in your circle taking on this Challenge, don't fret. Many folks have found success and reaped major benefits even when they're the solo participant in their otherwise shopping-focused household or social sphere. And what often starts as a pursuit of one becomes inspiring to others to the point where they want to join in as well. So don't be stymied by the naysayers or no-thanks-ers in your life. Just do your thing, remember that you're a badass with a good ass, and watch as your posse suddenly gains an interest when they see how calm, flush with cash, and stylish you are while buying nothing new. Don't say I didn't warn you.

I often say that No New Things is for anyone, but not for everyone. Embarking on the Challenge requires a little preplanning and access to some collective resources and networks. If you're absolutely burning the candle at both ends just to survive, you can certainly try your hand at elements of the Challenge, but by all means, don't stress yourself over doing every action item. If you live in an isolated area where you have little to no access to secondhand shopping, free groups, or sharing communities, you can still do bits of the Challenge, but it's going to be a lot more, well, challenging than it will be for someone living in a well-connected, bustling metropolis.

Moreover, No New Things is not intended to be a replacement for a debt repayment plan or professional financial intervention. I'm not a credit counselor or financial advisor, but I don't need to be those things to know that while the Challenge is not the answer to every money woe and bind out there, it can be an absolutely brilliant complement to any plan someone might already be engaging with. Like, I'm pretty sure any bankruptcy counselor would agree that, yeah, it would also be a good idea to curb impulse spending on new, nonessential items while regaining your financial footing. So, if that's you, you'll still find value and solidarity (and absolutely zero judgment) here.

While your mileage may vary because no two people are exactly alike in location, finances, life situations, and so on, everyone can still reap richness from No New Things, even if your journey looks a little different from the layout of the book. I am well aware that many people live in ways similar to the Challenge tenets not because they want to but out of necessity. So, being in a position to even try something called No New Things may feel like it comes from immense privilege, which is absolutely true. Some of us have the privilege of resources, or time, or access. In fact, I'd argue that overconsumption is largely a crisis of, or at the very least disproportionately fueled by, privilege. For instance, the Global Carbon Project estimates that the wealthiest 10 percent of people in the world contribute more than half of all global carbon emissions.[2] This Challenge is rooted in the belief that it's incumbent upon those of us with that privilege to use it responsibly, in a way that contributes positively to the greater good, and No New Things is a way to do this.

Week 1: The Foundations

So you've decided to take this No New Things journey. Congratulations are certainly in order. And though I was only a cheerleader the summer after eighth grade when I lost a bunch of weight on Jenny Craig and got my braces off (and even then, it was only for two games and I wasn't very good), allow me to pump you the hell up. I'm blasting the *Jock Jams*. I'm doing the Roger Rabbit because I'm way too old to attempt a Dallas Cowboys cheerleader–style jump split. I'm hollering your name until I'm hoarse. All that to say, I'm excited for you.

What I and others often cite as one of our favorite parts of No New Things is that it requires so little prep and zero start-up costs. Unlike other challenges out there that shall not be named, you don't need supplies; you aren't asked to spend your life savings on special groceries or equipment; you needn't defect from civilization while you engage in some fringy practice that makes it impossible for you to hang. And as far as preparation goes, most of it is mental and logistical. If you're the kind of type A baddie who packs their lunch the night before or sleeps in your gym clothes, you're totally welcome to do some of these before you start the clock on the thirty days. If you want to do a few days before you officially start the Challenge, I recommend doing Days 1–3, since the action items are mostly focused on list making and can be done in a few hours (or more quickly if you're fast like that).

The flow of Week 1 has been created to help you transition into the foundational No New Things tenets that you'll continually do throughout the Challenge. For instance, Day 5's Track Your Triggers is an activity I recommend you do every day for the next thirty days, as it's so much profounder than just writing down the timing and emotions associated with feeling spendy. Same goes for the Visualization, Love List, and Need Note you will create on Days 1–3. These are the low-lift first steps that are going to pack a big punch, so you'll be in the right headspace to rock the Challenge with confidence and, most importantly, joy. And it just so happens that approaching a challenge with positive feels sets you up for success by enhancing decision-making, cognitive flexibility, and emotional resilience.[1] Plus, it just feels way better to do something with joy rather than dread or apathy.

And while I firmly believe that a foundation of joy and excitement can really help you ace the thirty days, I'm also a human being rooted in reality. As with any habit-shifting journey, you are inevitably going to experience discomfort and resistance throughout the Challenge. And when you do, referring back to the action items from this week can be just what Dr. Deinfluence ordered. Most importantly, when you get discouraged or down, I want you to remember that these feelings are actually indicators of real change.

Besides, you're just starting out, and that on its own is something worth celebrating. You're learning how the Challenge will fit into your life in the short and long term. You're collecting data on yourself. You're laying the foundations to rewire new, healthier-for-you habits. None of those require you to be perfect or a No New Things purist right out of the gate, or ever, really. All you need to do is show up with an open mind and, at the risk of sounding terribly contrived, trust the process. This is a Challenge that drives profound habitual and attitudinal changes—that's the end goal; not whether or not you flawlessly execute No New Things for exactly thirty days. Unlike other popular challenges out there, there's no scolding or having to start over if you "mess up," and as we already covered, I don't even count supposed slipups as failures. So just throw that stinking thinking out right now. All righty, flash your brightest smile and get excited—your journey begins now! You're moving in the right direction toward overconsumption freedom.

Day 1: Visualize Victory

Okay, I get it. Not all of us had a childhood Lisa Frank Trapper Keeper obsession like I did and thus might have an aversion to journaling, doodling, daydreaming, and whatever other woo-woo stuff is often lumped in with the word *visualization*. But this is an exercise I do without fail almost every time I do the Challenge, because when I've done it, my experience is markedly smoother and more successful. I find that imagining how I want my life to be positively impacted by No New Things is profoundly motivating, and writing it all down allows me to go back and feel that optimism all over again when I need a boost. If you're still uncomfortable with this powerhouse practice, try reframing it. You wouldn't make your Broadway debut without having some dress rehearsals, would you? Right, so view this exercise as your No New Things dress rehearsal, and I'm your stage mom.

And if you are still feeling reluctant, maybe science will sway you. Recent studies indicate that visualizing ourselves doing something well can actually alter our brains' pathways, forging new connections that can help make our desired outcomes a reality.[1] In other words, picturing yourself being successful at No New Things (or anything, really) actually trains your brain to make it so. Hey, if visualizing is good enough for Olympic athletes, Oprah, and Tony Robbins, it's good enough for me. And as for writing our Challenge goals down? Data supports that too. Writing down your goals can lead to a 33–42 percent greater likelihood that they will be achieved.[2] So, if the juice feels worth the squeeze to you with that, set aside a few minutes to envision and record your Challenge aspirations—psychedelic rainbow-colored dolphin journal totally optional.

As with all prompts in this book, you can use a good old pen and paper, you can get Doogie Howser, MD, with it and have a computer diary, or you can use your phone's Notes app. People have even recorded voice notes for themselves that they then play back throughout the thirty days, and I'm obsessed with that idea. You can be long-winded (hi, me) and luxuriate over the descriptions of the life you want as a result of the Challenge, or you can keep it short, bulleted, and concise.

When I first did the Challenge, I recognized that my shopping habits were jeopardizing my financial future, my time, my health and fitness, my relationships (especially the one with myself), and were a deflection from me confronting the actual feelings that were bubbling below the surface. Addressing these through the Challenge, I hoped, would make me feel freer, fill my life with greater ease and joy, and allow me to be financially more secure. I hoped to have more time for the activities and people I loved and to live in a space that felt relaxing and open for creativity. Laying out and feeling into that vision was not only an exercise that got me seriously amped to start the Challenge, but writing it all down gave me a powerful reminder to refer back to when my resolve was waning or I was contending with tough emotions. And you know what? At the end of the first month (which was the original time frame I set for myself), I reviewed my notes and found that so many of the goals had already been realized. In just a few weeks? Wow. And having the Visualization to refer back to kept me happily sticking with No New Things . . . for nearly two full years.

So set aside some time, grab your favorite recording medium, and allow yourself to explore how doing No New Things will transform your life in the best of ways. Moreover, as you follow the prompts below and visualize your Challenge results, I'd urge you to use first person (*I*, *me*, *my*, and *mine*), as that point of view has been shown to cultivate a greater sense of personal investment and motivation. And maybe I don't need to say this, but just in case, there's no one looking over your shoulder. No one to judge your fears or aspirations here. So in the words of Prince, "Let's go crazy; let's go nuts"—no need to put the mental restrictor plates on your hopes for this Challenge. If you hope the next thirty days will be a springboard for you to wrangle spending and debt so you can eventually start your own business or launch your acting career, shucks, I'll be in the wings cheering you on. As you've probably already gathered, No New Things has yielded benefits far beyond participants' wildest expectations, so there's no reason you can't dream big.

Action Item 1: Using the prompts below, take some time to visualize how your life will benefit from engaging with the No New Things Challenge (using first person whenever possible), and then record those aspirations.

Question	Rationale
1. Why do I want to better understand my impulses around spending and stuff?	This prompt is intended to help you see and unpack how your acquisition of stuff is potentially creating difficulty or stress in your life.
2. How is my life negatively impacted by these habits?	Participants have cited that their shopping impulses have sucked up their time that could be better spent on other pursuits, have made their homes cluttered and stressful, have drained their finances, and so on. What are your experiences with your current relationships to spending and stuff?

Question	Rationale
3. *How will buying fewer items make my life better and easier?*	How will embarking on this Challenge ease some of the aforementioned burdens? How do you foresee your life being simpler and better during and after the Challenge?
4. *What are some words that describe how I want to feel during and after the Challenge?*	Start with five words that you'd like to reference to guide and define your No New Things journey. If you're feeling inspired, select as many words as feel right to you. Here are a few that recur for participants: *freedom, productivity, ease, everything in its place, purpose, create, calm, enjoyment.*
5. *What do I hope to gain from this Challenge?*	This can be more general, like "More time" or "Wasting fewer resources," or more specific like "Paying off $5K in credit card debt" or "Organizing my closets."
6. *What about doing this Challenge makes me anxious or afraid?*	Here we begin to address what you're foreseeing that may be a hurdle for you. Are you worried the Challenge will be difficult? Will it socially isolate you? Will it be unfun? Write those fears down here so that you can then begin to differentiate between fear and excitement (which sometimes can feel like the same thing).
7. *What about doing this Challenge makes me excited?*	Harking back to what you wrote above, are you excited about getting to those milestones and feelings?

Action Item 2: Keep this Visualization somewhere you're able to easily access it, and refer back to it when you need some motivation, as well as at the end of each week during your Weekly Reflections to track your progress.

Day 2: List Your Loves

Remember when we touched on what happens to your brain while you're shopping? Yeah, I'm still recovering from that. In case you missed it, here's the redux: When you're shopping, your brain's frontal cortex lights up like a freaking Christmas tree, and a hypnotic cocktail of dopamine and endorphins floods your body, making you feel, well, really good.[1] Until it abruptly leaves and then you feel not so good. So if we're trying to move away from buying new things, we need to find replacement activities that make us feel just as good, even better, or at least steadier. For instance, you can get a near-bioidentical rush to buying clothes as you can from eating, having sex, exercising, getting a massage, and, hell, even smelling cookies baking.[2] So the excellent news here is that there are oh-so-many healthier habit replacements during the Challenge, and many of them are fun and free.

And this is where what I alliteratively call a Love List comes in. No, it's not a rattling off of all your celebrity crushes (though I have a list like that too). The Love List is a brain dump of all the activities that are Challenge-compliant that really fill your cup. And you're going to keep this list handy so you always have alternative activities, or what I like to call *treats* at the ready. I don't know about you, but even though I'm a grown-ass woman, I stand by my need for a treat after doing something decidedly adult, especially if it's something I really don't want to do. Got my nethers inspected at the gynecologist? Little cappuccino and pastry for me. Did my taxes? It's zone-out time with that word game I love. Had a hard conversation at work? I get to shake it off at that fancy Pilates reformer studio I've been eyeing. Treat, treat, treat. You get the idea. So, fill your Love List with happenings that give you that delicious, treat-like thrill but aren't things. This isn't just because I like treats or want you to like me. Studies suggest that we are a whopping 79 percent more likely to keep at something if we have a celebratory reward or acknowledgment for our progress—and I don't know about you, but I am digging those odds.[3]

Your Love List is entirely personal to you and can contain any non-thing activities that bring you good feelings and are easily accessed. The easily accessed part is especially important here because while, sure, you will probably reap euphoric levels of joy from going on a luxury vacation to Capri, to the point where you yell "To hell with shopping, you peasants!" while you zip away on the back of some gorgeous specimen's Vespa, such an activity is not easily accessible for most of the general population. I'm not saying it'll never happen; I'm just saying for the purposes of the Love List, we gotta keep it real.

Your list can also contain activities or things you have already purchased or that were given to you. So say you were gifted a massage, pottery class, or a day on the golf course for your birthday last month. Well, put 'em on your list so you can use them when you really feel like tucking into something good. And there's nothing too simple or too silly to make it on the list. I've seen participants note everything from "Going to CrossFit" and "Making and sipping a latte" to "Masturbating" (not kidding, but also, respect) and "Staring into space" (a surprisingly common one among busy parents), to more applied hobbies like crocheting, drawing, writing, or playing an instrument or game.

I find that many of my Love List activities not only make me feel awesome once I get going with them, but they also fulfill some of the other benefits I hoped to cultivate during the Challenge that I'd envisioned in Day 1's exercise. So instead of buying that tempting, shoddily made product I saw an influencer hawking on Instagram, I'd go on a catch-up walk with a friend, and presto! I've 1) deflected my shopping impulse, 2) spent meaningful time nurturing a relationship, 3) engaged in joyful movement, and 4) talked through and received trusted insight for some life dilemmas. Now picture me marketing this like an '80s infomercial: *A limited-time walk with a friend! Costs nothing! FREE therapy! Get the blood pumping! Spend quality time! Share some laughs! Feel damn good! Fresh air and sunshine! FREE!* If only all activities that didn't involve buying crap were marketed so enticingly to us with such honesty.

When I was pressed for time and just needed a quick fix, I'd clean out my wallet or fire off a short gratitude list, and boom! Small steps toward a more contented and organized life. For real, these activities may seem itsy-bitsy, but both have been proven to lift your spirits.[4] Even taking a five-minute stroll outside can dramatically alter your mood and headspace.[5] When you're crafting your list, you might find that these are the activities that give life meaning—the free, simple, sumptuous things we often forget are at our disposal pretty much whenever, as long as we can carve out the time. And for that reason, the Love List also serves a bit like a gratitude list, reminding you of how many fulfilling, life-affirming, mood-changing happenings are already at your fingertips. Maybe in the hustle and bustle of a busy workweek, you forgot how freaking fun it is to blast an upbeat song and have a dance break with your kids (or just yourself)? Or perhaps the "Ugh, I have to make dinner" narrative made you lose sight of what a joy and privilege it can be to have the time and resources to make a wholesome, delicious meal for yourself and others? Did you forget how transformative a humble hug can be, how therapeutic it is to cuddle your old-man cat, or how fabulous it can feel to set your bare feet on the grass? Like, seriously, just peep the abundance of joy-giving choices in the example list below. How freaking lucky are we?

You'll want a wide variety of good-vibe activities to fit the bill depending upon how you're feeling in your moment of need, so make this list comprehensive, with plenty of low-lift, quick activities, as well as the more involved ones. And as a veteran Love Lister, I have some formatting recommendations that will make your list extra effective:

1. As with your Day 1 Visualization, use first person (*I*, *me*, *my*, and *mine*) when writing out your Love List to further bolster investment and motivation.

2. Keep your Love List positive. The items should focus on what you *can* do versus what you can't. While this Challenge does have a "don't buy new stuff" element, your Love List is about what you *can* do rather than what's supposedly prohibited. And for the love of all that's holy, don't be mean to yourself in your list. "Go to the gym, you lazy bum" isn't going to make you feel stoked when you're just trying to avert a consumerist impulse. So make sure you're addressing yourself kindly and in a way that will make you feel, ya know, good, because that's kind of the whole point of this exercise.

3. To enhance ease of access, format your list with one column dedicated to "Quick Hits" and another for the "Longer & Luxe" activities. And if these titles aren't your thing, feel free to change them to whatever works for you (and if they're especially clever, tell me about them!).

4. Alphabetize each column so you can easily find an activity that's on the tip of your tongue. If you'd prefer to number listings or rank them based on your favorites, get wild with it. It's your list, and it needs to work for you.

And of course, if you're fresh out of ideas, I've got you. Here are a few items that have recurred on participants' lists, as well as some novel standouts I knew had to be included (if you add "Do thirty sit-ups" to your list, well, you're my hero):

Quick Hits	Longer & Luxe
Clean a small space or item, like my wallet or my car's center console	Call [insert name of loved one / funniest, wisest friend] for a chat
Create one new outfit from clothes I already have (see Day 18 for more guidance on this)	Crochet, knit, paint, draw, make music, some creative hands-on hobby
Cuddle [insert name of pet]	Curl up with a good book, or savor an episode of a favorite TV show
Do thirty sit-ups (no joke, some probably flat-stomached genius/ masochist had this on their list)	Go work out (use my awesome gym membership!), or get outside for a walk, jog, swim, bike ride, etc.
Do a ten-minute meditation or engage in prayer	Journal or freewrite
Get the blood pumping by doing jumping jacks for one minute	Learn something new on YouTube or from a book
Go down to the fancy ice cream parlor and grab a scoop	Make a meal from scratch
Hug my kids / partner / friends / self	Sexy time (with self or others)
Make a playlist of my favorite music	Take a bath or everything shower with all the self-care goodies
Stretch	Take a long drive, preferably with good music blasting
Take a dance break	Take a nap

Quick Hits	Longer & Luxe
Write down five things I'm grateful for	Tend to my garden / flowers / plants
Write someone a quick, uplifting text, voice note, letter, email, or postcard	Volunteer or do something good for others

Action Item 1: Grab a pen and pencil, your Notes app, or whatever else you like to make lists with and in, and create your Love List. Consider it your lifeboat whenever you're feeling yourself getting sucked down by the eddy of overconsumption.

Action Item 2: Throughout the Challenge and beyond, add to your Love List whenever a new activity sparks joy. You can also do a continual ranking of your favorite activities, or add notes for how an activity came in clutch when you really needed it.

Day 3: Note Your Needs

I know it sounds wildly unfair, but life doesn't stop simply because you've tasked yourself with doing this Challenge. Like all humans, you're going to need to procure some things throughout the thirty days. And foreseeing and planning for those in advance via what I call a Need Note (there's that alliteration again) is an important part of setting yourself up for success. For instance, gifting occasions like weddings and birthdays that occur during the Challenge are going to require you to get a little creative while still maintaining that thoughtful vibe gift-givers always strive for. Back-to-school or equipment-intensive sports will certainly require some forethought around needs that may crop up. And if you've got out-of-the-ordinary circumstances like moving, a big trip, welcoming a new family member, starting a new job—you catch my drift—these might necessitate last-minute or extraordinary items (hello, extension cords and puppy pads) that can be made easier by planning ahead. Everything you think you'll need within the next thirty days (with the exception of the categories listed on page 28–29), I want you to write down in your Need Note. Then, next to each item, I want you to put a symbol (or many if you feel there are a few avenues for procurement) from the SUPER System to indicate the ways you might be able to acquire said item. As a refresher:

S	Shopping secondhand (thrifting, consignment, online resale)
U	Using, upcycling, or reimagining stuff you already have
P	Paying nothing (using store credit or memberships you already have, items you get for free via free groups, finding them, like in the alley or on a stoop, or from your networks)
E	Experience, donation, and monetary, non-thing gifts (used mostly for gifts for others)
R	Renting, borrowing, or sharing

Let's use the system to code a few sample scenarios:

Scenario 1: Your kiddo will be entering Algebra II next month and needs a graphing calculator. You add the item to your Need Note and determine that you can get one by: borrowing from a neighbor or friend whose kid no longer needs the calculator (R), buying the item secondhand (S) or by putting out an ISO ("in search of") in your local Buy Nothing or free groups to see if anyone has one they're willing to give you (P).

Scenario 2: Your best bud from high school is getting married and you know a wedding gift is in your future. If you know specifically what you want to get the happy couple, you can look for that item in new-with-tags condition secondhand (S) or buy the item with a gift card or store credit balance you already have (P), or you can opt for non-thing gifts (E) like an experience, a donation to their favorite charity, or straight-up cash.

Scenario 3: Despite wearing sweatpants and a tattered sports bra during most of your home time, you've been invited to a fancy gala for work. You obviously want to look hot as shit, but you're doing No New Things, so how do you make the glow-up happen? You put a gown, heels, and a clutch (or a tux, patent shoes, and a cravat, if that's more your vibe) in your Need Note. You can acquire these items by asking your friends if you can shop their closets or renting from one of those companies that has jaw-dropping special-occasion ensembles (R), or you could peruse secondhand marketplaces like ThredUp, Poshmark, or your local consignment or thrift stores for duds that might fit the bill (S). If those avenues don't bear fruit, you can always get some elevated items in your closet tailored and create a stunning ensemble from those (U). Either way, you're gonna look foxy as heck.

Scenario 4: You're holding a little dinner party to celebrate, well, being alive and learning how to cook a few meals. That said, you don't have a ton of plates, champagne flutes, flatware, and serving dishes for all your intended guests because you live in a three-hundred-square-foot studio apartment. And you're not gonna buy a bunch of plastic disposable stuff because 1) the planet and 2) you're throwing a civilized, real-forks-clinking-against-real-plates kind of shindig. So you add those items to your Need Note and determine that you can shop secondhand either at your local thrift (a great place to find these items, in my experience) or via a marketplace (if you're looking for a specific brand) (S), put out an ISO in your free groups to see if anyone is giving what you need away (P), ask friends and neighbors if they have these items you can borrow, instruct your attendees to bring their own utensils, cup, and a serving dish (scoff all you like, but I've been to absolute ragers that made this request and nobody cared or thought less of the host for it), or if you're very swanky, you can rent these from a local party supplier (R). Renting or borrowing will probably be your preferred methods because you really don't want to find storage for five serving dishes in the already packed area your landlord has the nerve to call a kitchen. In the end, you may decide that while you needed to acquire enough plates and flatware, your guests will be totally chill swilling booze from one of your existing mason jars, so you upcycle those (U). Sounds like a bitchin' No New Things party no matter how you go about getting what you need.

The Need Note is a living document, so add to it throughout the Challenge as needs crop up. Moreover, the Need Note is like blending spinach into your kids' pancakes—a sneakily awesome exercise that gently nudges your brain to create the neural pathways that make thinking circularity first a more automatic process. As you add to your note and code alternative ways to get said needs met, that simple categorization will have you thinking differently from the business-as-usual muscle memory of adding new stuff to your cart and hitting Buy. And that in and of itself is a radical, life-changing gesture you can and should feel damn good about. If you want to get an even more detailed idea of how this might look, here's my Need Note from a recent monthlong Challenge:

Item	S	U	P	E	R	Notes
Trekking Poles			x		x	Will post ISO in Buy Nothing first. Can also rent on-site.
Gift Mom				x		Treating her to a ThredUp gift card.
Baby Shower Gift	x			x		Giving gift card to local kids' store, along with some secondhand baby books.
Rain Jacket for Hiking	x				x	Going to ask some friends if they have one I can borrow; otherwise, will look for preferred brands secondhand.

Item	S	U	P	E	R	Notes
Brown-black Mascara	x					Will look for it NWT on Poshmark or Mercari.
Base Layers for Hiking	x	x				I have a few shirts I can tweak and upcycle to fit the bill. Will also look on Poshmark for specific brands secondhand.
Muffin Tin			x		x	Will post ISO on Buy Nothing, but will also ask my network if I can borrow since I only need for a few days.
Toaster	x					Will look on FB Marketplace.
Containers for storing batch cooking		x				Going to upcycle some glass jars and plastic tubs from ingredients I'm about to finish.
Birthday Gift for MR	x					Already found a dope vintage MCM glass trinket tray + vintage vase with plant cuttings.
Frame for Giclée Print	x		x			Will post ISO in Buy Nothing first. Will look at thrift store.
Laundry Detergent		x				Will use shampoo or liquid soap I have but am not using.
Housewarming Gift for DE	x			x		Will either find an item from her home wish list NWT secondhand or will give her a gift card for her fave restaurant.
Cat Carrier	x		x			Will put ISO on Buy Nothing. Will buy on Poshmark/Mercari/FB Marketplace as an alt.
Polished outfits for TV segments	x	x			x	Doing one-month trial of clothing rental service to mix it up. Also borrowing some items from friends and shopping my closet. Open to finding some pieces secondhand too.

And before you go thinking that I'm some magical ascetic who needs very little in life, please bear in mind that I've been doing this for a long time, over a decade, so my Need Note might be shorter than yours. And that's completely okay. Some participants have notes that are pages and pages, while others only contain a few entries. And both scenarios, or anywhere in between, are totally fine. The Need Note is intended to 1) help you plan for the thirty days, and 2) reengineer your thinking and habits around acquiring items, so creating it in the first place, no matter the length, is a main driver of positive development.

Action Item 1: Using whatever medium appeals to you that allows for easy access, create your Need Note by writing down every item you think you will need to acquire during the Challenge.

Action Item 2: Code each item in your Need Note using the SUPER System. You can add just one or many letters to each item to indicate how you plan to get that need fulfilled. Add notes to lend further detail to your procurement method.

Action Item 3: The Need Note is a living document, so feel free to add needs that crop up as you move through the Challenge.

Action Item 4: You might find gift cards (a little foreshadowing of Days 6 and 7), store credit, or other Challenge-appropriate goodies during the thirty days. Be sure to add the appropriate coding and note for those, should they help you fulfill a listed need.

Day 4: Connect with Community

Lone wolves look cool howling at the moon on novelty T-shirts, but being one is probably not going to make doing No New Things very easy . . . or very fun. You see, along this bumpy road to becoming an overconsuming society, we've also become more isolated. Gone are the days when borrowing a cup of sugar from the neighbors was the norm. Heck, even calling someone on the actual phone is starting to be considered strange these days. And while societal expectations may be different, our human need for trusted and meaningful connections remains unchanged. Community is a key ingredient in the No New Things way of life, as well as to one's general health and well-being.[1]

A post-pandemic survey conducted by health care giant Cigna found that 58 percent of Americans report feeling consistently lonely. And when we look at these rates across different demographics and situations, the results tell a very sobering story. For instance, young adults are twice as likely to feel isolated as seniors, which is unexpected because the sixty-six-years-of-age-and-over crowd are typically the ones to report the highest instances of disconnection in these types of studies. Income also has a bearing on our feelings around connection, with those making less than $50,000 per year or receiving government assistance reporting significantly higher levels of isolation than their wealthier counterparts.[2] And some of this makes sense with everything we've covered so far, right? Despite having more mediums for virtual, on-demand "connection" than ever before, as we moved toward capitalism and consuming, society has become increasingly more focused on the individual, leaving collective values of community care in the dust. And that isn't just a sad reality but one that also robs folks of well-being. Strong community connections directly correlate to lower rates of anxiety and depression, and 50 percent increased longevity—a.k.a. nurturing strong social ties can actually help us live longer, better lives.[3]

The good news is that low-consumerism communities already exist, and they're waiting for you to join up and share your light. And today, you're going to put the wheels in motion to get connected to those. Now, I can't guarantee that No New Things will automatically win you friends, but by connecting with groups that center values of sharing, borrowing, and taking care of the planet and one another, you'll inevitably encounter some kindred spirits, or at the very least feel fortified by interactions that are aligned with the principles of No New Things.

Moreover, you're also going to cultivate support within your existing networks so you can thrive during the Challenge. I mean, it's probably a good idea for you to give those with whom you share a home a heads-up that you're not gonna be buying new stuff for a month—we don't want to leave a trail of pissed-off spouses and kids in our wake. But beyond just informing them, perhaps you can inspire them to join you?

Some seriously powerful results have emerged from couples, families, friends, and affinity groups and clubs joining forces to do No New Things. A testimonial that stands out was from a young couple who, together, embarked on the Challenge and after three months had saved money and organized their lives enough to begin the process to adopt a child, something they'd desperately wanted but had been putting off for years. And what's more, having an accountability buddy can increase your likelihood of Challenge completion by 65 percent (up that to a whopping 95 percent if y'all have regular check-ins).[4] Virtual and IRL teammates can also boost your focus, calmness, and productivity during the thirty days.[5] So, on this day, you have two related action items that will help you stoke community in two different but vital ways:

Action Item 1: Get connected with circular and sharing communities in your area that will enable you to more seamlessly borrow, acquire, and responsibly off-load stuff while also building like-minded connections. These are the online and IRL groups and apps that will be vital resources on your No New Things journey, so spend some time enrolling and learning about how they work. While resources vary widely depending upon where you live, here's a handy checklist of the types of groups (and some personal favorites I use all the dang time) as they correlate with the SUPER System to consider joining during your No New Things adventure, should they be available to you:

S   Shopping secondhand

Thrifting, consignment, online resale

For clothes, accessories, and smaller home goods and décor:

- IRL: Consignment stores, thrift stores, charity shops, flea markets, and garage and estate sales
- Online: Poshmark, Mercari, the RealReal, Vinted, Vestiaire Collective, Depop, ThredUp, Geartrade (outdoor gear), Gem (allows you to search multiple platforms at once)

For furniture, appliances, home goods and décor, and other larger items:

- IRL: Thrift stores, charity shops, antique stores, flea markets, and garage and estate sales
- Online: Facebook Marketplace, OfferUp, Chairish, Kaiyo, and AptDeco (furniture), Back Market and Decluttr (tech), ThriftBooks (books)

U   Using, upcycling, or reimagining stuff you already have

- Local sustainability groups, neighborhood committees, Facebook affinity groups, and Meetups that encourage or have activities around creative upcycling and reuse
- Upcycling resources like YouTube and IG channels and influencers, blogs, and books that offer inspiration and tutorials

P   Paying nothing

Using store credit or memberships you already have, items you get for free via free groups, finding them, like in the alley or on a stoop, or from your networks

These are the groups whereby you can post looking for items for free, responsibly rehome items you no longer use, or just get solidarity and education from like-minded folks:

- A No New Things Challenge group in your area (if you don't have one, you can always start one)
- Areas of your neighborhood (alleys, stoops) where you know people put stuff out and social media accounts that alert to stooping finds
- Buy Nothing Groups (via Facebook, as well as their proprietary app) for your neighborhood or city. If you don't have one, you can always start one in your area per the Buy Nothing Project guidelines
- Free Box and Back-to-School Supplies share groups on Facebook
- Freecycle
- Groups and influencers who focus on financial fitness, frugal living, deinfluencing, and low- and no-buy challenges
- Little Free Library boxes in your area
- Meetup groups for folks interested in minimalism, organizing, and low-consumerist lifestyles
- Nextdoor free sections, as well as local neighborhood pages

E   Experience, donation, and monetary, non-thing gifts

Used mostly for gifts for others

Connect with groups that promote experiences over things
and provide opportunities for volunteerism, charity, and
intentional gifting.

R   Renting,borrowing, or sharing

These are places, apps, and sites by which you can rent or
borrow items you might need during the thirty days:

- Businesses that rent project- and occasion-related items
  and tools, like Home Depot
- Clothing rental companies like Rent the Runway, Nuuly,
  Haverdash, ModLux, Stitch Fix, Gwynnie Bee
- Clothing swaps near you (or plan yourself!)
- Furniture rental companies
- Stuff and tool libraries in your area
- Your local public libraries (and get to know the other
  resources you can rent via traditional public libraries
  because there are many)

Action Item 2: Tell your people—your family, your friends, your
coworkers—that you're doing the Challenge and entreat them to
join you by sharing your *whys* with them. Perhaps your partner will
want to participate if they understand how you'll fast-track your
savings goals in the thirty days, which gets you that much closer
to your dream vacation? Or your kids may want to get on board
if they understand that less crap (they usually end up forgetting
about anyway) will mean more money and time to go do fun
things, like hitting up the amusement park or ganging up on each
other at laser tag. And if your beloveds cannot be swayed, don't
fret. You can certainly succeed at doing No New Things without

the participation of members of your household; it's just easier if you have accountability buddies or, at the very least, folks who are aware of and support your goals over the next thirty days. So have the conversations and lay the foundations for your closest folks to either join forces with or support you as you embark on this exciting journey.

Day 5: Track Your Triggers

The word *triggered* has gotten a bad rap of late, often being misused to communicate that someone is too sensitive or fragile. But understanding what triggers us, however we're feeling, is perhaps one of the most important and enlightening parts of this Challenge and of dismantling our overconsumption compulsions. As you've hopefully gathered by now, marketing pulls a variety of persuasive emotional levers to make us buy. Uncovering how you feel when you've seen certain advertising or when you are compelled to shop are paramount to you outwitting coerced consumerism. Tracking your triggers creates intentional friction and promotes a pause in the purchasing process, which really pisses retailers off. It might not feel like it when your heart is yearning for that new phone or mattress, but our desires are extremely transitory. While research is scanty on urges as they relate to shopping, studies on similar phenomena like food cravings show that the intense longing for something usually only lasts for about three to five minutes.[1] Isn't it staggering to think that we can blow hundreds of dollars, that likely took us hours or even days to earn, on random stuff in a matter of only a few fleeting minutes? Moreover, studies show that 70 percent of items are returned because someone "changed their mind,"[2] which hits home how not well thought out our buying behaviors are.

Tracking your triggers gives you something to do during those critical minutes and creates the space you need to determine if an item is a mere want, influenced by marketing, or a legitimate need. If it's the former, you can keep it moving, now armed with the conditions that tripped the impulse to buy. In the rare case that you determine that item is a legitimate need, put it in your Need Note and code accordingly, or wait to buy it new after the thirty days. Abandoned cart data suggests that if we can just bust through the initial urge, 70 percent of us will resist buying the item altogether.[3] And remember when I told you that marketers track all sorts of elements of our lives like time of day, temperature, and even the amount of sunshine your area gets? Well, tracking your feelings helps to turn this low-level surveillance on its head.

Action Item 1: So, when I say Track Your Triggers, I mean that I want you to do just that. Be it in a notebook, spreadsheet, or your phone's Notes app, create an easy-to-access sheet whereby you document the following whenever the urge strikes:

1. *The item:* This one is kinda important. What is the thing you're lusting after in this moment? Is it new (N) or secondhand (S)? Get as descriptive or not as you like. Some folks even include photos of and links to the item so they remember (and maybe laugh about) it later.

2. *Where and how you encountered the item:* Ah, the place where you first laid eyes on that must-have kitchen appliance or hair-growth supplement. Who can forget? Well, don't forget—track it! Were you in a brick-and-mortar store or perusing online? Was someone wearing it on the train, or did you see it in an advertisement? Again, where and how you see an ad is a marketer's cosmic wet dream—they know you're more likely to buy something on Instagram or TikTok, for instance, than from a neighborhood flyer. For me and for most of my Challenge participants, our triggers are often stoked by social media or when receiving a sale email or text. This makes sense because social media platforms

are basically infomercials, so even when you think you're just watching someone do a kooky reel, they're low-key selling you on the trappings of their look, environment, and activities.

3. *Time of urge:* This is important because you're not likely to be wanting to hit the Add to Cart button when you're engrossed in a book, a yoga class, or a deep chat with a friend. You are, if you're anything like me, however, very likely when you're lying in bed scrolling on social media instead of going to sleep. Timing matters more than you know. Believe me, marketers know that *when* you see something is a key deciding factor in whether or not you'll buy it. And I promise within one week of tracking, you'll see incredible intersections of time of day and your buying impulses.

4. *How you are feeling in that moment:* This can be anything and everything. Perhaps you're feeling stressed, tired, or mad because your date from the other night hasn't texted back or your kid did something boneheaded. Or maybe you're kinda hangry and uncomfortable because your boxers are cutting into your bum. *Be specific.* You'll be surprised how seemingly simple things trigger a shopping response and the incredible patterns that emerge. When I look back at my entries in my Notes app, I see that often when I felt the strong urge to buy something random, I was 1) bored, 2) procrastinating, 3) sad or feeling not good enough, and 4) chilly. Yes, I wanted to buy things because I was chilly, guys. Which actually makes sense because there's a reason why malls, grocery stores, and movie theaters are cold as hell—it's scientifically proven that we're more likely to make emotions-based, as opposed to rational, purchasing decisions when we're uncomfortably cold.[4]

5. *Cost of item:* You'd be surprised how much these momentary urges add up—a $32 shirt here, an $8 vegetable peeler there. After just *one month* of No New Things and tracking her triggers, participant Ally tallied that she'd saved a whopping $36,581 just from items she wanted to buy, tracked, and didn't. And yeah, I consider that actual savings because she literally saved herself from spending that amount. It's worth noting that these were relatively small items, as well—it's not like she added a moped or hot tub to her tracker. In fact, there were 258 separate items just

for a single month. That's a lot of impulses thwarted and money saved, and for those of us who are especially empirical and like tangible evidence of progress, the dollars give you that eye-opening evidence.

Some folks choose to get very detailed with this and include screenshots of the ads and photos of the items. If you want to do that, by all means, proceed—you are your own data-collection lab. Others have referred to this as their shopping "parking lot," or a place where they chronicle what they want in case they wish to revisit later and actually purchase. At first, I thought this was counterintuitive to the Challenge, but then I realized it's a great psychological hack. If you treat this list as one of possibility, rather than prohibition, you may 1) more enthusiastically engage with this step, and 2) actually want the items less, as tends to happen when something forbidden becomes permitted.

This doesn't need to be onerous, and you don't have to make it weird and be glued to your phone tracking every impulse. Doing this for even a day can give you incredible insight into how marketing deftly strokes and stokes your shopping psyche. When you've found patterns—for instance, like the link between stress or feelings of low self-worth and the urge to shop—you can refer to your Love List for accessible things you can do right now to turn the tide on your feelings and actually engage with something free and satisfying that doesn't involve consuming more stuff. Because, as we've discussed many times already, stuff doesn't fix, or even offer meaningful reprieve from, these feelings.

In the spirit of transparency, here's a day of tracked triggers from a recent Challenge I did, and it's . . . embarrassing? And yes, I am constantly searching for the perfect vintage Bobby Brown shirt (I'm a size small, by the way). A few caveats here: I've been doing this Challenge off and on since 2013, so my mindset on and, in turn, my attitude toward how I shop and shopping in general has changed dramatically. I also don't receive many advertisements because I've done all the rigorous unsub, mute, unfollow stuff that you'll be tackling in the coming days. I also don't watch much television, and the little I do usually doesn't have commercials. All this is to say, I am not exposed to nearly as many ads on a daily basis as the average American, and the quantity of listings in my tracker probably reflects that. So please don't compare and despair as you get voyeuristic into my spending psyche, but also, please do let me know if you have a Don Henley shirt you want to get rid of.

What	N/S?	Where	When	Feels	$
Eames bentwood coffee table	S	Instagram, then FB Marketplace	7:10am	Upon waking, scrolled my phone and saw a similar table on a design IG. For some reason felt like I needed a coffee table RIGHT NOW, was def procrastinating on working out and getting after the day.	$500.00
Amazon Swirly Shirt	N	YouTube video; Amazon	1:15pm	Procrastinating, feeling stressed and kinda miffed I haven't gotten a reply to an important email yet.	$35.00
Dior transfer-proof red lipstick	N	IG Reel	2:04pm	Feeling fugly, like I need newness.	$49.00
4 Old Navy sweaters and sweater vests	N	Google sidebar ad about a sale	2:12pm	Def procrastinating on work, chilly because it's freezing outside and my heater is struggling.	$112.32

What	N/S?	Where	When	Feels	$
G.H. Bass Lug-Soled Fisherman Mary Janes	S	Poshmark	2:20pm	Feeling tired and procrastinating.	$165.00
Metal lemon juicer	N	Amazon	2:40pm	My old one broke, and now I'm just scrolling to scroll because I don't want to unload the dishwasher.	$15.00
Vintage Bobby Brown shirt	S	Depop	11:02pm	Tired, felt unproductive today, bloated, kinda mopey.	$315.00
Vintage Don Henley Shirt	S	Depop, Poshmark	11:15pm	Went down a vintage shirt rabbit hole after the Bobby one, and I started actively searching for ones I want. Don was also one of my first childhood crushes, which I know is weird.	$75.00
Vintage "Don't Mess with Texas" shirt	S	Depop, Mercari	11:20pm	Rabbit hole search, procrastinating going to bed, maybe feeling anxious about stuff I need to do tomorrow?	$89.00
YSL Libre perfume	N	TikTok	1:55am	Couldn't sleep. Found fragrance TikTok and now I'm hooked.	$95.00
DAILY TOTAL					**$1,450.32**

That's just a single day and $1,450.32 I avoided spending that I really, really wanted to, at least in those ephemeral moments. And looking back on it, while I absolutely would love the vintage shirts and probably the Eames coffee table, the rest barely stirs me. All that said, though, I am a browser at heart. Like, I can spend a good three hours in a Marshalls or Walgreens and not buy a single thing. I just love browsing because it's an exercise in imagination for me. In the rare moments I'm in a store, I'll be like, "What if I could only outfit my entire life here?" and then I let my mind go off. Is that a totally implausible scenario? Of course. But it does make me someone you'll absolutely want to join forces with should you find yourself locked in a Walmart during a zombie apocalypse. Doing the Challenge routinely over the years has shown me how browsing, especially online, even though it rarely results in a purchase, is a huge time suck for me. See? Even I, city planner for No New Things Town, have habits I uncover during the Challenge that I'd like to amend. I evolve with every Challenge I do, which I hope serves as a good reminder that No New Things isn't about being perfect; it's about better understanding yourself and using that data to make healthier-for-you (and arguably, for the planet and others) choices.

And if you're finding you're hitting the tracker to log wants often, well, that's totally normal. Instead of beating yourself up about it, try to look at this activity as morally neutral—it's all data. There's a saying that "what gets tracked gets changed," and I like to remind myself that this is just a way of documentation so you can understand and get a handle on a much bigger phenomenon. Just imagine what this will look like in two weeks, or at the end of thirty days? Stay encouraged and be proud of how far you've already come in just five little days.

Day 6: Wrangle Returns

Returns are a tricky topic. For one, people generally hate making them (I can relate), and that's because retailers don't love giving you back your money, so they make the process intentionally difficult. Returns are also notoriously terrible for the environment, with one logistics firm estimating that the carbon dioxide cost of returns in the US is equivalent to the output of three million cars.[1] Yeah, big yikes. I'll get a bit more into both of these data points, but just know that we're entering into today's action items well aware of these truths, and thus, we're going to be judicious in our approach of wrangling yours.

The fact of the matter is that many of us have items that can be returned. One Challenge participant found that she had nearly $2,000 worth of unused clothing and accessories in her closet alone, tags still on and eligible for return. I don't know about you, but that's a chunk of change for which I could find a bazillion better uses. Anecdotally, we know this to be true in some measure. Perhaps a peek into your wardrobe shows what used to be my reality before I started No New Things—loads of brand-new items bought for an aspirational life, style, and physique that I hung up and then promptly forgot about. If you scroll secondhand marketplaces, you'll often find listings for brand-new items with the seller saying something along the lines of, "Didn't fit me and I missed the return window." Many of us have items that we intended to return, but for a variety of reasons, the packages are still on the kitchen counter staring us down, making us feel both stymied and like lazy sloth people who don't have their act together. While it's not that deep, languishing returns just mean more clutter in your life and less money in your wallet. So today is your lucky day because we're going to corral those items, research their attendant return policies, suck it up, and get them handled.

Before we get started, though, I want you to have a clear line of sight into the harm and waste associated with returns and, thus, why they should be treated as a last resort, as opposed to part of an intentional shopping strategy. The concept of no-questions-asked returns was pioneered by JCPenney more than a century ago, and even when word spread about the revolutionary practice, only about 2 percent of purchases were returned. This can likely be attributed to the difference in consumer attitudes and behaviors pre–World War II, when folks were more utilitarian buyers and largely only returned items if they were defective. Today, you could say we're a culture of certified returners who regard the practice as just another part of the shopping process. For instance, 70 percent of returns today are made simply because someone "changed their mind." Every year in the US, we send back 3.5 billion products, 80 percent of which are perfectly usable.[2] We return so much stuff, in fact, that "reverse logistics" is now a booming industry, with our returns totaling nearly $1 trillion each year.[3]

I get it—in our more isolated, convenience-focused world, it is incredibly tempting to order dozens of styles and sizes online, with the aim of returning the ones that don't work, instead of going to a physical store and trying them on in real life (I too shudder when I think of dressing-room lighting). But this approach hurts the heck out of the planet. When we shop in a brick-and-mortar store, we're significantly less likely to make a return, largely because, duh, we are physically there to determine if an item suits us *before* we make the purchase.[4] And that tracks because the act of shopping in person requires more logistical effort, thereby making the returns and waste associated less detrimental. The reality is that most online returns are trashed and never resold. Moreover, destroy in field (DIF)—or intentionally ruining returns, dead stock, and unsold items before trashing them—is an actual strategy luxury that name-brand merchants use to preserve their reputations. You may wonder what the heck this accomplishes aside from intentionally damaging otherwise totally usable merchandise. Well, because we ascribe status and worth to certain brands, the last thing those retailers want is to have that unreachable mystique compromised by us slobs sporting a Burberry coat or Louis Vuitton bag we found in the trash. So, many brands, even non-luxury ones, will instruct employees to cut, slash, stain, and otherwise render their returned merchandise unusable, thereby sentencing items to a lifetime in the landfill. As if these ethical and environmental impacts weren't enough, the buy-to-return approach is also a losing game of financial limbo, frustration, and wasted time for you.

I don't think I'm revolutionary in saying that returning stuff is a giant pain in the ass, and that's by design, my friends. As you can imagine, retailers are not stoked about refunding your money, especially if you're looking to have that balance go back on your credit card. Have you ever initiated a return only to have the retailer offer you way more money if you opt for store credit instead of a refund? Yeah, whenever possible, don't do that. Merchants are not high-yield savings accounts—you gain nothing by unnecessarily keeping your money with them. It's just another semi-attractive, last-ditch tactic to keep you spending money with a company forever and ever, amen.

Even commerce giant Amazon, often heralded for its smooth return process, can sometimes create unnecessary friction to deter you from opting to get your refund back on your card and out of their ecosystem. To test this theory, I took one for the team and purchased and subsequently opted to return a pair of leggings. And would you look at that? When I said I wanted the money to go back on my credit card, as opposed to lingering on an Amazon "gift card" (lol, how is this a gift when it's my money?), the return drop-off location options changed from a convenient stroll from my house to "Do I need to rent a car for this?" sites. So my options were to either keep my money with Amazon and return the leggings to a nearby location, or go on a *Lord of the Rings*–level trek across town to get $27.82 put back on my Visa? Got it. And don't even get me started on how retailers are in cahoots to tempt you to keep spending, even when you've just made a return. Like how you receive Kohl's Cash when you make Amazon returns at their store? Bro, I just got $50 back on my card, and you're trying to get me to make a purchase as I walk from the kiosk to my car? Brutal. Don't fall for these last-ditch efforts to get you to part with your money.

And then there's the general labor of finding and repacking items, researching policies and eligibility, trucking them to the store, and having to monitor your card days and even weeks after to ensure the reimbursement has actually happened (and if it hasn't, tack on extra time and frustration for contacting customer support for a resolution). The point here is there's just as much labor involved in getting rid of stuff you no longer want as there is with the items you keep. While I don't make returns very often, every single time I do, I am reminded how much I fricking loathe the process. When we make returns en masse like you're going to do today (or on another designated day if the calendar doesn't permit on this exact day), we are reminded of that inventory manager role I often cite, and how buying with the intention of returning is not a shopping strategy that serves us. The time you think you're saving by not going to the store dressing room? You're just robbing Peter to pay Paul by sinking time into making and monitoring your returns. So, yeah, you may shake your fists at the sky and holler my name with disdain today, and I'm okay with that. Because, in the end, you'll have some money back, a bit of clutter out, and most importantly, a reminder that you don't want to spend a day like this ever again if you can help it, which you can.

Action Item 1: Do a sweep of your home, car, and office, and devote some time to preparing, packing up, and actually returning your returns. Research the return policies for these items, and for those that are still eligible, map out your routes. Ensure you have all the emails, receipts, tags, and any other accompaniments you need to get a refund. And, if you need some motivation to get you from the house to the car / the train / putting your walking shoes on, tally how much money you will get back from these returns, and tee up a Love List item to enjoy once you've completed your quest. You're also definitely going to want to make yourself a good perk-up beverage and playlist to ready your spirit for the journey.

Action Item 2: For the items that can no longer be returned or are not eligible, create piles and sort by:

1. *Giving:* Your friends, family members, or people in free groups might really love that item you're not able to return. Consider bringing to clothing or item swaps, or sharing with local "stuff libraries."

2. *Gifting:* No shame here. Some items that won't work for you might make an amazing gift for someone, especially if they're new with tags. Add any applicable items to your Need Note and code using the SUPER System accordingly.

3. *Reselling:* Either at brick-and-mortar stores or online. Refer to Day 13 for guidance on where and how to sell secondhand like a magical thrift wizard.

Action Item 3: If any returns allow you to receive your refund on your original form of payment, do that. In some instances, you may only be allowed to receive store credit or a gift card, and for those, log the retailer and amount in your Love List for a future pick-me-up or for fulfilling items on your Need Note.

Action Item 4: Make a mental note of how much time you devoted to today's action items and how it all felt. Let today serve as a reminder that returning stuff absolutely sucks whenever you're feeling the urge to splurge. And vow to, whenever possible, shop more intentionally by doing so in person, rather than buying hoards online with the intention of returning most of the haul.

Day 7: Gather Gift Cards

What if, as you flipped to this page, a check written out to you for $187 suddenly appeared? Well, cover me with Mylar balloons and call me Ed McMahon from those 1980s sweepstakes commercials because that's the average amount that individual Americans are estimated to have in unused gift cards and store credit just kicking around their homes and in their inboxes. That's not chump change, people—those little $5 and $20 balances add up. And it goes without saying that retailers would love to keep that money suspended in limbo in their favor forever, to the collective tune of $23 billion a year.[1] But the joke's on them, because if you're among the 47 percent of people believed to have lingering store credit, gift cards, or vouchers, today's that day that you go on an Indiana Jones–esque expedition to find them and determine how much they're worth.[2] So ready your junk drawers, wallets, and glove compartments, because you're going hunting for found money, honey. And once you've unearthed it, no matter how puny or astronomical, you're going to get organized so you remember to use that dough once and for all.

Action Item 1: Search your email inbox, home, car, purses, wallets, backpacks, and drawers for virtual and physical gift cards, as well as store credit you might have.

Action Item 2: Organize your cards and credits by either 1) creating a folder for or printing out the virtual ones, and 2) checking the balances (instructions for doing this are usually on the back of physical cards and in the email accompanying e-cards). To make everything easier to remember, I use a Sharpie to write balances on the backs of physical cards.

Action Item 3: For cards that are to places you know you'll never go (sorry, Bass Pro Shops three hours from my house), you can post in your local free group or give to someone in your network.

Action Item 4: Add the gift cards and store credits in your Love List so you can use them whenever the mood strikes.

Action Item 5: Update your Need Note coding by adding *P* (with the specific amount you have to spend and where) for any items you might be able to procure with your newfound gift cards or credit.

Week 1 Reflection

I've got some encouraging news: You, my friend, have completed SEVEN WHOLE DAYS of No New Things so far, and that's . . . pretty epic. You've also done A LOT in those seven days. So how do you feel? Have you begun to see or experience some of the tangible benefits that other participants have reported during the Challenge? Let's unpack your experience by using the following prompts:

Prompts	Your Answers
How did the week feel for you overall? Did it go smoothly? Why or why not?	
Were there days or action items that were difficult for you? Which ones and why?	
Were there days or action items that felt amazing for you? Which ones and why?	

Prompts	Your Answers
Did you glean any insights or realizations about your relationship to shopping or stuff that you hadn't realized before? If so, what?	
What are you most looking forward to about next week?	
Tally your Trigger Tracker for the week. How much did you save?	

Did the tally of your tracked triggers make your jaw drop? Did you discover satisfying alternative activities to shopping via your Love List? No matter how successfully you feel you tackled this week, I think you deserve a little treat, so pick something from your Love List to do in celebration of your first official week of loosening yourself from the yoke of coerced consumerism.

Week 2: Your Habits

Now that you've become familiar with the Challenge foundations, this week focuses on two areas that are key to No New Things. Over the first four days, you're going to take steps to remove the temptations and conveniences that make it all too easy to answer shopping's siren song, like deleting automatic payment information from websites and unsubscribing from merchant promotions. These action items are like noise-canceling headphones, blocking out the marketing messages that saturate your life and sabotage your efforts to kick overconsumption to the curb. And with those hushed, not only is it much easier to resist buying new things, but you also get to enjoy some peace and freed-up time.

The last three days of the week are dedicated to getting you more comfortable with and learning tips related to upcycling, shopping and selling secondhand, and an eco-friendly rehoming practice I call *ethical off-loading*. These three skill sets are directly related to the SUPER System and are vital to how you'll acquire and declutter items, and even make and save some extra money, during the Challenge. So if you're new to shopping secondhand or you're stumped as to how to repurpose something, this is the week you get more confident in those practices.

As with Week 1, these action items are not just one-and-done. Each day's action is technically a habit you're trying to form. For instance, you won't just unsubscribe from merchant emails or text messages one time; you'll do this every time one creeps in your inbox. Your social media channels will require a little pruning every now and then to ensure the content you're consuming is aligned with your goals. And of course, you're not going to hit up a thrift store for one isolated occasion and then never again. The intention is that this week's actions eventually become regular practices that will support your less-consumerist life. You can concurrently do any of these, and likely will, with other action items, at any point during the thirty days. So get ready to mute relentless marketing and crank the volume on money- and planet-saving practices that will serve you long after the thirty days, because it's go time.

Day 8: Silence Spending

It felt like we'd been climbing uphill for about six hours straight. A check of my watch in between huffing and puffing confirmed that, yep, it felt like that because we actually had been. Cool, cool, cool. It was Day 7 of trekking to Annapurna Base Camp in Nepal, the extraordinary weeks-long journey that's as stunning as it is grueling, and we were in the home stretch. Despite unknowingly contracting a gnarly case of walking pneumonia (hence the tissues shoved up my nose) and the freezing hail pelting my skin like thousands of tiny needles, I was in excellent spirits. I knew that once my group reached base camp, I'd be awash in that golden feeling of accomplishment and forget all about the blood I coughed up that morning or the fact that I hadn't showered in a week.

When we'd made it over the final jagged pass, Annapurna, arguably the world's most dangerous mountain, laid out before us in all her mind-boggling scale and glory, I immediately began to cry. Granted, I'm a weeper, but holy crap, we'd made it! I'd done it—I went from pack-a-day smoker to someone who just trekked seventy miles up to fourteen thousand feet! Holy shit, was I proud. Interested in logging this moment for posterity, I went to stop the hiking timer on my watch, only to be distracted by—what's that? No. NO. Seeing it had me in disbelief. *What the heck?* I thought, *I'm high in the Himalayas.* But sure enough, there it was. During a trip when I barely had enough reception to let my loved ones know I was alive, I received an emoji-laden push notification from Walmart about their Black Friday sale. "Well, this is going in the book," I muttered to myself with a laugh, because if anything illustrates how pervasive marketing is, it's that a promo notification found me in one of the highest, remotest parts of the world, distracting me from being in the moment of one of the greatest physical accomplishments of my life.

The novelty of a mountain trek aside, we are bombarded by marketing in the form of emails; texts; push notifications; sponsored social media content; television, radio, and podcast ad breaks; and old-school signage and flyers nearly every minute of the day. Promotion is so ubiquitously embedded in the fabric of our experience that we actually have to *pay* to remove advertisements from entertainment. And while some of this exposure is out of our control (you can't help what billboards you see when you're driving along the highway or what ads are in the magazines you read, for instance), a lot of these interactions happen on a digital scale because, at some point, knowingly or unknowingly, we opened the proverbial doors and let retailers invade our devices and our headspace with their relentless salesmanship. The good news is that those doors can be closed, and that's just what we're going to do today.

During the 2022 No New Things Challenge, I received a message from an older gentleman who remarked in semi-jest, "I think I hear from retailers more than I do my family and friends." A pang of sadness hit me when I read that. And regardless of whether or not he was joking, he's not wrong. A 2019 study found that of the 121 average daily emails participants received, 49 percent were promotional in nature.[1] That's nearly half of all the emails we get on the daily. It's no wonder we're lonely, while also wasting so much of our precious time consumed by consumerism.

And that's just email. When we take into account the growth of push notifications, texts, and influencer marketing, well, you're being smothered by someone trying to sell you things constantly. In the case of notifications and texts, 66 percent of people globally interact with retailers via billions of messages each week.[2] And push notifications, those pesky little messages that you probably don't even remember consenting to receive, are fast becoming an industry darling, because you're seven times more likely to click on them than you are an email, and once you're in, you're nearly 30 percent more likely to buy something.[3] Look, you're not Banana Republic's emergency contact, so why are you allowing them to message you at all hours of the day? ASOS is not your kid, so you really don't need to be kept apprised of the fortieth shipment of new fast fashion this year, do you? I promise that you will survive without Temu or Shein texting you some hollow sentiment about how it's Mother's Day and "you deserve the world" (of stuff).

And let's get into another rant about how social media influencers are stealth marketing, because much like Lay's potato chips, this book clearly can't have just one. I've been called "ruthless" for encouraging participants to unsubscribe from social media personalities whose shtick is hawking products—as well as those who might not seem like they are, but trust me, most are. The latter can be difficult to ferret out because not only are influencer sponsorships a huge portion of many companies' marketing budgets, but "natural integration" has become a preferred product-placement tactic. What the heck is that? you might wonder. Well, think of it like this: We've been conditioned to consume content that's dedicated entirely or in part to promoting a product or service, like the YouTube video where the internet personality says, "And that brings me to the sponsor of today's video, [fill in the blank company]." It's called out. You know the hustle is happening. Natural integration, on the other hand, is the product folded into content that doesn't feel overtly promotional. And that's how they grab you. It's the social media personality who does a "day in my life" reel that just so happens to feature her downing a trendy drinkable greens supplement or donning a viral workout ensemble while shuttling her kiddos to school. It's that ripped triathlete whose seemingly educational TikTok on macros has branded pre-workout and an uber-recognizable "it" water bottle prominently placed in the background. The products, and thus the salesmanship, are folded into what feels organic, like content created to educate you, or a voyeuristic chronicle of an otherwise ho-hum everyday occurrence. More often than not, though, this content is creating discontent. It's stirring a desire in you for—fancy that—the exact stuff you're subconsciously viewing in the background. And the approach works. In a recent survey, 23 percent of Americans recently charged upward of $1,000 on items they saw on social media.[4]

Compound this sneaky tactic with the fact that an estimated 93 percent of influencers don't properly or prominently disclose sponsorships,[5] and it can be tricky to determine who's out to sway you. A good rule of thumb here is tapping in to how *you* feel when you consume someone's content. Does your spending finger start to tingle? Do you feel less-than and like you need to buy the items they're promoting so you can be better? Let those reactions be your North Star as you pare down your follows. Look, I respect that influencing has blossomed into a bona fide career (in fact, it's a top response among Gen Alpha when asked what they want to be when they grow up[6]), but let's be real—unfollowing is an act of self-care if someone is triggering you to overconsume or go into debt, or if their content just makes you feel like shit. And while online personalities are of course people, and thus are owed the same respect as anyone else, chances are, they're not your buddies. You don't owe them any more than you owe retailers your business. So if all that makes me ruthless, well, by golly, come with me as I get the forehead tattoo.

Moreover, many of us follow retailers' social media like they're family from whom we desperately need updates. Sure, some merchants have entertaining accounts, and if you can enjoy those without feeling tempted, keep on keeping on. But the purpose of all that engaging content is to keep you locked in as a consumer by building brand affinity. So if that's not a cycle you wish to perpetuate during the Challenge and beyond, unfollow. We often forget this simple truth: followers are currency, so in turn, that means that you are powerful. And thankfully, you also have agency to do with that power what you please. If a follow isn't serving you—or worse, it's harming your well-being or threatening your goals—get the heck out of Dodge and don't look back.

I'm going to really earn that "ruthless" face tattoo by also urging you to also extend this philosophy to the social media accounts of people you know. That's right, Cousin Susan, your rage-baiting posts are on the chopping block today. If that one frenemy from high school is constantly hitting you up to buy hair care or leggings from her MLM or that old coworker's posts about his flashy cars are making you feel like crap, well, you know what I'm going to say: You owe these cats nothing. Unfollow, or go for the stealth mute if you don't want to cause a ruckus by outright unfriending. You are the gatekeeper of the content you consume, and it should never undermine the contentment you're aiming to cultivate during this Challenge and in your life.

I found that once I curated my social media to actually support my goals and how I wanted to feel, little scroll breaks became affirming and fun again, as opposed to defeating, depleting, and full of temptations. So if you've unfollowed all the stuff-pimping, duck-lipped darlings and you're wondering where to go now, I'd encourage you to refer back to the five or more words you wrote down during Day 1's Visualization. Are there words that resonate with you? Well, use them to find tags and creators who focus on those spaces. For instance, I love clothes, but I don't want to be marketed a bunch of new fast fashion, so I follow cool people who style with only secondhand finds. I ditched the body-checking diet promoters for badass humans of all ages and sizes who focus on what their bodies can do, rather than on how they look. I traded hollow salesmanship and never-have-enough celebrities for deinfluencers, productivity experts, content that inspires me, and of course, raccoon meme accounts, because we all deserve joy. Once you recalibrate your social media feeds to serve rather than sabotage you, you'll glean so much motivation to keep going with your goals, and you'll just feel way freaking better.

So today, we're going to unsubscribe, mute, block, unfollow, and any other action that's going to restore some non-promotional peace to your devices and life. And if you're like other participants, you just might be floored at and delighted by the resulting quiet.

Action Item 1: Comb your email inbox. For promotional emails that are currently in there, scroll to the bottom and find the linked Unsubscribe button (it's legally required to be included in an email, but that doesn't mean they're gonna make it easy for you to find it), or you can use your email client's tools to unsubscribe, block, or report spam. Adopt this as a practice each time you receive an email you no longer want to receive. If you can remember retailers with whom you've consented to receive promotional emails, you can go to their websites to proactively unsubscribe as well.

Action Item 2: On your devices, determine which retailers are sending you push notifications. Delete those retailer apps (this is often faster than attempting to reconfigure settings for push notifications). If you're receiving text messages from retailers, unsubscribe or block them whenever they come in.

Action Item 3: Take inventory of your streaming services, such as television, movies, videos, music, and podcasts, and explore 1) whether you use them in the first place, and 2) if you do, what options are available to you for enjoying ad-free content. Then choose the plans that make sense for your low-promotion-exposure goals.

Action Item 4: While less favored by marketers these days, physical junk mail still makes its way to us, and it's annoying at best and bad for the planet and predatory to certain people (especially the elderly) at worst. Start by visiting the Federal Trade Commission's (FTC) "How to Stop Junk Mail" guidance on removing your information from these distribution lists.[7]

Action Item 5: Curate your social media to support rather than sabotage your goals and mood. Unsubscribe from and unfollow influencers and promotional accounts that tempt you to shop or make you feel crummy. Moreover, if you're finding that certain social media platforms are just too chaotic or monetized for your liking, delete those apps so you don't access them. Extend this approach to your personal social media connections as well, and feel free to simply mute these profiles if you think someone might start drama over an outright unfollow. Once culled, follow accounts and personalities that are aligned with your interests, goals, and desired vibe.

Day 9: Block the Shop

You know those clear, badge-holding lanyards you get at conferences or for work? Yes, the ones that, for some reason, people seem to leave on display around their necks or on their belt loops when they're commuting on the subway or having after-work drinks at a bar. Like, weird flex, but okay, Ryan P. who works at Deloitte, we see you. Literally. They put your personal info on blast, so you probably wouldn't slip your credit card in there for everyone to see, would you? Right. And yet 80 percent of us have our payment information saved on retailer sites and in widgets and apps on our devices that streamline the buying process with the touch of a button.[1] This is referred to as *stored payment*, and it removes those pesky buying barriers, which is exactly what merchants want.

Allow me to put on the old-man-walking-twelve-miles-barefoot-in-the-snow hat for a minute: It used to be if you wanted to buy something, you had to truck your ass to a physical store. This meant putting on out-in-the-world clothes and ambulating in some way to get to the destination. Some days, you even had to go to an actual brick-and-mortar bank or ATM to get cash first (the horror!). And even at the dawn of e-commerce, you'd at the very least have to get up off your duff to grab your wallet, dislodge your credit card, and tap-tap-tap that long series of numbers into the keyboard to complete a purchase.

Nowadays, you can literally be naked on the toilet, TV blasting in the background, and purchase everything from a yacht to a life-size soft sculpture made in your likeness with a touch of your finger. And because you're not going through the motions of retrieving the physical payment method, this way of spending can feel almost unreal, like you're playing around with Monopoly money. That frictionless experience sends merchants to their euphoric place, because streamlining the shopping process means you're less likely to abandon your cart in those critical moments when you'd usually be deterred by getting up to grab your card.[2] Moreover, these systems are getting so sophisticated that some will automatically update your payment information if your bank issues you a new credit card, ya know, to make it easy for you. And I don't know about you, but I really don't like the idea of a retailer knowing I have a reissued Visa before, or even after, I do.

So gird your loins, because today we are intentionally restoring shopping resistance by removing your payment information from basically everywhere. Yes, this will feel a smidge uncomfortable because you're so accustomed to buying stuff instantly, but you and your finances will be better for it. And as we touched on earlier, just going to get your wallet can help you pass the three to five minutes of urge and gain the purchase-killing clarity to remember, *Wait, I live in a three-hundred-square-foot studio—I don't need a freestanding infrared sauna.*

If you're someone who's prone to shop 'til you drop, I'd urge you to take this friction restoring further by using your browser's tools or designated website blockers to make it impossible for you to access retailer sites on your devices, forever or for a certain time of day. As I confessed on Day 5 (a.k.a. Bobby Brown T-Shirt Day), while I'm not big on buying, I am a chronic leisure browser who will waste hours just perusing retailer sites. I've found site blockers to be absolutely vital to curbing and redirecting this habit. If you can't get to Nordstrom's website, you can't buy something on Nordstrom's website. Who'd have thunk?

Also allow me to lay waste to those layaway programs that may seem convenient but are designed to keep you spending well beyond your means. The popularity of "buy now, pay later" (BNPL) programs like Afterpay, Klarna, and Affirm has skyrocketed by 1,100 percent in just a few years.[3] Especially online, with 25 percent of us using them as a primary payment method.[4] Retailers are absolutely sprung for these because they're estimated to boost sales by 30 percent and ratchet up the average spend by up to 50 percent.[5] But you need to know what these actually are: they're installment loans, and just like any credit mechanism, they're not without their catches.

Back in the day, these programs used to be reserved for big purchases, the kind that would require a decent amount of up-front capital. But today, you can finance everything, from small-ticket items, like a twelve-dollar burrito bowl at Chipotle, to astronomically expensive luxury trips to Fiji. At first blush, financing appeals to us because it enables purchases we can't currently afford, often with zero interest for the first year. Also, this financing is often referred to as *phantom debt*, because these programs don't usually report to credit bureaus, which can be a positive for folks who have shaky credit. Sounds cool so far, right? Well, as with almost every scenario where human beings are seamlessly encouraged to buy shit they cannot afford, 70 percent of users say they overspend because of buy now, pay later, and 42 percent report that they've missed and had to make late payments.[6] And the addition of these financing installments to social media platforms has made it even easier for people to get themselves in major debt by buying every influencer-inspired impulse item they cannot realistically pay off.

News flash: These BNPL companies are not charities dishing out free money because they give a rip about you. Their business model literally banks on you forgetting about and making payments in perpetuity. It's death by a thousand cuts, especially for those of us with a history of destructive spending habits. Moreover, this phantom debt is a double-edged sword because it means that you're also not building good credit like you would if you paid off a credit card balance. Now, before you brand me the "Buy Now, Pay Later Hater," allow me to clarify: I'm not saying these programs are entirely bad; in fact, sometimes they can be a lifeline for folks. I'm just urging you to exercise caution and, if possible, refrain from engaging with them during the Challenge.

And if all this isn't hard-core enough for you, you can try one of my go-to moves during the lower-tech origin days of No New Things. Brace yourselves because this might seem ... intense: If I went out, I'd leave my credit cards at home. Yep, debit card too. All forms of payment. If I stayed home, I'd make them very difficult to get to by freezing them in a Tupperware of water or stashing them in a very high cabinet (I'm five foot two). I know, I told you this was gonna sound intense. *But, Ashlee, how did you survive?* Pretty happily, actually. For one, I planned according to the specific demands and activities of the day. Like, I wasn't some jerk who'd leave all my money at home when it was a friend's birthday dinner or my turn to buy the office coffee. But on regular days where I didn't have to spend to get by, I'd either have a small amount of cash with me for emergencies, or I'd have everything I needed ready to go—packed lunch, thermos of coffee, and train pass reporting for duty. Is this slightly extreme? Yes. Is it also an extremely simple way to block the shop? You bet your sweet ass it is. I know this is going to blow your mind, but if you don't have a way to pay, you can't buy shit. And if that absolutist, old-school approach appeals to you, by golly, do it. And if it sounds terrible, I'd encourage you to explore that aversion and still give it a go.

Action Item 1: Remove your automatic payment information from retailer sites and apps across your devices (computer, tablet, television, watch, phone, EVERYWHERE).

Action Item 2: Use site and pop-up blockers to make it difficult to access websites that tempt you. Delete retailer and shopping apps and widgets from your phone and other devices.

Action Item 3: Vow to not use layaway and installment programs, at least for the duration of the Challenge. This will help to strengthen the mindset that, unless something is an out-of-reach need or emergency situation that you're confident you can pay off, you will not make a habit of buying things you cannot afford right now.

Action Item 4: If you want to go especially hard, leave your payment methods at home or in a difficult-to-access place for a day or longer.

Day 10: Slash Subscriptions

"Oh, man. Sorry," Amy said as she kicked aside packages to make room for us to access the front door. There, in front of her house, was a cardboard-colored pyramid of dozens of parcels, just roasting under the hot Texas sun. For the next hour, we unpacked it all: glass bottles and tablets to make home cleaners. "Subscribe and Save" restocks of deodorant and dog food. Bougie air freshener cartridges designed to make your house smell like a luxury hotel. Two size *small* workout ensembles. "I'll have to wait awhile before I can wear these," Amy said, rolling her eyes, patting her seven-month-pregnant belly. A year's supply of razors and shaving cream. Themed subscription boxes stuffed with international snacks, magazine editor–picked cosmetics, hair care bundles, and wardrobe pieces for her husband curated by a department store.

"Ugh, it's all too much," she yelped, gesturing at the floor, now covered with boxes and mailers and Bubble Wrap. It was obvious that she was overwhelmed by the very subscriptions and memberships she thought, at one point, would make her life easier. And ain't that the irony of much of our stuff? Like any friend worth their salt, I sent her upstairs for a nap and cleaned up the carnage. When she woke up, we then spent an hour finding, going through, and canceling the sneaky subscriptions and memberships she no longer needed. When we finished, we'd cut $712 a month and a whole bunch of attendant clutter and overwhelm from her life.

So today, you're going to do just that. You may be wondering how these relate to the Challenge since many subscriptions and memberships are not technically things. Well, while they seem super convenient, these often encourage us to spend more, while also ushering unnecessary stuff into our lives. Similar to layaway programs, 42 percent of us frequently forget that we have a lot of our subscriptions in the first place,[1] and about 86 percent of them go unused.[2] And because signing up for these is so simple and forgettable, our perception of how many we have and how much they cost us is incredibly skewed. Most of us think we only spend about $62 per month on these perceived conveniences, when in reality, it's closer to $300.[3]

These services can also entice us to buy and receive more stuff than we actually want. Amazon Prime and other memberships incentivize buying with up-front discounts, different rates, auto-ship options, free and faster shipping, add-ons like access to movies and audiobooks, and hell, even designated days where members enjoy just-for-them sales. All to keep you engaging with their ecosystem, thereby buying more than you otherwise would without the membership. And it's not only Amazon; they're just one of the biggest. SO many companies rely on subscription models to turn a profit. When I worked at one such company, the internal mantra was *Easy, Easy, Hard,* as in *Easy to join, Easy to forget, Hard to cancel.* So the sign-up process was designed to be simple and seamless, while the cancellation process was, though FTC-compliant, an absolute pain in the dick by comparison. And because no sane company is going to waste energy and resources on sending promotional messages to customers who are already fully locked in, it was pretty easy for people to forget they had subscribed. I know, sneaky.

To make today's task more manageable, let's break these subs into three categories: 1) services, like your streaming entertainment or gym membership, 2) restocks, the items and services you actually use (or used regularly at one point) that you have automatically shipped at a predetermined cadence, and 3) everything else, like stuff discovery and novelty boxes. Services in the first category are less the target today because, well, they're not things. But if you want to take inventory of those and put them on the chopping block along with other memberships that may be unused and siphoning funds, by all means, get after it.

Let's look at restocks, the beloved "Subscribe and Save" stuff. Humans freaking love this concept because our base operating system runs on scarcity. So the promise of never running out of something, even if it's just dish soap, really comforts our primitive brains. Automatically receiving personal care, cleaning, and home supplies that you actually use up each month can be pretty convenient. But because we have such a skewed notion of what qualifies as an essential, these restocks can quickly bleed from needs to nice-to-haves. Pet food delivered each month? Helpful. Eco-friendly toilet paper mailed to your home? Awesome. Now you don't have to schlep a big pack home on the subway. Organic convenience meals and smoothies? Okay, a bit indulgent, but you have to eat, right? Oh, but you forgot to pause and you're going out of town and now two shipments have spoiled? Oops. Monthly toy deliveries for your dog? Sure, he loves 'em, but is that a need? New perfume automatically sent to you each month? Okay, now you're just rage-baiting me. This is definitely not a need, especially since you have fourteen half-full fragrances already. Do you catch my drift here? Like much of consumerism, these auto shipments are a slippery slope. Chances are you're automatically getting sent (and charged for, of course) tons of stuff you do not objectively need or regularly use.

And then there's this very modern phenomenon of "stuff" subscription boxes that basically drop-ship curated clutter straight to your door in the name of novelty and discovery. And, boy, do they have all the niche interests covered. Are you into beauty? There's a monthly box of the latest goodies available to you, whether you're a natural products enthusiast or you want a certain celebrity's latest picks. Oh, your kids sometimes get bored (as all small people do) with their toys? Enter services that will ship a steady stream of new ones every few weeks. There are subscriptions that'll send you a parcel o' crap for just about every hobby and affinity, from bourbon and gadgets to sex toys and camping gear.

There are also more generalist boxes that will deploy dozens of items at a time. If you've ever engaged with these, you know how this goes: The first shipment is hotly anticipated (hello, dopamine!) and contains some stuff you like. Awesome! But subsequent packages start to become a bit of a letdown, full of stuff you're not that keen on, that sits in your home, requiring you to figure out what the heck to do with it all. And usually when this happens, you're like, "I need to cancel this," and then the day gets busy, or someone is throwing up, or you're rushing to your next meeting, and you forget until you receive the next month's underwhelming box. And so on. These companies' business models rely on you forgetting that you have their subscriptions in the first place, or at least on you getting so distracted that you never get around to actually canceling them. Like, no joke, companies credit customers' absentmindedness for 200 percent increased sales.[4] If you've ever tried to get rid of these subscriptions, you're often met with interstitials that waste your time by asking, "Would you rather pause instead of cancel?" or that offer you discounts in an attempt to deflect you from putting an end to this madness.

So today, you're steeling yourself and handling these once and for all. You're going to take stock of all your memberships and subscription services, determine which ones you're using and which have completely eluded you, you're going to unsubscribe, tally up your savings, and get excited about a doorstep less obstructed by boxes of crap you don't actually need.

Action Item 1: Using your brain or an app designed to find repeat charges, take inventory of all your subscriptions and memberships across the three categories:

1. *Services* (streaming entertainment, gym and club memberships)

2. *Restocks* (Amazon Prime membership; "Subscribe and Save" orders; companies that auto-send shaving needs, personal care, supplements, home and laundry care, food items and meal delivery services, pet supplies)

3. *Everything else,* specifically stuff shipments branded as discovery or novelty curations

Action Item 2: Cancel or pause the ones you don't use or have forgotten about.

Action Item 3: Tally how much you've saved each month from canceling these. Walk taller knowing you're the captain of your financial ship again.

Day 11: Delete On-Demand Drains

When I was doing the No New Things Challenge in the summer of 2022, I made a disconcerting discovery. You see, while I was following the tenets of the Challenge to a tee, I wasn't seeing the savings I usually would. I was perplexed. Was it a heavy month of bills? Nope. Did I pay for big-ticket items like flights or something? Nope again. Then what the heck could it be? When I opened my bank statement and saw a slew of payments to Door-Dash, Grubhub, Uber Eats, and the like, to the tune of nearly $928 for just July, the answer hit me like a ton of take-out containers. Hi, what? That's almost enough money to get a mini facelift in Tijuana (don't do that).

But the evidence was right there: $42 for some iced coffees and vegan doughnuts to nurse a hangover (follow me for more nutrition advice); $153 for a Friday-night pasta feast while my Mom was visiting; and six separate orders from my favorite Ethiopian place. SIX. In the span of a single month. There I was, the Dame of Deinfluencing (nobody calls me that, but please feel free to start), the Overcomer of Overconsumption (same goes for this title), and I was engaging in the same bullshit behaviors I was shepherding thousands of folks to manage, just with food delivery. Look, I'm not proud of it, but I promised I'd be honest with y'all about my own challenges during No New Things, since we all have them. And this is most definitely one of mine.

"But, Ashlee, I thought food delivery was okay during the thirty days!" Yep, you're correct; food delivery, pickup, groceries, and going out to eat are all totally permissible during the Challenge. But this habit was clearly a runaway train for me that was sabotaging my goals. You may be surprised to find that these on-demand services, while permitted during the Challenge, can actually undo a lot of your shopping mitigation and habit replacement work. After all, it's all consumption. A quick internet search results in countless Reddit threads of folks desperately looking for strategies to overcome their "food delivery addiction," lest they go broke or turn into a human taquito. Fact is, the convenience of these on-demand apps gives us the same hypnotic blip of dopamine as online shopping, and thus, they keep us in a cycle of overspending, overconsuming, and coming back for more.[1]

When I examined how I could wrangle online shopping impulses so well but fell like a house of cards when it came to food delivery, it was really just down to something I did not want to admit: my being lazy. Like, my first book boasts an entire cache of me-created recipes that are properly scrumptious, so your girl knows how to cook. So many tasty places are a literal five-minute walk from my apartment. And because this happened during the summer, I didn't even have the excuse of the occasional blizzard to cover my tracks. This was simply a bad habit I picked up during the pandemic (like so many of us) and never properly offboarded. Was my institution of late-night ice cream parties, whereby we'd order cones and various pints from our favorite parlor, a cute distraction from the April 2020 scaries? Unquestionably, so cute. Are ice cream parties a habit that serves my health, financial, or behavior goals four years later? Probably not.

So today, you're going to examine your relationship to on-demand apps that peddle convenience but not necessarily stuff, and determine whether they're helping or hindering your healthy habit-building work. Look at the grocery, alcohol, and drugstore delivery retailer apps (that you haven't yet said goodbye to from

Days 8 and 9), couponing apps, gaming apps, and any other convenience portals you can think of that are consumption-adjacent. If you have excellent restraint with these types of on-demand drains, well, I salute you, and feel free to do nothing but pat yourself on the back today. For the rest of us mere mortals, I suggest deleting or hiding them, or at the very least, removing your payment info. Determine where and how you can create friction so you engage less, or in a healthier way, with these conveniences. Perhaps you can keep the apps, but institute a rule that instead of doing delivery, you'll only do pickup? Or maybe you can reserve delivery for special occasions where you've earned a little slothing, or extenuating circumstances, like when you're down with a bad cold.

To this day, I still struggle to resist the gratifying magic of pushing a button and having fresh falafel delivered to my doorstep. And because I know this about myself, I institute constant resistance by not having said apps on my phone, and habit replacement by always having appealing meals prepped in my fridge and pantry. Yes, I'm a toddler when it comes to this. It's a journey, but I've found that by being more mindful about how I engage with these on-demand drains during and beyond the Challenge, my ability to resist overconsumption in all its forms is that much stronger and more automatic.

Action Item 1: Delete retailer apps from your phone and other relevant devices if you haven't already done so completely from Days 8 and 9.

Action Item 2: Delete other on-demand apps that you find sink your finances and time. These can be for Challenge-permitted items like groceries, activities, food delivery, couponing, gaming, and other apps that keep you in an impulse-feedback loop.

Action Item 3: If you trust yourself to engage with these apps responsibly, insert whatever level of friction you deem appropriate.

Remove your payment information or put an app blocker or limiter on tempting apps (your devices usually offer settings for this).

Action Item 4: If food delivery apps are tough for you, create contingency plans like having groceries or a meal-prep schedule that ensure you have convenient access to satisfying food throughout the week, especially during trigger times when you feel especially tempted to fire up delivery apps. You can jump to Day 22 for guidance on how to stage your food and make quickie meals.

Action Item 5: If you find that on-demand delivery apps like these are tempting triggers for you, begin logging them when you track your daily triggers. You'll likely get a slightly sobering pang when you see how much money you've saved by creating some friction.

Day 12: Understand Upcycling

Now that you've spent the past few days blocking and shushing those pesky shopping temptations, we're shifting to cultivating some mind- and skill sets that will benefit you throughout the Challenge. Because, while you're familiar with the SUPER System, you might be wondering how the heck you're going to shop secondhand or repurpose stuff for thirty whole days if you've never really done so before. Well, fear not, because the rest of the week is dedicated to you honing the practices that are essential to the No New Things way of life. And I promise, they're actually incredibly useful and really freaking fun. And today, we're focusing on reusing what you've got, which you'll sometimes hear referred to as *upcycling, repurposing, reimagining,* or, my personal favorite, *making shit from other shit*—you get the idea.

How many times have you raced to the store, convinced you need a particular item, only to find a few days later that you already have something super similar that could've been repurposed to meet your need? As you can imagine, our preference for buying new, even when doing so doesn't make sense, creates a ton of financial and environmental waste. And the muscle memory toward buying new before exploring our own stuff is usually just that: a force of consumerist habit—we keep doing it because it's what we've always done. And yet, it wasn't always this way. In an earlier era, nothing went to waste. People largely met their needs by repurposing items until they practically disintegrated, and even then, I'm pretty sure our ancestors would've found a way to turn the particles into something. Folks had to reuse and repair because money and new items weren't as plentiful as they are today. But upcycling wasn't born solely out of necessity; it was a point of pride, a way of showing reverence for hard-earned stuff.

And today, you get to try your hand at honoring and repurposing what you already have. And while, sure, repurposing can save you money and stem unnecessary waste, it also packs the added benefit of making you more creative. You see, we've been fed this consumerist myth that endless choices equal unbridled possibilities, but true creativity requires conditions. Yep, the limits that No New Things imposes on how you get your needs met are also exactly what our brains need to push against to generate fresh ideas and approaches. Consumer culture has starved us of that imaginative process, making us dependent on marketing suggestions, rather than our own resourcefulness. So, when we're entrenched in overconsumption, we miss out on the satisfaction and well-being benefits that accompany creative pursuits.[1] Learning to see reuse as a first port of call can also enhance your cognition, as well as your kiddos' healthy development if you let them in on the fun.[2] Once you start, you'll begin to see all your things through a multipurpose lens. You'll also begin to see how so many items that we've been told have a single use actually have many—and you already own those items.

So today, we're giving your resourcefulness a workout by fulfilling an item on your Need Note through upcycling. For instance, you might need new cleaning rags, but could you make some by cutting old sheets, towels, or tees you already have? Could orphaned socks be used as home dusters (just slide 'em on your hand and go to Swiffertown)? Did you know that broken hangers can store rolls of tape, ribbon, and yarn just as well as the expensive store-bought solutions? Or that your sanity can be saved by upcycling rigid plastic produce containers to corral all those tiny LEGO pieces or Barbie accessories? If I tried to enumerate the possibilities, well, we'd be here all night. And that's the beauty of getting the creative juices flowing—the options become endless. If you need some guidance, the internet is replete with blow-your-mind tutorials on everything from wrapping paper and bird feeders to car organizers and self-watering planters.

In my house, I do all the requisite sustainable maneuvers, like saving and using jars for damn near everything, but I also have some fringe reuse habits that you may find inspiring (or horrifying). For instance, instead of buying whatever plastic contraptions are marketed to keep food packaging closed (remember chip clips?), I use cleaned rubber bands (like the ones that bundle your mail) and fifteen-year-old binder clips from my college days to reseal anything kitchen-related that needs resealing. I don't buy new plant pots, because old serving dishes, empty candle vessels, and glass spice jars look rad and work well. Instead of buying those spools of supposedly biodegradable pet waste baggies (they're not), I use those difficult-to-recycle soft-plastic food bags and shipping mailers we all already have loads of. So, if you've seen a blonde around town picking up poo with an empty baby carrots bag, yes, yes, that was me.

If you need an occasion to get into the repurposing spirit, might I suggest Halloween? I mean, 1) don't get me started on the excess of Halloween, but 2) I'm gonna get started on the excess of Halloween, sorry. It's crazy that a tradition rooted in imaginative dress-up usually results in us going online and buying some cheap-shit, sweatshop-made analogue of whatever we're attempting to cosplay. And you know what's really scary? Each year, Americans drop $4.1 billion on costumes, only to turn around and toss thirty-five million of them in the trash. Yes, thirty-five million costumes hit the landfill every year, creating around two thousand tons of plastic waste.[3] Forget *trick or treat*; we're acting like *trick or trash*.

My friend Hollie is a great example of how the holidays can be a fun money- and planet-saving time for you and your littles. Her spunky son, Wilder, has THE most epic and inventive upcycled costumes I've ever seen, all thanks to Hollie's resourceful brain. Like, this kid is out here handily winning local contests wearing incredible ensembles made from stuff that was just kicking around the house. There was the year he went as a picnic, complete with a full-body red-checkered tablecloth dotted with paper plates and a basket from the kitchen, adorned with play food Hollie's kids already had (and still play with today). Or when he went as Chicago's beloved icon the Sears Tower (I'll never cave to calling it the Willis Tower), ingeniously made from old shipping boxes and LED string lights. I'm not expecting that after doing today's action item, you're going to immediately ascend to Hollie-level ingenuity, but the money saved and creativity exercised via upcycling will certainly have you seeing the previously ho-hum world of your existing possessions in exhilarating, expansive new ways.

Action Item 1: Identify an item from your Need Note coded with the letter *U* that you intend to repurpose.

Action Item 2: Scout your house for items that could be repurposed or reimagined, and do a little research to get inspiration on upcycle ideas and approaches.

Action Item 3: If applicable, ratchet up the fun and learning opportunities by getting your kiddos (or friends or family) involved in the upcycling.

Action Item 4: Once you've completed your upcycling project, look at your Need Note and see if there are other items you previously coded with another SUPER System letter but that you're now seeing could be upcycled, and code them accordingly.

Day 13: Slay Secondhand

It probably goes without saying that a Challenge that not only focuses on but is named for not acquiring new things relies pretty heavily on not-new things. And for some people, this spotlighting of secondhand items can stir a lot of feelings. There are so many stigmas around preloved goods that are pervasive, but also pretty unfounded. And it should come as no surprise that many of these are rooted in consumerist society's villainization of the poor.[1] If I had a nickel for every time someone who's never set foot in a resale shop proclaimed that "thrifted items are dirty and gross," I'd be rich enough to build a spaceship and zoom out of this hellscape. Other folks innocently wonder if even enough stuff exists to live a life that relies so heavily on the secondhand market. (Answer: absolutely.) I don't mean to toot my own horn, but about 98 percent of what I own is secondhand, and not only am I still alive, but I also have no bugs, rashes, or weird odors following me. So I think that qualifies me enough to unpack these assumptions and hopefully assuage some of your fears.

Let's start with the concern that secondhand stuff is grody or riddled with germs. I get that it can be a little strange to buy something that potentially had a prior wearer or owner. But let me ask in all sincerity: Have you ever been to a hotel? Like, think of how many people have rolled through and dried their crotches with the towels, slept and engaged in other activities in the sheets, and lounged on the furniture buck naked before you showed up. That's arguably a way higher body count than the thrift-store shirt you're considering. But most of us don't think twice about staying in hotels, because we're conditioned to associate them with luxury. And while humans have been sharing hand-me-downs for basically ever, the unfair assumption that secondhand goods are filthy can actually be traced back to a satirical story run by the *Saturday Evening Post* in the late 1800s. At the time, with limited opportunities for employment, it was common for Jewish immigrants to sell used clothing in pushcarts. So when the *Post* ran an anti-Semitic smear piece masquerading as a cautionary tale about a beautiful blonde whose social standing and good looks were ruined when she contracted smallpox from a dress she bought from a—you guessed it—Jewish-owned resale shop, used wares were unfairly vilified.[2] While you certainly want to use common sense when you shop secondhand and not drag a rain-soaked comforter you found in the alley home, a majority of preloved finds are solid and clean, or easily made clean with a little elbow grease.

And if you're worried that there's just not enough stuff, or not enough good stuff, on the planet to help you get what you need during the Challenge, well, hold my beer while I comfort you with some facts. Plenty of really great, useful, stylish items already exist on the planet. Secondhand clothing accounts for nearly 42 percent of the entire retail market and is expected to grow 127 percent by 2026 (that's three times faster than the apparel market overall).[3] New stores, apps, and platforms for finding everything preloved, from tech to baby clothes to sex toys, are popping up every day, indicating both overwhelming demand and an overflow of palatable merchandise. This makes sense when we consider that Americans toss twelve million tons of furniture and seventeen million tons of clothing each year, much of which is still totally usable.[4] The British Fashion Council estimates that there are enough clothes on the planet right now to dress the next

SIX GENERATIONS.[5] Because we are a society that consumes for novelty, we often get rid of perfectly good, sometimes never-even-used items simply because we're bored of them. In fact, each year, 65 percent of the one hundred billion garments produced globally are thrown out within twelve months of their purchase, much of which are in new condition.[6] These are incredibly unfortunate and harmful manifestations of the consumer mindset, but they also signal that enough fantastic stuff exists in the second-hand ecosystem to not only meet your needs but to delight your style and sensibilities.

Shop Secondhand First

Now that you're hopefully more comfortable with the idea of pre-loved, let's get you in a space to absolutely ace acquiring items you need in this way. Take a peek at your Need Note. Are there items you've coded with an *S*? Select the one that feels easiest for you to acquire and make it your mission to fulfill that need today. Literally anything can be found secondhand these days, so whether you're looking for furniture, décor, appliances, or clothing, the following steps will help you find exactly what you're seeking, in the desired condition, at the right price:

- **Determine your destination:** Use your communities and groups, internet searches, and reviews to determine which secondhand destinations will be the best fit for the item you're seeking. Is it on-line or brick-and-mortar? Does the retailer specialize in furniture, or is it more of a big-box resale center? Is the online marketplace reputable? If you're looking for luxury or designer items, does the destination do authentication as part of their service model? For instance, I've found that it's easier to find a specific item or brand through apps or online platforms that let me search and filter by brand name and other characteristics, rather than hoping I'll stumble upon a West Elm lamp at my local thrift store. Some brick-and-mortar resale shops will have a specialty like furniture or gown consignment, so determine which place is going to be the best fit.

- **Set your budget:** Research the item and know how much you want to spend. If you're looking for a specific brand or style, a quick

Google search will usually show manufacturer's suggested retail price, or MSRP, which you can then use to calibrate your budget based on the item's condition.

From there, the process forks based on whether you're shopping online or in-store:

In-Store:

• *Be prepared:* When I go to a physical store, I bring a mini measuring tape (as well as measurements of any relevant spaces in my home), a stain-remover pen, cash (some places are cash-only), and a generously sized reusable shopping bag. If I know the place has a bargain bin that requires deep and sometimes gnarly sorting, I might throw in some gloves. I also wear socks (if I plan to try on shoes) and clothes that are easy to slip items over, since most places don't offer dressing rooms. I also have my Need Note on my phone so I can refer back to see if a good find can fulfill something I've listed.

• *Be aware:* Thrifting is fun, but peak times can be frantic, so I try to go on less trafficked days to minimize stress. I also chat with employees to get a sense of the schedule and follow the shop's social media accounts to find out when sales are happening and when new shipments arrive.

• *Stay open:* Bring your creative brain and see the possibilities in items. If you're looking for a vase, expand your search to include pitchers, tall glasses, and umbrella stands, and remember that items never have just one use. And don't sleep on overlooked sections. For instance, if you're looking for fabric, check out the bedding section (who says you can't reupholster a cushion with a gorgeous, old pillow sham?). My favorite sweatshirt in the world, a super-soft '80s single-stitch dream, was found in the kids' section for one dollar.

• *Check the go-back rack:* This varies by store. This might be a dedicated rack near the dressing rooms, or it's basically anywhere near a mirror where the stuff that caught people's eyes, but didn't work out, ends up. Someone has already kind of curated these items, so sometimes this move yields really cool finds.

• *Know your limits:* In my experience, many cosmetic stains can be lifted (this is why I bring a stain-remover pen, to see if I can budge a stain in-store before I buy), buttons and hems can be repaired, knitwear can be shaved to remove pilling, but leather that's been marinated in a decade of cigarette smoke? Barring access to an ozone machine, that's a much tougher fix. For furniture and home goods, conditions like rusting, stained wood, crummy hardware, and wobbly joints can all be easily addressed with no special skills. But broken mirror glass? Not so much. So know what you and your cache of local carpenters, cobblers, tailors, and dry cleaners can do, and if something is just too arduous to restore or care for, don't buy it. For more guidance on identifying and making repairs to home and wardrobe items, check out Days 16 and 17, respectively.

• *Look for quality:* While you can certainly find plenty of today's fast fashion and furniture secondhand, older items tend to be better built. For clothing and accessories, look for natural materials like wool, cotton, non-stretch denim, silk, and leather, and solid construction like reinforced hems and lining. For home goods, opt for solid wood, stone, glass, cast iron, ceramic, and metal, and repairable elements like screws over glue.

• *Inspect an item:* This is a hands-on process, so pick up an item and look at its interior and exterior. Most secondhand retailers do not allow returns, so know what you're getting into before you buy. If you're stumped on what something is, snap a pic and let the magic of Google Lens inform you of its provenance, use, and market value.

• *Avoid overconsuming:* The same traps that lead to excess when buying new can happen when shopping secondhand. Don't let cheaper prices and the thrill of the hunt cloud your judgment or lead you to buy more than you actually need. For me, if something is not a hell yes, I don't get it.

• *Be considerate:* To the store and others. Treat a resale store with the same courtesy you would any other retail outpost by putting items back where you found them and not leaving piles of castoffs. Also, there's a very real shortage of plus-size clothing in the thrift world, so if you're not in that size range, avoid depleting what little stock there is.

• *Be patient:* It can take time to find what you're looking for in a store. If you're newer to IRL secondhand shopping, give yourself a cutoff time, or choose smaller, more curated stores so you don't get overwhelmed or disenchanted too early in the process.

Online:

• *Get familiar with functionality:* Many online marketplaces allow you to search and filter by brand, color, condition, size, price, material, and other attributes. Once you've found relevant listings, try sorting prices from low to high, so you see the best deals first. If you're searching for something to give as a gift (or that you just want in newer condition), filter by "New with Tags." Functionality varies across apps and marketplaces, so get schooled in all the ways they can help you more precisely find what you're seeking. For instance, some apps will let you set up an alert for keywords or items so you're notified when new listings are posted, while others will show you related items.

• *Know your specs and sizing:* If you're on the hunt for a piece of furniture, for instance, know the measurements your space can accommodate. For clothing and accessories, it's important to know how a brand fits you because many platforms do not allow returns. I'll often go to a brick-and-mortar store and try on the item or something similar so I can determine the size that will work best for me. Then I search for that size online.

• *Search misspellings:* This tip may seem kooky, but I have had amazing luck getting great deals on designer items simply because I searched a misspelled version of the brand's name. My favorite Helmut Lang suit was found by searching for "Helmet Lang."

• *Read and ask questions:* If a listing catches your eye, read the whole thing. Zoom in on and study the photos to get a sense for the condition of the item. If the listing only has stock or retailer images of an item, but not photos of the actual piece, request that the seller upload some. And if you've got questions about anything else related to the item, by golly, ask them! Return policies are rare on secondhand sites, so it's important to do your due diligence before you buy.

• *Read reviews:* Most sites will allow users to rate or review sellers, so use that information to ensure you're buying from a good one. And do your part by leaving reviews of your experiences.

• *Prioritize your security:* Only use established platforms that offer consumer protections like secure payment and authentication for items over a certain price. Moreover, never give sensitive financial or personal information out on these sites. While shopping online is a largely positive experience, beware of scammers, and if you're grabbing an item from online-to-IRL sites like Facebook Marketplace or OfferUp, always do the handoff in a public place.

• *Know when to negotiate:* By using image search and determining an item's retail value, you can often make offers on online apps that you cannot when shopping at a brick-and-mortar secondhand store. This is an opportunity to get a good deal, but also to be fair. So if something retails for $200 and a seller has it listed at $80, don't be the dickhead who offers $10 (there's always one).

Selling Your Stuff

I'd be remiss if I didn't mention how gratifying and lucrative it can be to sell your stuff secondhand, not to mention better for the planet. Whether it's via a consignment-type store, designated apps for niche categories, social media networks like Facebook Marketplace, or a good old-fashioned yard sale, selling your stuff is a rewarding way to rehome your items while maybe making a little coin. Now, we don't need to get too serious about this, because chances are, you're not about to transition careers to become a full-time Poshmark seller, but these steps make it super easy for me to determine what to sell, where to sell it, and what to do with items that don't sell.

- *Set your threshold:* Selling requires some time and monitoring, so I set a price threshold to determine which items are worth the effort and which are better given away in my local free group. This will be different for everyone, but I generally sell items online if 1) I know they're likely to sell, and 2) I can make $40+ on them. I bring items to brick-and-mortar consignment stores or mail to ThredUp, which are both less time-consuming than listing online, if I feel they'll fetch $15+. That's my personal rubric, and only you can define yours.

- *Batch listings:* If you have a critical mass of items you want to sell online, I recommend taking photos, measurements, and researching pricing and brand information in advance, and compiling that information in your phone's Notes app (this makes it easier to copy and paste into the listing). Then set aside some time to batch your listings.

- *Avoid overvaluing:* An emotional bias happens when we own something, even If we don't want or need that thing anymore—we overvalue it. This is called the *endowment effect*, and it can lead us to overprice our stuff. Research the going rate for what you're selling, price it fairly or competitively to move, and be open to reasonable offers.

- *Be specific:* Take quality photos and offer measurements and specs in the description because buyers will ask you for that information. If you've a flair for salesmanship, you can do like I do and add a little narrative to really sell the item and help potential buyers see how it will fit in their wardrobes or lives.

• *Stay vigilant:* Reply to messages and inquiries, repost your listings (as is the case with Facebook Marketplace, where they automatically expire after a certain time period), and offer promotions (most apps let you make offers to interested likers, as well as discount shipping) to maintain buyer interest. And when you have a buyer and the price is right, let no moss grow on the transaction— get the piece mailed out or schedule an in-person handoff of goods ASAP. People's online attention spans are extremely short, so time is the enemy of a swift secondhand transaction. The whole point of this is to efficiently rehome your unwanted items, not have pen pals.

• *Be nice:* This should go without saying, but you're going to be interfacing with people, so be cool. When mailing an item to an online buyer, I like to throw in a little note on a repurposed card and sometimes a little sample I have kicking around that I'm not going to use. Reviews are helpful in getting eyes on your listings, and these little touches make shopping secondhand feel like a personalized, thoughtful experience for folks. Plus, I'm of the belief that the more positive we can make the secondhand shopping experience, the more likely folks are to opt for preloved over new items.

• *Consider seasonality:* When consigning in person, ensure items are appropriate for the current season (a.k.a. you won't have much luck consigning a wool topcoat in July). This is less of a consideration for online selling, where the market is more evergreen.

• *Supply the sale:* Selling online will likely require 1) a way to print the prepaid shipping label, 2) mailing supplies, and 3) access to a post office. I have a printer I got secondhand that works fine for this purpose, but local libraries often offer free printing. I also save every scrap of packing material that enters my home to reuse when mailing customer orders. And don't count out your local free, neighborhood, and Buy Nothing groups when it comes to stocking up. I've picked up rolls of packing tape and Bubble Wrap from members who didn't need them.

Many apps and consignment stores will offer you more money if you do a trade and keep your money in their ecosystem over cash or depositing that money in your bank account. It's important to remember that these marketplaces, though great alternatives to traditional consumerism, still bear resemblance to it. So do with this information what feels right for you. If you actually need some things, by all means, keep a balance so you can put your proceeds toward purchasing them. But if you're trying to limit the flow of new-to-you items in your home or you're just trying to shop less generally, putting your earnings in the bank is a boss move.

Action Item 1: Find an item on your Need Note that you've coded with an *S*.

Action item 2: Tap your networks and resources to determine the best-fit secondhand destination for buying your Need Note item. Is the most appropriate marketplace an app or site, or a brick-and-mortar specialty consignment store?

Action Item 3: Once you've determined where you're going (physically or metaphorically) to find your Need Note item, use the tips above to ensure your trip is as smooth and enjoyable as possible.

Action Item 4: Try your hand at selling some items you no longer want or need, be it online or in person. And if you didn't get a chance to list or sell anything this week, fear not—next week's action items will probably leave you with some pieces to sell.

Day 14: Ethically Off-Load

I have many dreams, but chief among them is to one day host a fun, *Queer Eye* meets *The Home Edit*–type television show (if you're a producer, hit me up) that doesn't 1) involve buying a billion new plastic organizers, or 2) result in dozens of trash bags stuffed with usable items getting thrown away or "donated" to who knows where. Because while those shows are super inspiring and fun to watch, I cringe at how cavalierly the message of "just get rid of it" reinforces disposability culture in the process. It's important to remember that there is no such thing as "away" on planet Earth, so while we have been misled to think that trash collectors transport our waste to some alternate universe, few things actually ever biodegrade.

Look, it may make us feel warm and fuzzy inside to drop bags off at the big-box collection site, but the hard truth is that donation centers, wonderful as they are, are still businesses. And like any business, if there's no aftermarket for something (looking at you, tatty old boxer shorts), not enough space to merchandise said stuff, or too few employees to sift and sort through the billions of pounds we donate each year, there's a high likelihood many of your donations are going to the landfill. The EPA estimates that only 16 percent of donated items actually get resold, so you can probably guess where the remaining 84 percent goes.[1] And how often do you hear someone say, "I'm Goodwilling that stuff," or "That bag goes to Salvation Army"? Indiscriminate donating is so ubiquitous in American culture that we use the company names interchangeably with the verb of donating. And when items like clothing or furniture are trashed, they don't biodegrade, because landfills are notoriously starved of the conditions necessary for items to break down—like sunlight, microorganisms, and oxygen. So when your stuff goes to the landfill, chances are high that it's just mummifying there, releasing a shit ton of harmful methane during its tenure.

Moreover, many donation collections—like those large metal self-serve receptacles—are just middlemen that ship our castoffs to under-resourced countries to become another community's problem. Most of our old clothes, for instance, are sent to countries in South America, Africa, and Asia to be resold, but an estimated 40 percent arrives in such poor condition that it must be trashed.[2] In Ghana's capital of Accra, fifteen million pieces of our unwanted clothing arrive EVERY WEEK. The surplus is so excessive that an escarpment at the banks of the Korle Lagoon is almost entirely made up of Westerners' discarded clothing.[3] You read that right—a literal landmass mostly made up of the items we are too lazy to responsibly rehome. Chile's stunning Atacama Desert, believed to be one of the oldest deserts on Earth, is so littered with thirty-nine thousand tons of dumped fast fashion each year that the piles can be seen from space.[4] FROM SPACE. I don't need to tell you why this sucks for so many reasons.

This process of pawning our overconsumption off on historically oppressed areas is just another form of colonialism. Until manufacturers take more responsibility for the extended and end life of their products, our possessions are our responsibility, and I don't think most of us want to foist harm and pollution on others. The best antidote to this harmful cycle is to, first and foremost, buy less. And since you're doing the Challenge, I think it's safe to assume that you're doing that. The second is to take a more intentional approach to getting rid of your unwanted items by identifying recipients who will use or destinations that will recycle them. It's a process I call *ethical off-loading*, and it's actually way easier to do than you might think. Some examples of ethically off-loading are:

- Donating items to organizations that have explicitly requested or stated a need for those types of items
- Giving pieces to folks in your network who will use them
- Posting things you no longer need in free groups
- Selling unwanted items via online marketplaces, apps, consignment stores, and yard sales (yep, Day 13 is a form of ethical off-loading—rejoice!)
- Taking harder-to-off-load or broken items to specialized recycling programs

The commonality is that there's an intended recipient who will get utility from or a service that will recycle these items, instead of sending them to the trash heap. Besides being better for the planet and your community, it feels so freaking good to know that the stuff we've little use for can serve others. That box of maternity clothes can help a mom-to-be feel supported. That bundle of old blankets can provide sweet shelter critters waiting for their forever home a cozy place to rest. And just like when you made a buttload of returns on Day 6, this exercise is a potent reminder that our items require more time and attention than we often consider when we're adding them to our carts.

Action Item 1: Are there any items in your home or wardrobe that you can ethically off-load? Maybe you have a pile of things you were going to dump at an indiscriminate donation center, but reading this chapter changed your mind (hell yeah!). Begin researching options in your area that allow you to more responsibly rehome or recycle them.

Action Item 2: Identify at least one item you were going to drop off at a big-box center, and instead, take it where it can be ethically off-loaded or recycled. Rinse and repeat for more items if you're feeling inspired.

Action Item 3: Continue cultivating the mindset and practice of ethical off-loading whenever you're faced with unwanted things. Make and regularly update a list of more intentional donation options in your area (new ones crop up all the time!), and refer to it throughout and beyond the Challenge.

Week 2 Reflection

Fourteen days. FOURTEEN DAYS! You are officially halfway through the Challenge. How do you feel? I'm personally a bit partial to Week 2 because, while every week features valuable themes and action items, there's something so indispensable about 1) taking the steps to mute consumerist messages and 2) honing better, more responsible ways to interact with our stuff. These action items will hopefully become joyful, beneficial habits for you.

For instance, every month, without fail, I scan my social media and cull any accounts that aren't serving me. It's an easy activity to do when on the go, like when I'm commuting on the train or clocking some steps on the stair climber, that reaffirms that I am in control of what I consume. I also instantly unsubscribe from salesy retailer messages whenever they slip through the cracks to my inbox. And through repetition, I'm building those strong neural pathways that allow me to enjoy fewer promotions and comparison traps, and more peace. When I do find myself needing a general item, I see if I already have something that can be repurposed. If I want a specific thing, my instant response is to see if I can get it secondhand first (and I'm usually successful because the circular economy provides!). This habituation to circularity keeps me flexing my creativity and away from traditional retail traps. It's my sincerest hope that in trying and refining this week's action items, you're already feeling more freedom and contentment.

So go ahead and get after the prompts below. And for a fun twist, you're going to tally your savings from this week as well as from last to get a mega total of money you've saved by not caving to consumerist impulses. I'm high-fiving you right now! And as with every week, make some time to treat yourself by engaging with a luxe Love List activity, because you deserve it.

Prompts	Your Answers
How did the week feel for you overall? Did it go smoothly? Why or why not?	
Were there days or action items that were difficult for you? Which ones and why?	
Were there days or action items that felt amazing for you? Which ones and why?	
Did you glean any insights or realizations about your relationship to shopping or stuff that you hadn't realized before? If so, what?	

Prompts	Your Answers
What are you most looking forward to about next week?	
Tally your Trigger Tracker for this week. How much did you save?	
Total your savings from Week 1 and Week 2. How much have you saved since starting the Challenge?	
Did you sell anything secondhand this week? If so, list the total amount you made here.	
Add the totals from Week 1, Week 2, and your sales.	

Week 3: Your Space and Stuff

While much of No New Things is about acquiring fewer or no, well, new things, it's also about cultivating that all-important attitude of gratitude for the things you already have. And one of the fastest ways to accomplish this is by taking stock and care of those things. It's pretty difficult to feel appreciation for your stuff when it's haphazardly flung around the room, forgotten about in the recesses of your home, eclipsed by other stuff you barely use, and left in dirty disrepair. This week, you'll be paring down to only the items you love and use and providing those things with some much-needed TLC in the form of cleaning, repairing, organizing, and actually using the items that make the cut. You're also getting an extra bonus day this week, but alas, this doesn't change the fact that you have the same twenty-four hours in a day as Beyoncé.

Though decluttering is often seen as procedural and trendy, I'd argue that it's a process that can be pretty profound. Time and again in real life, I've seen a simple declutter literally shift someone's trajectory and spirit. Science supports that organizing our spaces boasts unexpected benefits like healthier bodies, better sleep, enhanced cognitive function, and even fewer accidents.[1] Taking inventory and care of your possessions also provides tangible evidence of the abundance you already enjoy. And gratitude for and attention to our existing abundance is a remarkable antidote to feeling the lack that is weaponized against us in a capitalistic society. Like, how can you feel out of touch with trends when you have all these kick-ass clothes? You're way less susceptible to feeling not-enough when you're hyperaware that you live in a home that has everything you need to be cozy, comfortable, and safe. Holy crap, man, you have five different kinds of bodywash? You're freaking rich! Sure, we'll always have needs and varying degrees of plenty, but most of us are, to quote a favorite Southern homily from my youth, "riding a gravy train with biscuit wheels"—and we don't even recognize it.

So today kicks off a week of steps that nudge you to break through the fatigue-and-freeze that accompanies a stuffed space (and that only gets worse and more difficult to surmount the longer we put it off). Sure, embarking on a full week of focusing on your things in a very hands-on way may feel daunting, but many participants have noted that this is the week when things begin to radically shift. In fact, I'll bet that your simplified, sparkling, snatched spaces and stuff are going to have you feeling freaking fantastic. When we realize how much we actually have by opening our dang eyes and taking care of our possessions, we put asunder the marketing narrative of never having enough that drives us to overconsume. So instead of bullshit retail therapy, look at this week's action items as majorly meditative moves that yield real, lasting therapeutic results, not just in your spaces but in your psyche.

Day 15: Unstuff Your Space

U nless you're a minimalist monk or ascetic, you probably have a living space that contains a lot of stuff. There's nothing necessarily wrong with this, but if you're anything like the average American, all that clutter isn't doing you any favors. The average US home is estimated to contain more than three hundred thousand items,[1] and yet 59 percent of us say a lot of that is stuff we "no longer want or need."[2] And because "mess equals stress," we often just want that broken or unwanted stuff out of sight. So, we push our closets, basements, attics, and garages to the limit to hide our stressors away, often only to buy more stuff in the now-hidden stuff's place. Think I'm exaggerating? Oh, no. Because of our stored crap, 32 percent of Americans who have a two-car garage can only fit one car inside, and 25 percent can't even fit one, not even a tiny Smart car.[3] And once we've maxed out our residential options, 20 percent of us will opt for a self-storage facility, which, as a result, has become one of the highest-performing sectors in commercial real estate.[4]

A bit of a turning point between people and possessions occurred during the pandemic. As you can imagine (or you likely don't need to, because you lived through it, as well), sheltering in place within the same four walls every day had 78 percent of us thinking, *Holy crap, I have way too much stuff.* Now, did this realization drive us to buy less stuff? No, no, it did not. While the zeitgeist was one of being overwhelmed by our possessions and, thus, donations skyrocketed, many folks were also engaging in what I call *boredom buying*, spiking sales of nonessential goods like athleisure and home décor by an unprecedented 65 percent.[5] It goes without saying that we likely have enough fucking stuff, but you know, I've gotta say it.

So the first order of business today is to tackle the stuff that's no longer of use to you. I'm not a professional organizer, but I know enough about people to know that you probably have piles or bags of things you've already vowed to take to donation, to the special recycling center, to the animal shelter, to the Little Free Library, that have been loitering in your hallway or the trunk of your car for weeks. Today, you're going to tackle those. And because determining which of your many possessions go and stay is both a big undertaking for most households and a step that will enable you to better handle other days during the Challenge, you're going to do this space by space throughout the Challenge, with the end goal of having it all done by Day 30. Yes, at the end of this, you're ideally going to have all your spaces and stuff decluttered, repaired, and working for you like never before. Can you imagine how that will feel? And if this sounds incredibly daunting, don't freak. Many days, especially this week, feature decluttering as part of the action items, so consider those win-win opportunities to keep the momentum going.

How you tackle your castoffs is up to you. A lot of participants dig the whole Marie Kondo thanking-items-before-you-bid-them-adieu approach, while others pile the entire contents of their closet or dresser in the middle of the room and emotionlessly go about the cull with a quickness. The objective today is to tackle the items you already know you no longer need, for which you have intended ethical off-loading destinations in mind. So start with the low-hanging fruit, the comparatively easy stuff—the stuff that's already in your mind, in piles or bagged up, and ready to go. And, no, if you haven't needed or even noticed an item was absent for the past four months, you're not going to miss or need it in the near future. Then load 'em up and get 'em gone.

And while the main objective for today is to get rid of the stuff you don't need or use, I'm also going to encourage you to go a step further and use the information you gleaned from Day 14 to target destinations for your items that are more intentional than just dropping off at big-box donation centers. If you're like me, organizing stuff is a drug of choice, and you might want to keep going. By all means, do—I won't stop you. The goal today is to tackle the low-lift stuff, while emerging with a thoroughly un-stuffed space by the end of the thirty days, and the pace at which you get there is ultimately up to you.

Action Item 1: Take inventory of the items you've already targeted and bundled for donation. Ya know, the ones that have been languishing in your foyer or the trunk of your car. Today's the day they're going to their intended destination.

Action Item 2: If you don't already have more intentional donation spots for your items, or you were planning on dropping them at a big-box donation center, revisit Day 14 to learn about ethical off-loading and why it's so important for you, your community, and the planet. Research more responsible destinations for your donations whereby they can be either given a new lease on life by recipients who actually need and will use your items, or properly recycled.

Action Item 3: While you're bundling donations and castoffs, if you see other clutter-related tasks that need to be tackled—like handling the trash, recycling, or compost or culling junk mail and piled-up papers—do those for some extra credit.

Action Item 4: Continue the decluttering process throughout the Challenge. Many of the coming days' action items dovetail nicely with this continuous decluttering, so take advantage of those win-wins.

Action Item 5: Take a moment to look upon the items you're donating. Those things required money and time to enter your life. Can you feel gratitude for them, the items that remain in your life, and the resources that made them possible? Can you look around and feel simultaneously grateful for the space you've created and the stuff you have? Stuff doesn't define our worth, but it can serve as a tangible example of our abundance. And when we feel abundant, we're less likely to overconsume.

Day 16: Polish Your Possessions

Amid the uncertainty and despair of the pandemic, I sought comfort in the warm embrace of pure, unadulterated wholesomeness. No, I'm not talking about a weighted blanket but rather the BBC television show *The Repair Shop*. I adore this series so much that if I ever meet someone who doesn't feel the same way, I'm going to automatically think they're a sociopath with no soul. The premise is this: In the idyllic countryside of West Sussex resides a beautiful structure called, you guessed it, the Repair Shop. On the outside, it looks like something out of a children's storybook, like you just know little mice are wearing aprons and baking strawberry pies inside. But past the doors, the place is bustling with charmingly obsessive master craftspeople at the ready to fix beloved but broken keepsakes. Each episode features patrons who mosey in with their grandpa's watch that survived D-Day or an inherited Japanese vase rumored to have belonged to Winston Churchill, in such bad shape they're seemingly destined for the scrap heap. The team of restorers gets to work mending everything from torn lace to upholstery, restoring twisty metalwork, and imperceptibly putting broken porcelain back together. Witnessing their process is a privilege that hits home how repair is an art form all on its own. And when the patrons are reunited with their fixed possessions, well, bitch, just hand me a tissue already. It is moving. The show perfectly captures how our things can be way more than just things; and the craftspeople at the Repair Shop aren't just repairing stuff, they're rekindling memories, reestablishing legacies, refining histories, and changing lives.

Unfortunately, these days, for a variety of reasons, repairing our possessions is largely a lost art. For one, we're offered so few truly accessible repair options. Like, when was the last time you saw a brick-and-mortar vacuum or television repair shop, or called a company to seek resolution for a broken small appliance, only to have them offer to send you a brand-new one instead of the replacement part? And when repair options do present themselves, they're often deemed "way too expensive" because our sense of fair pricing has been skewed by items made ridiculously cheap by sweatshops and forced labor. The truth is that you cannot produce a six-dollar throw pillow without significant collateral damage, usually in the form of exploited humans forced to work eighteen-hour days without a freaking bathroom break. So duh, of course our first impulse is to scoff when the cobbler quotes forty dollars to resole those Zara loafers when a new pair can be had for thirty dollars. And this "ditch it, don't fix it" attitude has us seeing everything as disposable, which, as we've covered already, is a farce—nothing is ever really disposed of on planet Earth.

The fact is that so many landfill-bound items could've been made useful again with super-simple repairs—a tightened screw, a reglued joint, a replaced handle. The US Environmental Protection Agency (EPA) estimates that most of the 85 percent of used textiles that are trashed each year could have been easily repaired or repurposed. And that's just clothes. What about furniture? Don't worry; we don't discriminate against large, unwieldy items. Americans trash twelve million tons of furniture each year, which is 450 percent more solid waste than we produced just sixty years ago.[1] None of these items biodegrade quickly or easily, instead producing a fuck ton of methane, a greenhouse gas with a global-warming potential twenty-five times that of carbon dioxide. Ten out of ten would not recommend the landfill as a destination for your furniture and home décor. And most of this detrimental waste could've been avoided by just getting out a screwdriver. Sheesh.

On this day, and throughout the Challenge, you'll be sprucing up the stuff in your home—like furniture and home décor (you can table—pun intended—wardrobe and tech items, as they have their own dedicated days this week). Today, you're going to give your home goods attention like never before and diagnose what needs to be done to render those items more beautiful or functional. Does that kitchen chair annoyingly wobble and squeak because it's absolutely useless, or do you just need to tighten two little bolts? Is your cast-iron pan a rusted mess beyond help, or does it just need seasoning? What about your mangy-looking couch? Is it forever lost, or could a once-over with the electric de-pilling machine and some spot treatments have it in suitable condition for future movie nights? Make note of the items in your home that need some lovin' and, well, give them said lovin'. I keep a running list of items in my apartment that are crying out for some TLC, and these repairs often require so little effort for such a positive result that I lol as to why I'd put the tasks off for so dang long.

In most instances, the fixes are small and well within your tool and skill sets. In some more niche cases, you may need to send something out to be cleaned or repaired by an expert, and since you're doing No New Things, those expenses are absolutely permitted. Because most of us haven't been conditioned to think of repair as a natural first port of call when something starts acting wonky, you may overestimate what you need to outsource and underestimate your abilities to actualize these repairs yourself. But I'm here to tell you that you absolutely can rent a carpet cleaner and get your rugs fluffy-fresh again. You can borrow some Goo Gone and wood conditioner from your local free group or a friend and save that maple dresser from your kids' sticker assault. Nothing's stopping you from using a complimentary hotel sewing kit to fix the small snag in your duvet cover. These repairs needn't be perfect. *Architectural Digest* is not rolling up to your front door unannounced to assess how well you've polished your possessions. The point here is that you should feel major pride in taking the simple steps that breathe new life into your beloved things, and in turn, those steps will love you back by restoring utility to your life.

Not only does this sprucing extend usefulness and keep the landfill at bay, it also imparts that feeling of freshness that we're often seeking when we buy new items or replacements. If Day 15 has worked its grateful-for-my-stuff magic, this will likely resonate and get you in the right headspace: you are the steward of your stuff. With that lens, washing your throw pillowcases, fixing a wobbly table leg, or buffing a water ring from your wooden nightstand will feel like second-nature expressions of appreciation for all the comfort and convenience these items bring to your life.

Action Item 1: Go through your home (and car and office, if you have those) and make a list of items that you wish to keep that need some attention. Determine which repairs or refreshing you can do yourself and which you need to outsource.

Action Item 2: For items you can tackle in-house, borrow, rent, order, and ready any parts, supplies, or tools, and get after it. Set a timer and spend an hour making little fixes, cleaning, and freshening up your possessions for optimal functionality. Do this throughout the Challenge as needed until you've tackled your entire list.

Action Item 3: For items that require outsourcing to expert tools or talent, make any appointments necessary and get the ball rolling. Do this throughout the Challenge as needed until you've tackled your entire list.

Action Item 4: As you take stock of repairs, you may find it naturally dovetails with decluttering stuff that you no longer need—books, décor, kitchen gadgets, and the like. If you don't get utility or joy from them anymore, ethically off-load them where they'll be useful and appreciated.

Day 17: Care for Your Clothes

Now that you've given your home perhaps more attention than ever before, it's time for your wardrobe to have its own designated day in the sun. Often when folks tackle their closets, they're bombarded with guidance on how they should curate a capsule wardrobe or "uniform," and you can absolutely do that if it feels right for you (and you'll do a little bit of that on Day 18), but today we're focusing on winnowing down your wardrobe to only your favorites that fit and feel great, giving those items some much-needed TLC, and finding new homes for everything else.

You might be surprised to find that even the most minimal among us only wear about 20–30 percent of our closets 80 percent of the time; and despite enjoying gobs of options, 61 percent of us experience "wardrobe panic" on the regular.[1] You already got rid of the tags-on, returnable items on Day 6, and today's action items build on that progress to ensure that when you go to get dressed, you need only select from quality, clean, good-condition pieces that fit your life, style, and bod.

Clothes hold so much more gravitas than we think. I once heard someone refer to our stuff, and specifically the stuff we wear, as "the company we keep," which kind of shook me. Using that lens, what does your wardrobe say about you? Is it crammed with items bought for an aspirational life or style? Perhaps it's full of luxury logoed goods that you hope communicate wealth and exclusivity but really just magnify your waning feelings of worthiness? I'm not trying to go all psychologist with this, but what we choose to outfit ourselves with is actually pretty deep. Most of us, for instance, have kept pieces from years ago that used to fit, or we've recently purchased newer items in "someday" sizes that we haven't been able to wear even when we were in freaking middle school (points to self). You see these items nearly every day, so what are they conveying to you? That you wish you were smaller, taller, or more jacked? That you long for your pre-baby or post-P90X body instead of celebrating your current form? That your day, which is mostly spent on foot commuting or wiping snotty noses and sticky hands, probably isn't going to get much utility from the fifteen pairs of stilettos you used to wear to the club in 2012? Yeah, been there. Heck, sometimes I'm still there.

Case in point, I have never, in my entire life, even when I was a flat-chested, prepubescent girl, worn an outfit that could not accommodate a proper brassiere. No judgment or propriety here; I just feel my most comfortable and confident when the bosom is properly holstered in. So tell me why I've bought and tried FOR YEARS to wear supposedly "bra-friendly" dresses from a popular brand that feature necklines so comically low it looks like I'm about to wet-nurse a village? I keep getting these dresses because 1) I see all these "it girls" wearing them on the socials, and I'm human and wanna be that cute, damn it, and 2) I lobotomize myself into thinking that the next one will be different, or maybe I'll suddenly be different and wake up with a body that fits? Neither scenario has ever materialized, and when I do a scan of my closet, I realize I need to get real and stop wishing away my money. Or what about the size 4 Levi's I got from a very petite friend at a clothing swap that I was able to wear (while standing up and not moving) for a hot second after a vicious bout of food poisoning? I've never comfortably been that size ever, and seeing those jeans taking up precious and prominent real estate in my closet every damn day just made me feel ... like crap.

The truth is your closet is full of aspirations, both realized and unrequited, and if you give it some time and attention, you'll tune in to which items make you feel fantastic versus those that make you feel like a failure. And life is just too damn short to have any stuff that makes us feel like we're failing at it.

Moreover, whenever I help folks detox their closets, I see so many items that someone absolutely adores that, like our home goods and furniture from yesterday, just need a little spiffing to live another day. Instead of relegating the shirts missing a button or shoes that need resoling to a sad jumble, we're going to tackle them and get them wearable again—and the great news is that many of these fixes can be done at home in the time it takes to watch an episode of your favorite show. In my experience, a few hours and a killer playlist can yield a ton of life-bettering benefits like:

- Discovering forgotten items that make you feel absolutely awesome

- Feeling more confident and comfortable physically, mentally, and emotionally because you have a wardrobe that serves and celebrates your today body and life, as opposed to a ton of pieces that remind you of what you were or are not

- Making more informed future purchases (and saving money and time) because you have a better sense of what you actually like to wear

- Making money by selling or consigning items you no longer want

- Marked reduction in stress, wasted time, and dressing-related decision fatigue

- Reducing visual overwhelm and clutter with a freshly cleaned, organized space

- Saving money by repairing and refreshing what you already own instead of buying new

- Uncovering your true personal style by weeding out the stinkers and spotlighting the goodies that feel authentically you

Unless you're living in a nudist colony, the odds are good that you're going to enjoy at least one of these benefits from doing today's action items. And look, I'm a realist. I know that life's busy, and taking a block of however many hours you estimate to do this right isn't always feasible for many of us. That said, you can tackle this in installments or one fell swoop; whatever makes the most sense for you.

So gather up some (repurposed) bags for sorting, grab yourself a delish drink, pump a playlist that keeps the vibes high, post up near a mirror, and maybe even solicit the help of an opinionated but kind person in your life to help you determine your best looks. Once you're set up, try everything on. Sure, focus on fit, but more than that, focus on how you feel. Is the piece comfortable? Does it lay right, or is it constantly riding up? Does it require a lot of complicated underpinnings to make it work with your style? Or perhaps there's only one scenario in which you'd wear said piece (which is why you haven't worn it in six years)? Maybe those ivory silk trousers are stunning but so precious and easily stained that you're afraid to wear them? Are you holding on to something because it's designer, you once upon a time spent a lot of money on it, or it's sentimental for you? Ask yourself some of these questions when trying each piece on (and this includes accessories, seasonal items, and basically everything wearable):

- Can this work with different pieces to create a variety of looks?

- Do I already own something very similar or identical to this that I like?

- Do I need it for my job, school, sport, or some other life situation?

- Does this feel good on my body?

- Does this fit in a way that I like?

- Does this move comfortably with me throughout the demands of my day?

- How do I emotionally feel in this piece?

- Is the care required to maintain this piece something I'm willing to commit to, or is it too expensive or arduous?

- When was the last time I wore this? If it's been a long time, is it because the item is more special occasion or because I forgot I owned it?

- Would this work better for someone else in my life?

- Would this work for me with some tailoring?

These questions will usually give you the concrete intel you need when you're not quite sure about a piece. You're then going to use this intel to put your pieces into one of five categories:

1. **Keep:** These items feel great, fit well (or they're items you must keep because they're a school, work, or sports uniform), and need no repairs.

2. **Keep and Repair:** These items are keepers, but they need a repair, tailoring, cleaning, or other spiffing to serve you best.

3. **Sell:** These are items you no longer want but are in a condition or are from a brand that you know you can successfully sell at your local consignment store or online marketplace.

4. **Give:** These are items you no longer want, but you have an idea for ethically off-loading them. You may wish to give these items in your local free group, a clothing swap, or to someone in your network or a charity organization you know will get use from it.

5. **Recycle or Repurpose:** These are items you no longer want that are beyond repair, so you plan to either send them through recycling programs or repurpose them to have different utility in your life.

Once every piece has been categorized, give your wardrobing spaces a thorough clean because, let's be real, it's probably been a while. Then you're going to make a plan to tackle your five categories as completely as possible before the end of the thirty days (you can do it!). Keep items are cleaned and put back where they belong. Repairs are made or scheduled for keepers that need some TLC. If you're wondering what kinds of repairs are even out there, allow this list to inspire you to give your pieces top-notch care. As with all the charts in this book, these are suggestions, not a prescriptive or exhaustive list, so you'll likely uncover other maintenance activities and items along your spruce-up journey.

Items	Types of Repairs
Cloth Textiles *Cloth bags, scarves, hats, gloves* *Most outerwear and soft clothing* *Underpinnings*	• Bleach whites • Darn holes and tears • Dye (great for concealing stains that can't be removed, or making an item like a bridesmaid's dress more wearable) • Dry cleaning • Get underpinnings sewn into items (like gowns) • Lace, tulle, and crinoline repair • Lint and hair removal (if you have pets, you know this life) • Remove pills (with a fabric shaver) • Remove tags and open pockets and back seams (tailored items like topcoats and suits, and any clothing that has pesky tags that make you itchy and annoyed) • Replace and repair buttons, clasps, zippers, and snaps • Steam • Tailor alterations
Shoes	• Add inserts and pads for comfort / anti-chafing • Clean and polish • Resole (or adding more practical soles) • Replace laces

Items	Types of Repairs
Shoes (continued)	• Replace or add taps (to prevent wear on high-impact areas) • Replace or remove loose stitching • Stretch (to create a more generous fit) • Weatherproof
Leather and Harder Textiles *Bags* *Belts* *Leather, pleather, and suede garments*	• Condition and polish • Clean and wash (bag lining, cloth bags) • Create additional holes (for belts, fastenings) • Patch tears • Remove stains • Replace straps, handles, buckles, and loose stitches • Tailor • Treat and weatherproof
Outdoor Gear and Sports Equipment	• Clean • Patch holes and tears • Replace or repair zippers, buttons, and clasps • Treat with insect repellent • Wax or seal (or removing these) • Weatherproof
Jewelry & Other Accessories *Cufflinks and tie clips* *Eyeglasses and sunglasses* *Hair clips and adornments* *Metal belts and chains* *Necklaces, rings, earrings, bracelets* *Pins and brooches* *Watches*	• Clean and treat lenses (eyeglasses and sunglasses) • Polish and clean metal and gems • Remove or add links • Replace or buff face (watches) • Reset loose or outdated pieces • Solder and repair chains, links, and clasps • Tighten screws and springs (eyeglasses and sunglasses) • Untangle chains and charms

I know I sound like a broken record, but you'll be flabbergasted by how much you're capable of repairing at home. I don't own a sewing machine, nor am I terribly coordinated, but I'll be damned if I can't repair buttons perfectly with a needle-and-thread kit I snagged from a Holiday Inn many moons ago. Stains can usually be removed with products you already have at home (looking at you, baking soda and hydrogen peroxide), a Reddit search, and a prayer to the fabric gods. And don't get me started on the incredible therapeutic thrill I get from using my electric fabric pill remover (a.k.a. the best thing I got from my Buy Nothing group ever) on everything from sweaters to the inner thighs of my workout leggings to my couch. If you have pets, bless them, you know that a session with the lint remover results in not only a more vibrant, less shabby garment but also enough fur to make another five creatures. The point is, if you want to give it a whirl, you very likely have the skill and supplies you need to spiff up your wardrobe items all on your own.

And if the DIY route is not for you, call in the real MVPs: your local tailors, dry cleaners, and cobblers. For instance, when I recently brought a thrifted dress to be taken in, my tailor told me she could also patch my favorite pair of jeans. My cobbler not only stretches my beloved boots to accommodate thicker socks in winter but can also repair broken handbag straps and add more holes to belts. Magicians among us, I tell ya. And what's more? Enlisting their services usually means you're supporting a small business and artisans' craft.

Okay, so you've handled your repairs and they're on track to get finished before the Challenge ends. Doesn't it feel freaking amazing to restore the utility and beauty of your stuff? I'll answer that for you: yes. Let's keep that good feeling going. For the items you're putting back into your closet or drawers, should you be craving those seemingly cure-all organizers you see on TV and being hawked on social media, allow me to encourage you to look around your house and see if you already have stuff that might fit the bill. For instance, all sorts of boxes, including the oft-overlooked shipping boxes, make for great storage. If you're balking at the gnarly exterior of some of the ones you have, consider recruiting your littles to give them a coat of paint, or cover them with wrapping paper. The point here is that you have loads of organizers in your home right this very second—you just need to see items differently to spot them. And if you simply MUST HAVE designated organizers, peep your local free groups, thrift stores, and Facebook Marketplace. Organization overhaul is a regular pursuit for folks, and I constantly see people off-loading bins, baskets, drawer dividers, shoe racks, and so on. Give 'em a good clean and they're ready to revolutionize your wardrobe.

For the items you have slated to Sell or Give, set aside time to list them online, bring them to a consignment store, or give them to the intended recipients or organizations. And last but certainly not least, get creative about what pieces can be upcycled and repurposed in your home. It's important to remember that it's estimated that each one of us sends nearly eighty-two pounds of textile waste to landfills every year (and that's not even counting many of our non-textile wardrobe items). So for pieces you can't realistically repurpose, you're also going to research the myriad recycling programs available for everything from shoes and lingerie to old athletic gear, and ensure those end-of-the-line pieces don't become another landfill statistic.[2]

Action Item 1: Go through your entire wardrobe, including clothes, seasonal and specialty items (think: hiking or skiing gear, ballet slippers, snorkels), outerwear, shoes, accessories, jewelry, undies and underpinnings, socks—basically anything you put on your body to get dressed for all of life's occasions. Remove everything from drawers, closets, and storage bins.

Action Item 2: With access to a mirror (that one is pretty helpful) and perhaps a second opinion, try everything on. Using the prompts above, pay attention to how pieces feel, fit, and function in your life. Then put items in the five categories outlined above.

Action Item 3: Since they're emptied, give your dresser drawers, closet or wardrobe, shelves, and any other areas you keep wearable items a good clean. For items in the Keep category, fold, hang, or store them in their newly freshened space.

Action Item 4: For Keep and Repair items, peep the list above to determine if any of the suggested spiff-ups are in order. Then research which fixes or cleaning you can do in-house versus those you'll need to outsource. Schedule appointments for specialty care, and set aside time and supplies needed to actualize the repairs you intend to do at home. Once complete, hang, fold, or store those newly repaired items in their space.

Action Item 5: For items in your Sell category, set aside time to consign them in person or list them online at your preferred marketplaces. For more detailed guidance on selling your items secondhand, visit Day 13.

Action Item 6: For items in your Give category, take the appropriate steps to post them in your local free groups, notify your family and friends that you think said item might be great for them, or identify organizations or donation centers that will actually use the items. Then drop off and unite these recipients with their intended items. For more detailed guidance on ethical offloading, visit Day 14.

Action Item 7: For items in your Recycle or Repurpose category, get your creative thinking cap on. Silky scarves and neckties can be upcycled as purse handles and belts. Tees and other soft-material pieces make great cleaning cloths. Orphaned earrings can make cute keychains or purse adornments. Busted jeans can make cool shorts. The options are endless, but for further repurposing inspiration, visit Day 12. And for the items that cannot be repurposed, look into textile and accessory recycling options. There are designated recycling programs for shoes, bras, clothing, and beyond.

Day 18: Shop Your Stuff

Phew! This week has already been a big one, and you're only three days in! If you've followed the calendar, you're hopefully starting to enjoy a less cluttered, more organized and functional home and wardrobe. And though the goal is to continually engage in these action items throughout the Challenge and get them completely ticked off your to-do list by Day 30, I think you deserve a little midweek break. So today, you're going to celebrate the space and serenity you've created in your wardrobe by shopping your closet. The benefits of this are twofold: 1) creating a single new-to-you ensemble from items you already own exercises all the right muscles to make making do a habit, and 2) you can enjoy the same good feels that happen when you're shopping in an actual store, except you'll also be flexing your oft-neglected creativity. It's estimated that we purchase 60 percent more clothes than we did in 2000, and many of us buy new pieces when special occasions arise.[1] Today's exercise provides that hit of novelty we hope to get from shopping, without feeding into overconsumption and overproduction.

By now, your closet contains only what you love, feel absolutely electric in, and all those duds are en route to being repaired and raring to go now, so this should actually be really freaking fun. I want you to find an outfit online, on TV, or in a magazine that draws you in, and re-create it using items in your wardrobe. If you want to really splash out with this, you can create Pinterest boards of your favorite looks and then pull similar pieces from your closet to re-create them your way. Even if the attempt isn't an exact match, you're training your brain to see and explore a trend without buying a single stitch of new clothing. And if you're worried that your current duds are too outdated to create the "now" aesthetics, let me remind you of how cyclical fashion is. For instance, the criminally low-slung flared denim of my early-adulthood clubbing days borrowed from the 1960s and '70s. And judging by my students' rain- and street-soaked jean legs and exposed bellies, that look is very much back. In the immortal words of Yves Saint Laurent, "Fashion fades, style is eternal," and you can cultivate fantastic personal style with just the pieces you have right now. Promise.

During this exercise, you may decide to add some items to your Need Note because you're missing a foundational piece. That's cool, and fortuitous because secondhand shopping for clothing is a vast, well-established universe of gorgeous, affordable options. And for gosh sake, you're trying to replicate the joy of shopping, so pantomime this as you see fit. Grab a beverage and a reusable shopping bag. Play the John Tesh radio station in the background to conjure that authentic shopping mall Muzak vibe. Get gussied up so that everything you try on feels like it's part of a finished look. Crank the AC and set up a horrifically unflattering light above your mirror (kidding). Hell, if you want to put a smock on your dog and set him up behind a makeshift register so you can really scratch the "I'm shopping" itch, I'm not gonna judge you.

Is there an area of your life for which you are in need of more outfits? Is there a style you're curious about exploring? Are you just seeking some freshness in your daily rotation? Once you've found the ensemble you'd like to re-create, tally up how much it would cost if you were to go to the store and buy it today. So often, the looks I'm into are on celebrities and, thus, cost a bazillion dollars. Being able to replicate that look for zero monies is gratifying as hell, gives you major confidence, and makes you feel proud of how versatile your little wardrobe is.

Sometimes, an item just needs a little modification to fit the look perfectly. For instance, I had been wanting a suiting vest forever but didn't want to drop dough on the generic, shoddily made new ones in the stores. I did, however, have a menswear blazer I thrifted that fit beautifully along the body but had sleeves that were about a foot too long for me. Well, you can probably guess what happened next. I busted out the shears, cut the sleeves off (and saved them for another project), and folded and tucked under the shorn edges with some fabric tape I had. What resulted was a perfectly oversized vest arguably of higher quality than if I'd bought a new fast-fashion piece. What's more, the style is so authentic. I feel like a cast member of the 1980s hit show *Night Court*, which is exactly my desired personal aesthetic. Beyond saving money and not feeding into overproduction, this was actually really fun.

Don't just take my word for it. There are influencers and stylists who make absolute magic from what they already have, and they're a constant source of inspiration. If you feel this is too far afield from your creative comfort, call in a favor from an inventive friend. They'll be able to look at you and your wardrobe with fresh eyes, make recommendations, and put together combinations that might never have occurred to you. If that's not your bag, there are also apps that generate new outfit ideas that you can then re-create or that catalog photos of your pieces and then mix and match those items into exciting new combinations. Your options are endless, so approach this with an open mind and an attitude of adventure. This is supposed to be fun, and if you do dress your dog up as a cashier, please, PLEASE send me photos.

Action Item 1: Identify an area of your life for which you need new outfits, a general style you'd like to explore, or an exact look you want to re-create.

Action Item 2: Once you've found your target look, tally up how much the look would cost if you were buying brand-new items.

Action Item 3: Then in whatever simulated shopping conditions make you feel the most excited, shop your wardrobe for the items you'll need to re-create the target look.

Action Item 4: If you need inspiration or help, check out influencers who style from their closets, apps that generate new combos and looks, or solicit the help of a creative friend.

Action Item 5: Create one outfit you're excited to wear. Keep going if you're feeling inspired.

Action Item 6: If you've uncovered foundational gaps in your wardrobe, add those items to your Need Note and code accordingly. If you need guidance on how to acquire these items second-hand, refer to Day 13.

Day 19: Groom Your Grooming

One Valentine's Day, I was alone. No, this isn't the opening line of a Jane Austen novel; it was my truth in 2005. And 2006. And probably for quite a few years, but who's counting? Anyway, on this day, I decided to brave the crimson-clad, bouquet-holding couples and ride the bus to the Prudential Center Mall. Once there, I had a plan: I would treat myself to a little spree at Sephora, which no doubt would make me feel way better and much less single. And treat myself, I did. I spent $322 that night, only to return home and find that I'd bought two things that I already owned, like a complete bonehead. And these weren't even products I was planning on repurchasing because they were so not-vital to my routine that they lived in a box in my hall closet, and thus, I'd forgotten all about them. Incredible. While self-care can be fabulously restorative, I ended up feeling even more like a stooge than before, and a broke stooge at that, because I had overdrawn my fricking account and payday wasn't for another two weeks. So my awesome plan meant that I'd spend the rest of the month subsisting on Dollar Tree ramen and office peppermints while sporting $35 lip gloss—which didn't speak too highly of my financial survival skills.

From then on, I vowed that I wasn't going to shop for another life-changing mascara or serum until I used what I already had. When I first instituted this, I realized pretty quickly that beauty hauls had always been my go-to stress reliever. Bad day? In I'd sashay to CVS to get some hopefully happy-making cosmetics. Hot date? I'd roll up to Ulta with a quickness. If there was a new product drop or promotion, I was on it. In fact, one year, I tallied up that I'd spent nearly $6,500 on beauty products alone, which is especially unhinged when you consider that I was making $45,000 a year, paying $950 and $650 per month, respectively, toward rent and student loans. Did any of these items make me markedly more beautiful? A scan of old photos I found in a mementos box recently says no. In fact, my skin was more chaotic and reactive than ever due to product overload, and my hair was absolutely fried from at-home bleaching (who else survived bleach blindness of the early 2000s?). And when I looked around at my stuffed cabinets and makeup bags, I realized that in my entire life, I'd never even finished a single lipstick. The truth is that for many of us, we have a stockpile of personal care products that can keep us looking and feeling great during, and well beyond, the Challenge.

While it's difficult to quantify the scale at which we waste grooming products, we can look to the risk associated with buying these items to get an idea.[1] When you go to a store to get a pair of shoes, you try them on and can reliably determine that they're going to fit. When you purchase cosmetics or skin and hair care, items that require longer-term, applied use to determine effectiveness, you're trusting that they'll work without much guarantee that they actually will. Does this sound familiar? You buy an item you think will rock your world, only to find that that beard grooming oil gives you a weird rash or that conditioner makes your hair greasier than before you showered. In less extreme cases, it's more a matter of "the thrill is gone," and we fall out of love with a color, scent, or user experience long before we've made a dent in the product.

Common sense dictates that this disenchantment would deter us from buying more things only to be let down again. But no, instead, we're motivated to keep buying more (to the tune of nearly $4,000 per year for each of us), in the hopes of finally discovering the mythic products that make us look like supermodels.[2] But like, supermodels don't even look like supermodels, so where do you think that desire came from? Oh, right. Marketing. So today, and throughout the No New Things Challenge, you're going to use what you have, and by use, I mean use it up before you even think of buying another.

Not only are these hit-or-miss buys clogging up your cabinets while emptying your wallet, they're also pretty shit for the planet: 70 percent of beauty waste is attributed to packaging, like the annual 7.9 billion units of rigid plastic created for the industry in the US alone. And while some intentional beauty recycling programs have popped up, it's still estimated that only about 9 percent of all plastic actually gets recycled.[3] Moreover, traditional cosmetics packaging is notoriously difficult to recycle or even disassemble for reuse. Think of a bottle of face cream or a tube of mascara—many different materials like metal, glass, and plastic come together to create those containers. And most municipal recycling systems cannot handle mixed-material items, like those pesky soap pumps and spray nozzles that seem to be on everything these days. So, as you move through this process of grooming your grooming, I urge you to adopt the mindset that when you do need a replacement item, you'll upgrade to more eco-friendly options, like those with low or no packaging, compostable or reusable components, no animal testing, and refill options.

I'm also not trying to turn anyone into a beauty or grooming minimalist here either—if this is a joyful hobby for you, you needn't worry about leading a product-less life. But I do want to tempt you with some of the bona fide benefits of paring down and not buying any new lotions or potions until you've run through everything you have. For one, a streamlined routine can actually make your day easier and faster, with less of that pesky decision fatigue we touched on in previous chapters. Moreover, I've personally found that a simpler, consistent routine, that doesn't involve me constantly adding the latest treatments and acids, has actually helped me look and feel healthier.

So go through your beauty and grooming products and determine your must-haves and backups versus what you don't use and what doesn't work for you. For items in the former categories, arrange them in a way where they're easily accessible and get used. For products from the latter categories, first determine if they're safe to use and unexpired. Many products will feature on-package use-by dates (like the number inside the little jar icon on a lot of skin care) or have that info on the manufacturer's website. If you don't see any use-by guidance or a product formulation is separating, do a patch test or dump it, clean the packaging, and recycle or upcycle appropriately. For the still-good items that remain, consider offering to friends and family or in your local free groups. For less-used or unused, more prestige items, consider selling online. Yes, you can ethically off-load all price points of cosmetics and grooming products, even if they've been used— happens all the time. If you think this is crazy talk, let me tell you that a beauty bundle (a.k.a. me throwing a bunch of products I don't use into a bag and snapping a photo) gets snatched up within minutes in my local Buy Nothing group. And I regularly sell skin care or fragrances that haven't worked for me on resell apps with great success.

Should you have a product you definitely use for which you need a replacement, add it to your Need Note, and see if you can acquire it for free or secondhand. If acquiring makeup secondhand sounds gnarly, remember that most platforms let you sort by and search for new-with-tags or new-in-box items. You can also use a gift card or store credit, or repurpose something you already have. For instance, lipstick can be used as blush. A bronzer can be used as eye shadow. Can that face lotion that wasn't quite right for your sensitive skin be used as a hand or foot cream? On a manufacturing level, so many products that we've been told are specialized for different body parts and applications are actually remarkably similar. What I'm trying to say here is you're not going to die if you refill your hand soap bottle with bodywash or use shampoo as laundry detergent—I do it all the time, and I'm alive enough to be writing this book.

In addition to paring down and using what we have, we're going to follow this week's spruce-up principles and take care of what we're keeping. This is a great time to wash your scuzzy makeup brushes, sweep the little stubbles from your electric razor, remove buildup from your trusty hairbrush, wipe down your makeup palettes, and give your medicine cabinet, makeup bag, dopp kit, and shower organizer or caddy a good once-over. As with many of this week's action items, giving your beauty and grooming regimen some TLC will reinvigorate your appreciation for and the utility of them and might even have them scratching that "new thing" itch again.

Action Item 1: Go through your beauty and grooming products and organize into five categories: 1) Use, 2) Backup item I could use, 3) Doesn't work for me, but can repurpose, 4) Doesn't work for me, and 5) Never use.

Action Item 2: For categories 4 and 5, consider offering the items to your friends and family, posting in Free groups, or selling on secondhand sites. If the items are expired, separated, or just plain grody, clean and appropriately recycle or upcycle the containers.

Action Item 3: For categories 1 and 2, clean and arrange your items, as well as the spaces in which you keep them, to give your regimen a fresh feel.

Action Item 4: For category 3, see if you can repurpose these items in innovative ways. Can the bodywash or shampoo you didn't love be used to refill your hand, dish, or laundry soap? Maybe the beard oil you didn't jibe with can be used as a cuticle oil or leather conditioner for your boots? When it comes to creative reuse, you're really only limited by your imagination.

Action Item 5: Regarding items for which you need replacements, add to your Need Note and code accordingly.

Action Item 6: Adopt a mindset of upgrading items for which you need replacements with eco- and animal-friendly options that feature low or no packaging, compostable, reusable, and easily recyclable components, absolutely no animal testing (keep your peepers open for the PETA Beauty Without Bunnies, Leaping Bunny, or Vegan symbols for maximum confidence), and refill options.

Action Item 7: If you want extra support during this process, search online for "project pan makeup" to find loads of groups and advice threads dedicated to folks using up their beauty and personal care products.[4] If you've always wanted to post a photo of yourself with an empty compact of foundation or bottle of shampoo, this is your chance.

Day 20: Tune Up Your Tech

Remember early in the book when we talked about Alfred P. Sloan's introduction of planned obsolescence, or the manufacturing of items with an intended, artificially short lifespan, to the Western world? Well, there are few areas of industry that demonstrate planned obsolescence more than the technology sector. And boy, do we love our tech. Our electronic device consumption is six times what it was in 1950, even though the world's population since has only doubled.[1] And most of our devices cannot be repaired by design because manufacturers make it virtually impossible to replace components and parts. Companies further trap us out of repair options by intentionally using nonstandard screws, sealing or soldering parts together, and developing software that slows or glitches for older or repaired devices. And despite these practices being branded unethical, they know they can get away with it because we're often so wedded to and dependent upon their products.

And it goes without saying that this planned obsolescence is terrible for the planet. Electronics are already some of the most taxing items to produce, due to their reliance on mined and rare materials, which also makes them difficult to properly dispose of. And dispose of, we do, to the tune of nearly fifty-four million tons each year, because we don't really have other options.[2] To compound the awfulness of this practice, much of our e-waste, just like our unwanted clothes, is disposed of in under-resourced areas, where it leaches toxic substances and pollutes communities. And while some fantastic and effective buy-back, take-back, and recycling options do exist, only about 17 percent of discarded electronics globally are properly recycled.

You'd think, knowing this, we'd do our best to keep our tech in check and make the most of what we have. But here comes marketing to squash that dream. Think about it: nearly every week, we're bombarded with advertisements for new releases of phones, computers, gaming consoles, watches, and so on, that make us feel like silly Luddites if we don't upgrade our only year-old device to the shiny new version. And we're so moved by this messaging that new releases of, say, an iPhone can mean that hordes of people are practically guaranteed to be lined up around the block for hours in all kinds of weather to grab theirs, even though their current phone probably works just fine. And the data supports this marketing-kindled social frenzy; 77 percent of Americans feel it's "essential" to have the latest tech and gadgets, with 28 percent admitting to prioritizing this pursuit over true essentials like paying bills and rent.[3] Moreover, the expenditure associated with chasing the latest tech leads to individuals amassing an average of $1,500 in debt each year. Of course buying new gadgets feels essential when we have few feasible repair or recycling options. But there's a lot you can do to keep your stuff running smoothly that doesn't involve trashing what you have or going into debt buying something new.

Now, if you're a tech enthusiast or reviewing appliances is your job, I'm not coming for you. But if you're someone with a perfectly functioning tablet who is just being lured by the siren song of one with a *slightly* better camera that now comes in rose gold, I'd urge you to do today's steps in earnest and *then* revisit the prospect of buying the newest iteration. At the very least, these steps will help your tech run better, for longer, with you getting more utility and joy from your items while saving money. At most, these steps will do all of that, as well as show you that you didn't need the new version after all—you just needed a tech tune-up. And we love that.

So first, we're going to corral all of your tech and electronics. And I want you to think beyond just your phone here. Like, yes, of course your phone, but I'm also coming for your earbuds and headphones, computers, printers, televisions, monitors, vacuums, toasters, air fryers, automobiles, chargers, hair dryers and flat irons, gaming consoles, cameras, even that sound machine that plays rain when you go to sleep—you get the idea. Ask yourself, *Do I actually know how to work this?*—which, yes, I know may sound ridiculously basic, but I'm writing my second book and I rarely, if ever, read the instruction manuals for anything. And I'm not alone—surveys have shown that 75 percent of us simply don't read the dang instructions, like, ever.[4] So if you're in that camp and think your existing items are broken and thus need replacing, hear me out: Could it possibly be because you haven't read the manuals? Doing so can unlock functionality you didn't know existed and mean the difference between an appliance becoming a landfill landmark or a world-changing contraption you can't imagine being without. And don't freak out if you trashed or can't find the paperwork; most manuals are accessible online.

Once you know what you're working with, literally, we're gonna clean those devices up. Forget true-crime shows—if you want to chill yourself to the bone, look no further than scrubbing the mesh speakers in your earbuds. Like, you've been putting those in your ears for months, my dude—what did you expect? The options for cleaning are endless, but here are a few ideas: remove the crumbs from your keyboard and toaster, rinse and dry your vacuum canister, tighten the screws on your blender container (yes, many have screws that keep the blades tight), add fresh batteries to or charge your remotes (and gather spent batteries to be properly recycled), give your washer and dishwasher a dedicated clean, remove the dust that clogs the filter and accumulates behind your fridge (seriously, it's scary back there) or on your clothes dryer, fix the wonky setting on your car stereo, organize your charging cords and cables, and change burned-out light bulbs. These pursuits are extremely rewarding, boost our gratitude, and restore the joy associated with using our things, which is a similar feeling to buying something new.

During this process, you'll likely discover devices and components that you haven't used in a dog's age or that require some expert repairs. For the items you wish to off-load, spend a little time researching their next destinations. That's right; just because planned obsolescence is the manufacturing strategy of the day does not mean that every piece of older tech is doomed to the trash. In fact, many options exist for giving your devices a kick-ass afterlife. For instance, where I live, there is a program that will gladly take donations of computer components and parts in all conditions and ages, which are then used to teach people from underserved areas computer engineering and repair skills. Domestic violence programs and shelters will often accept functioning phones (yes, even non-smartphones) to serve as lifelines for victims attempting to escape dangerous situations. Organizations like Habitat for Humanity will often welcome older but functional large household appliances. And specialized recycling programs exist for everything from charging cords and bricks to broken and burned-out light bulbs. Moreover, some of the items you don't want can be donated to thrift stores, offered in your local free groups, or sold on secondhand sites. My boo off-loaded a broken vintage turntable in his local Buy Nothing group to a woman who wanted to surprise her teen son with something complex to take apart and put back together. While this would be a nightmare surprise for me, the kid reportedly loved it. The avenues for responsibly stewarding your castoff tech to greener pastures really are plentiful, and next to none of them involve you chucking stuff in the garbage. For the items you use or would like to keep using that need an expert's eye, research your options, and set the wheels in motion.

Now that everything is sorted and cleaned, we're going to further enhance your gadgets' utility and performance by deleting any unused programs and files, updating operating systems and applications, and determining if any items are in need of repair and what those options may be (remember that No New Things doesn't bar you from paying for repairs and replacement parts). Then explore those repair options and attendant warranties and schedule appointments to get the show on the road. And for the devices not in need of repair, don't be afraid to do a little extra and give them a new background or desktop pattern, a secondhand, new-to-you case, or a new alarm or fun ringtone (hi, 2005 called and it wants its "Candy Shop" by 50 Cent ringtone back). Sometimes those little enhancements alone can sate the need for newness, which marketing so often has us craving.

I'm admittedly a disappointing and derelict tech person. Not only do I basically never read instructions or manuals, but I also once (lol, like two weeks ago) had 1,200 files, not in organized folders but residing atop one another, on my desktop—and then I'd wonder why my computer was always hot to the touch, making a disconcerting whirring noise, and would move at a glacially slow pace. Devoting just forty minutes to tossing the old stuff, organizing the files I wanted to keep, cleaning the screen and keyboard, and yes, slapping on a cute, inspirational desktop pattern not only made me excited to do my work but also made a huge difference in its operational efficiency. Like, my sputtering Yugo had become a sleek Ferrari, and using it became thrilling again. Same goes for my phone, which is more time capsule than streamlined convenience device most days. For instance, my contacts list is like reading a cryptic ancient scroll (who the heck is "DO NOT ANSWER [poop emoji, barfing emoji]"?) with a few familiars' names sprinkled in to throw me off. Why do I have an app on my home screen that I used exactly one time to get into a Tears for Fears concert in 2016? How many videos of one's pet sleeping is too many? Psych, the limit does not exist. Excellent questions. Let's cull those for both operational efficiencies and to reduce the visual clutter that we're confronted with every day.

These may seem like silly little tasks, but 1) cleaning, organizing, and updating an item can make it more delightful to use and scratch that itch of getting a new thing, and 2) will often extend the life of your devices and appliances, which is an Ashlee-approved middle finger to an industry whose kink is creating flimsy things that break and can never be repaired so we'll buy crummy replacements.

Action Item 1: Corral and clean your devices and ensure you know how to actually work them by familiarizing yourself with their instructions. You can round up and read the physical manuals or find them online.

Action Item 2: Make system upgrades, update apps, delete unused apps, clean up your desktop, and generally help your devices help themselves.

Action Item 3: Wrangle and organize your cords and charging cables, put fresh batteries in, and power up your devices so they're ready to rock.

Action Item 4: For items that you never use and don't plan to use, research and set in motion rehoming and recycling options like donating to organizations, electronics recycling and upcycling services, selling secondhand, and posting in your local free groups.

Action Item 5: For items you plan to keep, explore repair and refurbishing options should items require a more involved fix or a replacement.

Action Item 6: Make it cute. Sometimes a fresh desktop pattern, screen saver, or even a secondhand new-to-you phone case can give your tech the upgraded feel you need to keep the love alive.

Day 21: Rearrange an Area

This far into the book, I'm sure this will shock you, but I wasn't a very popular kid. Being an only child, I spent a good bit of time alone. And because of that, I've honed the talent of delighting in my own company, which means, yes, I can weather a four-hour flight with just the entertainment of my imagination, no sweat. So, on the rare occasions when I'd do something worthy of punishment, my parents had to eventually find an alternative to grounding me, because I actually really liked being confined to my bedroom. One particular instance known as "the Pool Pump Incident of 1990," after I'd fibbed about emptying the pool skimmer baskets (the negligence of which led to the entire pool pump getting backed up with leaves and thousands of dollars in repairs), I was grounded. Fair. Fine by me. A few hours into my confinement, my sweet mom came to check on me only to find that I'd completely rearranged my room. Like, shelves, bed, desk—everything heaved and pushed around by little old nine-year-old me. I was having a freaking blast and feeling way better than one should when in trouble, and it became clear to my parentals that this punishment wasn't yielding the penitent contemplation they'd hoped for.

Research shows that I actually wasn't that odd after all (at least not in this instance), nor was I spinning my wheels in house-arrest purgatory. Rearranging your space has remarkable cognitive health benefits. Whenever I read up on those, I think, damn, what a sophisticated little mammer jammer I was, lovingly relocating my Jordan Knight poster and neatly arranging my *Goosebumps* books, just following my bliss.

The science behind rearranging is actually pretty darn interesting. Our brains are remarkable pattern-making machines that can become accustomed to our spaces, and that monotony sometimes leads to distracted thinking. Thus, shifting or changing elements of an area stimulates our brain to find new focal points, thereby stoking and enhancing concentration. And literally seeing things from a new angle can get the creative juices flowing, so much so that a common hack for writer's block is to change environments (hence, the prevalence of idyllic writers' and artists' retreats), or at the very least, move one's desk.[1]

In addition to enhanced focus and creativity, mixing up a space has been shown to improve your mood, enhance sleep quality, kick lethargy to the curb, and spike motivation. Numerous studies actually support decluttering and rearranging as powerful prescriptions for folks struggling with depression. And on a very basic level, retooling a space that maybe isn't working well for your needs means you'll likely get more seamless function from the new arrangement.

Jennifer, a Challenge participant with four kids (bless her), realized the staircase by her front door was a tripping hazard, piled high with shoes, keys, tiny toy cars (that could make a regular stumble worthy of an emergency room visit), and other casually flung items, and it was making her—in her words—batty. For today's action item, she created a system using stuff she already had with the addition of a charming thrift store find. An overlooked cabinet that had been collecting dust in another room was made functional next to the staircase, where each member of the household now had an assigned cubby for their shoes and stuff. She topped it off with some décor items she already owned: a lamp, a pretty plant, a mirror so everyone could check their teeth on the way out the door, and a little bowl for keys. Items that needed to go upstairs but perhaps hadn't made it there yet would go into an ingenious vintage step-shaped wicker basket she found at her local secondhand store. Now, the clutter is mostly corralled, and someone takes the basket up each night and rehomes the errant items that were previously strewn about the stairs. A small rearrange, a little repurposing, and a huge win for the sanity of parents everywhere.

Another participant, George, also refreshed some small elements of his work-from-home space with outsized results. An eyesore of a printer that once took up half of his desk was moved to a lower shelf, which meant he had more workspace and less visual clutter. He anchored frequently used charging cables to the back of the desk (using an upcycling hack he saw on YouTube), which meant he'd be spending less time fishing them out from behind the computer when they'd fall (so annoying) and more time enjoying his always-powered-up headphones and tablet. Even simpler enhancements, like moving a drink coaster from the living room and placing a postcard he found inspiring on the wall, meant his notebook wasn't getting damp from his iced latte's condensation, and he had something new to gaze at when he needed a little zone-out break. Small tweaks like these cost George no money and took about twenty minutes total to make happen but dramatically increased the ease of use of his workspace, and in turn, his productivity.

So today, you're gonna get that free and fun mood boost that can be had from rearranging a space. This can be as grandiose or humble as you like. If you want to really get after it, rearrange an entire dang room, furniture, décor, and all. If you don't have that kind of time or energy, just tackle a drawer or a shelf you regularly encounter. You can also use your frustrations as a guide for which spaces might need a tweak. For instance, if you're having difficulty sleeping, maybe you'll benefit from moving the ornamentation, books, photos, and whatnot from your nightstand? If your utility drawer has become an abyss of junk and you're constantly searching through sundry crap to find what you actually need, maybe that's where your attention is most needed. See, part of what we're seeking when we shop is freshness, that hit of delight that comes from newness and novelty. The same feelings are sparked when your eyes tell your brain, "Hold up, something's different here," and you can enjoy that impact whether you tackle your entire living room or your nightstand drawer.

Action Item 1: Target an area of your home and radically or nominally rearrange the space by decluttering, repurposing items you already have, and acquiring items secondhand.

Action Item 2: Pay attention to the functional frustrations you experience within your home and with your stuff. What's not working? Are certain arrangements slowing you down, creating unnecessary friction, or getting in your way? Could those areas benefit from a changeup? Then target those areas and spaces for future rearrangement.

Day 22: Focus on Food

I see you, friend. One day, you've got it all together, hitting the grocery store like a boss, only to get home exhausted the next night and order delivery. And then one evening turns into many, and you've now got a fridge full of rotting produce and take-out containers on your hands. It happens an awful lot, especially in the United States, where around 32 percent of our well-intentioned grocery buys go to waste.[1] That's like lighting $152 on fire every month, which I'm pretty sure is not an activity on your Love List.[2] And while No New Things doesn't have any parameters around eating out or buying groceries (we're very pro-food around here), showing the food you have some love by actually eating it strengthens the habits that help us sucker punch overconsumption.

America has a food waste problem. Our convenience-obsessed culture has put us ahead of every other country when it comes to tossing food, to the tune of forty million tons each year, or nearly 40 percent of the entire US food supply. Yeah, that's a lot. And when you break that down to an individual level, that means that you likely waste about a pound of food every single day. Which might not sound like that big of a deal, but when you consider that forty-four million people right now in the US are food insecure, thirteen million of whom are children, that 32 percent of wasted groceries feels almost criminal.[3]

And much like our clothes and other possessions (are you

noticing a common theme here?), a lot of the food we trash is actually perfectly good. We can chalk this up to two phenomena: 1) we misunderstand expiration dates, which are more sugges-tion than edict, and throw items out because we wrongly think they've gone bad; and 2) we don't consistently prep ingredients or meals, so there's a lot of friction and work staring us down when we're hungry but lacking energy. Let's be real right now: food waste is just another epidemic of excess, a product of over-consumption.[4] So today, I'm tasking you with giving your gro-ceries some love in two ways that will make 'em easier to eat and harder to waste.

First, you're going to take stock of all the goodies currently in your pantry and fridge. This can be you just getting a visual on everything by snapping a pic, or writing out an actual list so you buy only what you need the next time you hit the store. Clean out the obviously gnarly stuff, and while you're at it, give your shelves and fridge a good wipe-down for that fresh-start feeling. Determine what will get eaten if you just put in a little prep. And I don't mean this in a full-blown Instagram influencer meal-prep way, though you can certainly do that. Think of this as staging your food for success, whether that means just readying ingredi-ents or batch cooking components to easily add to a meal. Like, that pineapple makes a way more convenient snack option when you actually cut it up, and those fresh herbs will last longer if you store them properly. Some participants, especially those with kids, have found great success placing an "eat first" basket, full of on-the-brink food like fruits or veggies, at the front of the fridge or right on the counter. Just going through the food you have (and trust me, you likely have way more than you think you do) and staging ingredients for success will signal to your brain how freaking abundant you are. I also want to caution you to not fall prey to the trap of aesthetic organizing and decanting. We're aiming to extend the utility of the food you have, not enter your cabinets in a beauty pageant. Most participants have been able to easily make do with containers they already have or that, ya know, come with the food. If you find you're in need of meal-prep or storage containers, hit up your networks and free groups, or channel basically everyone's grandmothers and upcycle forty tubs of Country Crock.

For extra credit, I'm going to encourage you to look into composting options in your area, if you don't already partake in this magical practice. Just as furniture and clothing never really biodegrade when trashed, nor does most of our food, at least not very easily. Remember, landfills aren't large composting sites; they're mummy makers. And when food scraps go to those sad places, they release way more methane than they would if composted, thus accounting for 11 percent of the world's greenhouse gas emissions.[5] Who'd have thought your little food scrappies had such an immense environmental impact? Composting is easier, cleaner, and cooler than ever before, and a quick internet search or ask of your networks will likely yield options that work with your home setup and lifestyle. I live in a small apartment with no outdoor space and have used a compost pickup service for nearly a decade. No, it doesn't stink or attract bugs or require a lot of space or money or upkeep, but what it does do is significantly reduce my trash creation and my negative impact on the planet. Plus, I'm sorry, but once you see all the things you can compost, like pet hair, pencil shavings, and paper packaging, it almost becomes like a fun game.

Once you've staged your food for success and possibly joined the composting club, your second action item today is to make a meal from the ingredients you already have. Since you've taken inventory of your kitchen, you can either tap into your inner Emeril (BAM!) and get creative making your own recipe, or you can use AI or the many apps out there that generate recipes specific to ingredients you have.[6] You may not think you're the cooking type, but whipping up a meal has so many benefits beyond just getting you fed. Much like upcycling and other elements of the Challenge, cooking encourages creativity, eases anxiety, and fosters innovative thinking.[7] So if you have a eureka moment for a badass invention while you're slicing mushrooms, well, you can buy me that Bobby Brown shirt because I told ya so. You'll save money, ratchet up your resourcefulness, stem harmful food waste, probably eat something better for you than takeout, and maybe even feel a surge in gratitude for what you have and more confidence in the kitchen—not too shabby for a day's work.

Action Item 1: Take inventory of the food you already have and determine what's usable and what's not. If you want, make a physical list (I have one on my phone for easy access) or snap photos so you avoid duplicates and get only what you need during your next grocery trip.

Action Item 2: Prep and store the still-usable items in ways that keep them fresh and in places that will keep them on your radar. If necessary, upcycle old food containers to maximize your storage. Should you want to take this even further, you can batch cook ingredients or do a full-blown meal prep for the week. The kitchen is your oyster!

Action Item 3: Clean your pantry, cabinets, and fridge before putting everything back to give your kitchen that "I can't wait to cook here" feeling.

Action Item 4: If you don't already compost, look into composting options in your area. If you do, responsibly compost any food that didn't make the cut in Action Item 1.

Action Item 5: Once harmony has been established in your kitchen, make a meal from what you've got. You can get creative and wing it, or you can solicit the help of AI or the many apps that will take those ingredients and generate right-fit, mouth-watering recipes.

Action Item 6: Repeat these steps anytime throughout the Challenge to strengthen your make-do muscles and avoid food waste and overconsumption.

Week 3 Reflection

Y'all! Y'ALL! I'm shouting. Why? Because you're more than TWO-THIRDS of the way through the No New Things Challenge. Yes, I know you can count, but like the proud stage mom I am, I'm going to call out the obvious because, hi, twenty-two freaking days is a big deal. When was the last time you stayed the course with something for three weeks? If you've refrained from buying new items during this time, lemme just say WOW. In an overconsumption-saturated society, you've essentially stepped away from participating in the very hypnotic new-stuff cycle for a pretty long time. Think about that. Is this the longest you've ever gone without purchasing new things?

It's a pretty epic feat, and hopefully, you're 1) feeling incredibly proud of yourself, 2) finding that the No New Things habits are starting to feel a bit more automatic and comfortable, and 3) enjoying less intense and frequent urges to overconsume. And even if you did end up purchasing some new items, big whoop. What's important here is that you did so at a slower clip than usual, or you exercised more intentionality than you would have before the Challenge. All of that is what we call *progress*, my friend—and progress is the name of the game. So however you feel you fared this week, BRAG ON IT. What you're doing is powerful and literally changing your life, so you deserve all the snaps. And by the time we reach next week's reflection, you'll have completed the Challenge, which means you're in the home stretch.

The question I want you to really reflect on as you close out this week is: *Am I better now than I was at the beginning?* And I don't mean *better* in some judgy, worth-baiting way—I mean, do you genuinely feel better since starting the Challenge? If *better* doesn't feel like the right word, try swapping the question for *Am I experiencing a positive difference from Day 1?* Are you more aligned and in control, less driven by consumerism and marketing? Are areas of your life reflecting this liberation? Have you learned more about your shopping impulses and responses to marketing? Maybe you're just feeling a little more ease or steadiness. Do tell.

And in regard to this week specifically, did the daily prompts and activities have you feeling more gratitude or seeing new possibilities for the items you own? Are you appreciating your simplified, organized, and rearranged spaces and stuff? Maybe you're feeling absolutely triumphant because you finally knocked some long-lingering tasks off your to-do list. Log those emotions because it's all incredibly valuable data. Add up your savings, both for this week and the prior weeks combined, as well as any proceeds from secondhand sales, and prepare to have your mind blown by those digits. And no matter how you feel about your progress thus far, definitely treat yourself to something from your Love List.

Prompts	Your Answers
How did the week feel for you overall? Did it go smoothly? Why or why not?	
Were there days or action items that were difficult for you? Which ones and why?	

Prompts	Your Answers
Were there days or action items that felt amazing for you? Which ones and why?	
Did you glean any insights or realizations about your relationship to shopping or stuff that you hadn't realized before? If so, what?	
What are you most looking forward to about next week?	
Tally your Trigger Tracker for this week. How much did you save?	
Total your savings from Week 1, Week 2, and Week 3. How much have you saved since starting the Challenge?	
Did you sell anything secondhand this week? If so, list the total amount you made here.	
Add the totals from Tracked Triggers and your sales.	

Week 4: Getting Out There

O ver the past three weeks, you've forged the skills that have enabled you to wriggle out from the clutches of consumerism and confidently stride into better-for-you habits and activities. Man, that read like the back of a Tolkien novel. Hyperbole aside, now that you're basically an old pro at No New Things, this week will have you navigating the scenarios that crop up outside of your personal habits and home. This week's action items were directly informed by past participants' most recurring dilemmas when taking the Challenge to the streets, like:

- *How do I give good gifts and still follow the Challenge?*
- *How can I break up with the awkwardness I feel around borrowing stuff?*
- *I love living this way. How do I set goals for myself that reinforce this new way of life and don't revolve around consuming?*
- *Where does self-care fit into the No New Things way of life? Is that too . . . indulgent?*
- *How do I follow the Challenge while on the go or traveling?*

And just like last week, this week has an eighth bonus day, which incidentally is also your last day (if you want it to be, that is). On Day 30, you'll crunch the numbers and calculate, literally and figuratively, the impact of the Challenge in your life thus far. And while I don't have a crystal ball, I have a hunch both the savings and the impact are going to be magical.

Day 23: Borrow Before Buying

I remember doing a TV segment on No New Things early in 2020 where I said that if there's an occasion-specific item you need (like a power drill, for instance), consider asking someone in your sphere if you can borrow theirs instead of buying said item new. And let me tell you, the uproar. Like, shaking-fists-at-the-sky UPROAR. Now, granted, it was in the thick of shelter in place, so maybe folks had a lot of time on their hands, but I received no fewer than twenty emails from pissed people telling me that even deigning to ask a neighbor or friend to borrow their lawn mower or fondue pot instead of "buying your own" was tacky, cheap, opportunistic, and perhaps the nastiest barb of them all, shameful. *Shameful.* Shameful, y'all. What?

To be clear, I *never* suggested folks ask without offering, or take without giving, or gunk up someone's item and not, like, return it in pristine condition. After all, the shareconomy is all about respect and reciprocity. But to say that asking for help from someone in the form of borrowing a thing is *shameful* is just about the most perfect example of how capitalism has made us into monsters who value ownership over access, even when it comes to trivial consumerist trappings like weed trimmers and glue guns. In 2015, *Fast Company* proclaimed that "the sharing economy is dead and we killed it," lamenting, how the heck did "an idea that everybody loved so much . . . that made so much sense on a practical and social level, [morph] into the pure capitalism that it is today"?[1] To answer this, and also restore some of the shine to peer-to-peer lending, we need to go back a bit to when pooling resources was second nature.

The sharing economy of today tends to focus more on the use of idle assets, like renting out your spare bedroom on Airbnb, or driving someone to a concert in your Kia via Uber or Lyft. And while the reinvigoration of this type of pay-for-play sharing is useful and builds community, the *gift economy*, which refers to the *free* exchange of items or services, is what more closely resembles how borrowing was revered and practiced for centuries around the world.

Up until very recently, mass production of goods was not the norm. Items were either handmade by a skilled craftsperson or their creation took hella time, and pricing reflected this labor. Take the first iteration of the personal computer, the IBM 610 Auto-Point. This bad boy debuted in 1957 for a cool $55,000.[2] When adjusted for inflation, this so-called personal device would cost $615,000 today, which is a stark contrast to the $200 computers you can buy right now. So yeah, stuff used to be incredibly expensive compared to individual incomes, and thus it wasn't feasible for a person or household to own every item they might need or use. This meant that people shared resources as a way of getting their needs met. Gradually, as household incomes increased alongside mass production, which made goods cheaper, Western society began to favor individual ownership over that communal access that was so vital to our survival for generations.

Beyond losing the community ties that bound us, the focus on each of us owning one of everything we might ever use is an exercise in egregious waste—wasted time, wasted money, wasted space, and wasted resources. The fact is, unless you're a stuff archivist for the Smithsonian (not a real job), or curator of the World's Most Overwhelming Overconsumption Time Capsule (also not a real job), you don't need to own everything you might occasionally use. Your home is not a Noah's Ark of items you're preserving in the face of some biblical disaster. How often do we drop hundreds on an ornate twelve-person dining set from a couple's wedding registry, only to find a few years later that they've used it once, or never? What about the pandemic rise in amateur chefs that resulted in millions of enthusiastically purchased bread machines and pasta makers that are now collecting dust? Does every household really require its own pressure washer, bouncy castle, or riding lawn mower to be functional and societally legitimate?

Peruse your home for a second—is there stuff that you bought or were gifted that you rarely or never use, that could've been borrowed or rented? Many of these items become expensive statues in our garages, while others make their way to those indiscriminate donation centers or straight to the landfill. But, of course, all this collateral damage is way better than being branded as *shameful*, right?

I'll be honest—even I had a hang-up about borrowing. Chalk it up to the fear of aforementioned borrowing judgment, or it could be that whole women-being-conditioned-to-not-want-to-burden-or-inconvenience-others thing. I just desperately did not want folks to think I was a cheap neighborhood succubus. But once I got over myself, I found that people actually love sharing because it's a way to feel closer to and build trust with one another. In fact, helping someone can actually boost our positive feelings toward them by 20 percent.[3] If you're the "What's in it for me?" type, you'll be stoked to know that sharing can make you happier, less stressed, and even impart a sense of purpose. This is backed by data, but anecdotally, we've all experienced the joy of reciprocated action. I've had so many rich relationships start from my asking to borrow an item, someone generously offering theirs, and then when they ask to borrow something of mine later on, I am so hot-damn excited to provide the same kindness to them. And so on, until a helpful, mutually satisfying connection sometimes emerges. And even when it doesn't result in an "Are we best friends now?"–type situation, lines of communication are forged, whereby we express, intuit, and fulfill community needs together with our collective resources.

I see this phenomenon daily in my local free groups. Someone asks to borrow a standing mixer and, in kind, returns the squeaky-clean KitchenAid to the lender along with a batch of freshly baked cookies. Last year, I lent a gal who was fostering some kittens all the neonate supplies I had used when I took care of my then day-old, very smol (but now obese and rude) cat, Skipper, and in turn, she sent me daily photos of the adorable litter of calico orphans she nursed to robust health. And in my little corner of the world, there's absolutely nothing shameful about fresh cookies or kitten pictures. I stand by that.

Opening these lines of sharing communication has even emboldened my personal friend group to get over the initial apprehension of asking for help because we know it's a secure line. Now whenever one of us has an occasion or need, we will ask if we can raid one another's closets for an ensemble, or "can you lend me your legal eye" to tell me if I should sign this contract? And if no one is able to assist or the ask is too great, we're frank about it. With that understanding, I find I have more helpful and honest relationships across my life.

And not to get all gushy, but there's just something so cool about sharing. Have you ever lent someone a book that you just couldn't put down? That shared experience of enjoying the same gripping story, getting a whiff of the well-worn pages—it's special. The same experience can be had when you're wearing a friend's dress to accept a big award, or you lend an aspiring photographer your barely used Canon so they can take portraits of local senior citizens. It takes a little courage to step out of ourselves and make a borrowing request, but once you give it a go, you'll find it's a beautiful, community- and connection-affirming practice.

So today, you're going to embrace the mindset of borrowing

before buying, and either put a call out to borrow an item, lend something out, or both. Ideally, this will create a domino effect where you get more comfortable with being a part of the movement to democratize your community's access to goods. And if you're already a card-carrying member, well, today will be a piece of cake (made with a borrowed electric mixer).

Action Item 1: You know those sharing communities and groups you connected with on Day 4? Well, you're going to hit them and your personal network up and ask to borrow something that's on your Need Note. Pay special attention to how you feel during the process. Did you feel any trepidation around asking? How did others respond to your request? What was the end result?

Action Item 2: If you have nothing you need to borrow, you can scour said groups to see if someone else is in need of an item you have to lend. Easy-peasy. And then watch the magic of sharing pour in and make you feel all fuzzy in your heart. Take note of this, and remember that folks who get the opportunity to lend to you often feel the same pang of joy. Congrats! You're actively participating in positively nurturing your community.

Action Item 3: Adopt a mindset of borrowing before buying whenever you or someone in your network needs something.

Day 24: Get Good at Gifting

One of my vivid memories from childhood was my totally glamorous (think Joan-Collins-from-*Dynasty* fabulous), but also completely nightmarish aunt yelling in her delicate Southern drawl that if my uncle didn't buy her this fur coat or that emerald necklace, she would divorce him. "I'll divorce you!" would underscore practically every holiday and family gathering. It was so ubiquitous that I can call my mom today, totally out of the blue, and say without any preamble or pleasantries, "If you don't get me this [fill in the blank] . . ." and without missing a beat, she'll reply with, "I'll divorce you!" And we have a good chuckle because it's like a sound bite from a *Real Housewives* episode, right? But in a society where overconsumption is expected, of course we ascribe a lot of feelings, worth, and consequences to the presents we give and receive.

Undeterred by this grossly ungrateful display, I am naturally what you might call a "present person." If I see something someone might enjoy, I get it for them. If I know a pal is grinding particularly hard on a project, I'll surprise them with a tasty-fun snack. I never miss a birthday and often have gifts lined up for future occasions months in advance. I don't say all this to be sickeningly self-congratulatory either. I genuinely get so much enjoyment and satisfaction from the whole process. I recognize that this is not everyone's love language or area of comfort, and that's perhaps because gifting today is ridiculously high stakes. Of all the scenarios one might encounter during No New Things, gifting during the Challenge is THE one that seems to strike the most fear in the hearts of participants. And I get it. But allow me to bust through that anxiety and drop some truth: capitalism has tricked us into forgetting that truly impactful gifts have way less to do with money and newness and more to do with thought, investment of time, and another human being making the effort to understand you. That's right—thought, time, and understanding. Those intangibles pack way more emotional sustenance than the latest piece of must-have crap.

In an effort to reconnect to this truth, let's talk about your experience receiving gifts and why using that lens can help you reconnect with gifting from a place of thoughtfulness, rather than coerced consumption. Think back to truly meaningful gifts you've received in your life. Were they meaningful because they were just purchased for a king's ransom at some retailer? Or was it the friend who saw how burned out you were and said, "Hey, I'll watch the baby so you can have some time for yourself"? Or maybe it was your partner who took you for a day of trampoline jumping and ice cream cones when you were depressed. You may argue that these are gestures for every day, but in doing so, you're proving the point—they're gifts and can be freely given and enjoyed at any old occasion, and their impact is usually far profounder than anything that comes from a store.

For me, it's when my mother—who's both an incredible artist and whose love language is totally going overboard on gifting—has hand-painted something for me. Or when my dad, who admittedly doesn't like to fuss with emotional intimacy, sends me a card with some doodles of dogs that tells me how proud he is of me. Or the time my partner and best friend conspired to surprise me with her flying in for my fortieth birthday party. Those were gestures and moments, not things, that I'll cherish forever.

And when I think back on physical gifts I was given, the ones that stand out are not expensive or particularly luxurious. When my soulmate dog, Banjo, passed away a few years ago, I received such unexpected and thoughtful gifts from people, near and far, that I was overwhelmed. Mary, a gal I went to grade school with, whom I hadn't seen since we were teenagers, sent me a picture she drew of Banjo that she had her children color in. It was so unexpected and special that it's now in a thrifted gilded frame on my wall. My kinda-quiet student who brought me a pothos cutting and told me that he hopes it lives on like Banjo's memory? Yeah, that really moved me. Or my pal Kit, who painted a charmingly tiny folk portrait of Banjo that I display with pride. Sure, these gestures required work and time, but they weren't bought new-with-tags from a store, just for the sake of giving me something new from the store. They were rich in thought and care, and I'll never forget how they made me feel.

My great-aunt Hattie was a legendary gift giver. She was an adventurous, upbeat spirit who had a cache of life stories almost as impressive as her scarf collection. She was also an academic and writer, and as is often the case with both of those categories, was pretty skint when it came to money. But she still managed to give the coolest gifts. One year, you might receive a two-foot-tall wooden cowboy sculpture she found at a thrift store. The next, it might be an old book that she'd annotated in the margins just for you ("This part always makes me think of you, you naughty girl!"). For my twenty-seventh birthday, she mailed me a chic-as-hell art deco cigarette case with the most satisfying closure click (yes, I used to keep cigs in it when I was a young smoker person, but I've since kicked that habit), which I use for miscellany, and it always brings the biggest smile to my face. Now that I've shared some of my personal favorite gifts, think on yours. Which ones come to mind? Are there lessons from them that can inform your own gift-giving ventures? This reflection just might have you feeling more at ease with the true spirit of giving and take the dang pressure off already.

Gifting and relationship upkeep have become so conflated with consumerism that giving a present can sometimes feel hollow and transactional. And what else can we expect from an industry that rakes in $960 billion in November and December alone?[1] Like, okay, So-and-So is getting married, so we will have to get them this $400 Le Creuset serving dish on their registry. Or the baby is turning one and the party invite says he needs a $150 play mat even though none of us remember anything from when we were a year old. And because we don't want to disappoint our loved ones, or worse, come off as cheap, we robotically buy these prescriptions, knowing damn well that most of this shit will go unused and unappreciated. In fact, data supports this. Each holiday season, over half of Americans go into debt spending nearly $900 each on presents alone. But 53 percent of those gifts are unwanted, to the tune of $9 billion collectively wasted.[2] And that's just the holiday season—when we factor in the birthdays, anniversaries, housewarmings, weddings, christenings, showers, affinity days (Valentine's, Father's, Mother's), and basically every other gifting occasion, you can logically assume that if you're keeping up with societal expectations and marketing edicts, you're hemorrhaging money with little to show for it. Which tells me we're just buying to say we bought a bevy of new things for our people—and when we examine that, it means our giving is more about assuaging our fears than delighting the recipient.

So today, armed with the knowledge that consumerism corrupts, well, basically everything, but especially the spirit of gifting, I want you to find one of the present-type items in your Need Note. Or if you don't have any gifts on your Need Note, use the SUPER System to conjure a pressie for someone deserving on the fly. Can you brainstorm some non-new-thing presents that would fit the bill? If you're struggling to come up with ideas, don't sweat it. We've been so conditioned to send something from a registry or wish list that we've lost a bit of that imaginative, creative muscle that makes giving a gift so special. Hopefully, as you're further into the Challenge, you'll feel more connected to that magic, but in the meantime, here are some ideas that'll put a sparkle in your (and your recipient's) eyes:

S Shopping secondhand

- New-with-tags, nearly new, or delightfully gently used item from a brick-and-mortar or online secondhand, thrift, consignment, or vintage shop.

- Style an outfit for the recipient with entirely thrifted pieces and go all out with accessories to round out the look.

- Try your hand at personalizing a secondhand item, like ironing on patches, or embroidering your recipient's name on a vintage jean jacket.

- Vintage books, home décor, cookware, art, vinyl, magazines, clothing, jewelry, furniture from vintage stores.

U Using, upcycling, or reimagining stuff you already have

- Bake or cook tasty gifts like granola, baked goods, soup and spice mixes, accompanied by upcycled or secondhand containers or pans.

- Create scrapbooks, collages, vision boards, homemade cards, art pieces or objects, music playlists; write a heartfelt letter.

- Make self-care indulgences like sugar scrubs, body oils, body butter, candles, perfumes, air fresheners, home cleaners.

P   Paying nothing

- If you live in a large urban area or a college town, pay special attention to the stoops and alleys at the end of each month when people tend to be moving. During these times, people often put out perfectly good items that can be spruced up and just might be the exact thing your recipient has been needing or looking for.

- Put an ISO in your free groups for a specific gift you have in mind.

- Propagate plant cuttings from your own collection and plant in a thrifted or found pot or vase.

E   Experience, donation, and monetary, non-thing gifts

- Engage in a special experience with the recipient and make it a meaningful social occasion—like volunteering together.

- Gift memberships they'll love and use like a workout studio, sports league, streaming service, clothing rental, facials, massages, etc.

- Gift special experiences like restaurants, concerts, shows, movies, theme parks, trips and vacations, and adventure activities.

- Give them a thrill via a special message from their favorite celeb via apps like Cameo.

- Give them money, a check, or a gift card or voucher.

- Make a financial or in-kind donation in their name to a charity that is important to them or relates to causes they care about.

- Offer to provide or pay for helpful acts of service like childcare, house cleaning and organizing, cooking meals, sewing, massage, Reiki, yoga, color consultations, or lessons.

R   Renting, borrowing, or sharing

- Rent out a space and borrow party supplies from your networks and throw a little surprise shindig for your recipient.
- Rent equipment like a boat, paddleboards, kayaks, ATVs, mopeds, etc., and have a blast enjoying nature.
- Rent a flashy or classic car for the day and have a joyride.
- Treat your recipient to a change of scenery by renting a cabin, campsite, tiny house, yurt, or other out-of-the-ordinary accommodation.

Above all, remember it is indeed the thought that counts. Gifting has become so fraught with superficial expectations these days, but the impetus to give should indeed come from the heart, the desire to fill a need, the hope that what you provide will be helpful, healing, or happy-making for the receiver. With that as your North Star, in my opinion, you cannot go wrong.

Action Item 1: Think back on gifts you've received over the years that were of special significance to you. What made them meaningful or memorable? As you unpack this, add the common elements that emerge to your own philosophy on giving.

Action Item 2: Use the SUPER System to acquire a gift from your Need Note. Review the table above if you need creative Challenge-compliant ideas that will delight your recipient.

Action Item 3: If you don't have any gifts on your Need Note, pinpoint someone in your life and get them a just-because gift using the same process.

Day 25: Pay It Forward

Not too long ago, I was in the throes of moving, and as is customary when relocating, I was both overwhelmed by even my pretty minimalist stash of stuff and consumed by taking stock of all the new things I convinced myself I needed to make my next space homey. For weeks, I'd add items to a running list of crud to buy and curate Pinterest boards with décor inspiration images and product links. It was kind of insufferable, if I'm being honest. During this time, I also answered the call from the shelter where I volunteer to emergency foster two very adorable, very stinky eight-week-old puppies. And what a time we had, those little rascals and me. When it was finally time for Pedro and Celia to return to the shelter for adoption, my partner came along because wrangling these wriggly babies was a two-person job.

After I'd handed the little stinkers over to clinic staff and wished them lives of love and happiness, I said what I say any time I'm at any shelter: "Let's go upstairs and see the dogs and cats!" So upstairs we went. Now, as a lifelong animal rescue advocate, when I hit an adoption floor, something comes over me. I morph from regularly enthused Ashlee into the shelter's PR person, familiarizing myself with each sweet creature's personality and intake story and pimping them out to every decent-seeming human who crosses my path. Does this happen to anyone else? Well, lemme tell you, on this day, I was in rare form.

Random dude passes by, and I start in: "Hey, did you see that rottie mix with the cute eyebrows? He'd make such a great pal!" Lady walks in with her twins in tow: "Don't you just LOVE that big girl Molly? That face—AND she's great with kids!" Like, I was publicizing these dogs like it was my job. And those closest to me were not immune to my promotion. Oh, no, I was playing yenta between my boyfriend and the older pit bull, Tank. With the persistence of an Ibiza club promoter, I was sending pics of a little terrier to my friend Pete, saying, "Get your ass over here ASAP. He's your perfect dog son!" And not to toot my own unhinged horn, but some very rad things resulted from that marketing: 1) my boyfriend, who literally never makes snap decisions ever, brought Tank home (where he's now the most delightful eighty-pound couch potato); and 2) Pete rolled up to the shelter and adopted that little terrier, now named Rustin. What's more, when I saw the lady leaving with Molly, her kids excitedly hugging on each side of the gentle stray, I felt so much purpose and satisfaction wash over me. Was I officially on the shelter's volunteer clock that day? Lol, no. But my paraprofessional promotional activities in some small part helped these pups, some of whom had been there for months, snag loving forever homes. It's funny to think that in the weeks leading up to this day, I was so focused on myself and my bullshit shopping desires, but these few hours of people-to-pet matchmaking brought more fulfillment than any home décor purchase ever could.

The point here is that it's nearly impossible to not feel awesome when doing something that benefits others. And the data supports this. People who volunteer, even for short stints, report experiencing significantly higher levels of happiness, increased self-esteem, and reduced stress.[1] Older adults who give of their time reduce their risk of hypertension, dementia, and loneliness.[2] And when kids volunteer, the results can be truly transformative. Young volunteers are 25 percent less likely to experience anxiety and 50 percent less likely to engage in destructive behaviors like smoking.[3] And the rush you get from volunteering is far stabler and longer-lasting than the dopamine letdown that accompanies shopping because of the addition of steadier serotonin and oxytocin, which mitigate the stress response.[4] I don't want to get ahead of my skis here, but it's almost like being part of the solution can help us live healthier, longer, more meaningful lives. And the same cannot be said for shopping for new things.

I'd be remiss if I didn't mention another perk of volunteering: it redirects your focus to what actually matters and away from buying stuff you don't need. It's pretty difficult to browse for shoes or hit Buy on a brand-new guitar when you're playing bingo with cool elderly folks or teaching the tween you mentor how to hit a baseball. And because consumerism can, well, be all-consuming, these moments provide clarity and perspective on what really matters.

For a long time, I was like a majority of Americans—telling myself I was just too busy to volunteer.[5] But when I started doing No New Things, I quickly found that that was just bunk. I had plenty of time; I was just squandering that time zoning out into the shopping abyss. And when I began allocating just a few hours a month to causes I really cared about—namely, with animal shelters and with kiddos in the foster care system, I found that my cup, which I was previously trying to fill with stuff, joyfully runneth over.

For one, I was busy doing values-aligned things and feeling like I was, even in some small way, contributing to the rebalancing of the universe toward good. And secondly, I was constantly reminded of the intrinsic abundance in my life, just as it was. Hanging all day with a nine-year-old whose belongings fit in a single suitcase, who longs only for an adoptive family to invest in him for life? Yeah, that will make you feel an embarrassment of riches for your stocked, cozy home and supportive circle. And something else miraculous happens—you become recalibrated to life's richness residing in the experiences, the encounters, the DOING and BEING, rather than the HAVING. Your barometer for what matters moves away from stuff and more toward support. It's a beautiful thing, and usually, it costs you nothing but time.

I firmly believe that if more of us put down our phones and stepped outside of ourselves to offer assistance or an understanding ear to others, our world would be a much better, more beautiful, more nurturing place. And the good news is, this far along in the Challenge, you've probably uncovered pockets of your time that used to be devoted to acquiring stuff that you can perhaps reallocate to doing some good in your hood. And this doesn't have to be some big, formal thing. If an orientation or complex onboarding situation isn't in the cards for you, there's nothing stopping you from taking a repurposed shopping bag (oh, the symbolism!) and picking up the trash you encounter on your afternoon walk. Or what about calling a friend you know is going through a tough time and offering them encouragement? Maybe you want to treat the guy experiencing homelessness you see on your daily commute to lunch? If you think you have nothing to offer, I'd urge you to think again. Nonprofits often have gaping needs for practically any function you can think of, from back-office accounting to grant writing to making cat toys out of pipe cleaners and wine corks. You're useful, you are needed, and with a little time and an open heart, you can do some or a lot of good in the world.

Action Item 1: Identify pockets of time that have been freed up by doing the Challenge. How much of that time can you allocate to volunteering?

Action Item 2: Determine what organizations are a good fit for you based on 1) your interests, 2) your talents, 3) your time commitment, and 4) the onboarding formality. Then get after it.

Action Item 3: If a formal volunteer gig doesn't work for your schedule or situation, try finding moments in your every day to do something good for someone or something. The opportunities are endless, every little bit counts, and volunteering will keep life in perspective and your overconsumption habits in check.

Day 26: Socialize Sans Shopping

If you existed during the early aughts, you were probably dazzled by the portrayal of glam big-city living as shown in series like *Sex and the City* and *Gossip Girl*. Now, no shade to those shows, they're good fun, but I don't think it's earth-shattering to say that having an Upper East Side apartment and a never-ending rotation of couture clothing on a freelance writer's salary is not realistic. I'll admit that I recently indulged in a few episodes (seasons, actually), and one of the things that struck me the most, besides the revelation that I need to be wearing more headbands, is how nearly every scene of the characters socializing is set to a backdrop of shopping or browsing. And this is actually art imitating life, as opposed to the other way around. Socializing has become so conflated with shopping for women especially[1] that we sometimes require a little tune-up to remember that our true friends will hang with us whenever, wherever, no commerce required. My dad is full of memorable quips and homilies, and he always says that if someone wants to spend time with you, "Shoot, they'll help you organize your pencil case," which basically is just a more poetic way of saying your real pals don't need to shop to spend time with you.

If the last mic drop doesn't ring true for you, and you have contacts who make you feel less-than because they've got the latest flashy stuff and you don't, I don't think I'm revolutionary in telling you that those aren't your friends. No matter what capitalism tries to force down our throats, our worth does not reside in things. You deserve to spend time with humans who don't conflate your or their value with stuff. And if you're struggling to know the difference, No New Things will certainly help shed light on who's here for you and who's here to show you up or feel better at your expense. And that intel is priceless. If your social circle is full of people who guilt or enable you to spend beyond your means, it's time to have some frank conversations about your boundaries and goals. And if those don't do the trick, well, refer back to Day 4 for tips on how to connect with people and groups that value fiscal fitness.

When I had my first "big girl" job in Boston, my girlfriends and I would hit the mall or Newbury Street boutiques constantly. Did we ever actually need anything? Nope. We were browsing for entertainment, for suggestions, similar to when people zone out on retailer sites today, waiting for the stores to tell us what we should buy. After all, we thought this was just what grown city gals did in their spare time. Like 42 percent of Americans, we considered shopping a hobby.[2] On the weekends, we'd squander the sunny days perusing stores, which usually involved one of us sheepishly calling our bank from outside the boutique after our card got declined. "What? How can that be? Please run it again," one of us would say with our best wealthy-person-exaggerated-look-of-disbelief impression, knowing damn well we'd blown our last forty-five dollars on appletinis at the club the night before. Were some great conversations and laughs had during those times? Absolutely. But could we have had those good times elsewhere? Also, absolutely.

This philosophy should extend to all our relationships—dating, romantic partnerships, and familial. For instance, you shouldn't have to bribe your kids with stuff to get them to spend time with you. Read that again. You're setting a dangerous precedent when you promise your offspring—or anyone, for that matter—things as a reward for hanging out with you. You and your partner can connect without gathering stuff to buy as you move through Home Goods or Costco. A romantic date doesn't have to culminate in a teddy bear with a balloon or a pricey piece of jewelry. True connection exists apart from stuff. That's just facts. No New Things is not only a Challenge strengthened when done with your people; it's also a great time to find non-shopping ways to nourish relationships with those people.

So today, you're going to brainstorm ways and schedule rendezvous whereby you nurture camaraderie without the consumerism and prioritize connection over consumption. And because I want to support your dreams of being the most sought-after hang out there, here are some ideas for activities you can do with your friends and family that don't involve browsing and buying:

• Co-work	• Host a throwback-style sleepover or movie hang
• Cook a meal	
• Do a DIY wine tasting at home	• Prep meals for the week
• Do a free online workout class or meditation at home	• Play basketball, tennis, football, pickleball
• Garden or tend to your plants	• Play board or card games
• Go for a walk, run, bike ride, or hike	• Run non-stuff errands
• Go see a movie, show, or concert	• Set goals or make vision boards
• Grab some instruments and have a jam session	• Take a day trip somewhere new
	• Take a lesson or class
• Have a phone or video call	• Try out a new restaurant or coffee shop
• Have a picnic	
• Hold a clothing swap	• Volunteer

Action Item 1: Using the list above, an internet search, or your imagination, select some non-shopping activities to do with your friends and family in the near future, and get those appointments scheduled and on your calendar.

Action Item 2: When socializing in the future, opt for opportunities that maximize connection over consumerism, and note how these alternatives make you feel, how much money and temptation they've spared you, and how they've strengthened your bonds.

Day 27: Travel Thoughtfully

It was close to dusk in Kathmandu and we had ducked into one of the many little side street shops, mopeds and savvy stray dogs weaving around us. I needed to rent some trekking poles before we embarked on our Annapurna hike, but like any traveler, my eyes were also a little peeled for souvenirs. Our guide, Tikka, knowing I was from America, pointed to an enormous table clearly merchandised for tourists. "Asssslee, Jack Daniel! American whiskey!" he exclaimed with a huge smile. There they were—piles and piles of hats and shirts sporting gently tweaked logos (the merch literally said JACK DANIEL, minus the *s*) of the iconic booze house. Another row of shirts boasted images of Michael Jordan and Kobe Bryant. And still more featured slogans so hilariously altered (as to not spark copyright infringement violations, I gathered) like RED MULE GIVES YOU WINGS. As I looked them over, laughing at how far-reaching Western consumerist pollution is, I realized that most were marked MADE IN CHINA. And when we visited other shops and stalls, the merchandise was the same. Even high in remote Himalayan villages, the seemingly uniquely Nepali prayer flags and deity figurines being sold were mass-produced in other countries.

While my experience isn't always the rule, the tourism industry is replete with poorly made pseudo-sentimental bric-a-brac that we do not need. This is not to say that you must abandon your magnet-from-every-country collection if it really brings you joy. But buying things as souvenirs is not a requirement or an ethical imperative of traveling. In fact, the actual French word *souvenir* literally means "memory"—and memories don't require that you buy a single thing.

And for those who holler, "But stimulate the local economy!" My friend, I'm absolutely into doing that, but let me put you on to some facts: most souvenirs aren't even made in the country in which they're sold, with the merchants who sell them barely breaking even.[1] And because of this, the lore that buying souvenirs stimulates the local economy and community is just that: lore. You're much better off meaningfully supporting locals by choosing food, lodging, excursions, and occasional retail options that are small, independently owned businesses—and leaving them great tips and reviews, too, when appropriate.

While you may not be traveling today or anytime during the 30-Day Challenge, doing so the No New Things way is not only totally doable but actually incredibly freeing. Instead of browsing stalls for tchotchkes that'll probably collect dust later on, you can engage in activities where you actually explore and learn about the place you're visiting. Instead of body slamming your suitcase, praying to the zipper gods it'll close and accommodate all the crap you've bought (been there), you can enjoy returning home with a full heart and no extra baggage fees.

After saving up for many years (another perk of doing No New Things on the regular), I had the privilege of visiting Antarctica. On that life-changing trip, I encountered loads of seriously interesting people who'd been backpacking through South America for many months, sometimes years. I was inspired by the lightness of their packs juxtaposed with the richness of their experiences. Like, no joke, all their possessions for swimming in cenotes, hiking mountains, working at hostels, partying hearty, and basically every other activity, save for running a suit-and-tie board meeting, fit into a single backpack. Their souvenirs were not things but rather the experiences and people they'd encountered along the way. Stuff would've weighed down their ability to embark on the next impromptu adventure and couldn't have held a candle to reminding them of the good times nearly as much as actually having said good times. And as a result, these were some of the best people with whom to share some drinks and stories. I am not saying everyone can or should quit their jobs and trek the globe or that there's not immense privilege in these kinds of adventures, but as with everything, there's a lesson to be appreciated here, and that's the old adage "Collect moments, not things."

If you still have the yen to bring home a local treasure or you don't want to face the ire of your boss, who insists you bring them back the keepsake du jour whenever you go somewhere, consider hitting up the abundant secondhand options available in many destinations (looking at you, Parisian flea markets), or investing in a high-quality, legitimately human-made piece that will actually support an artisan. Also, this should go without saying, but please leave the nature where it is—don't go taking stones or plants or animals from natural sites. Leave areas better than you found them, and don't allow your journey to be burdened by mindless overconsumption, and you'll enjoy plenty of those true souvenirs—memories.

Action Item 1: While you may not be traveling on this exact day or during the Challenge, when you do find yourself traveling, adopt a No New Things approach to souvenirs by remembering to collect moments instead of things.

Action Item 2: During your stay, support the local economy in meaningful ways by patronizing independently owned accommodations, restaurants, activities, and shops. Make sure to tip generously, leave positive reviews, and give good word of mouth when appropriate.

Action Item 3: If you must get physical souvenirs, consider secondhand options or local, artisan-owned retailers that will genuinely benefit from your patronage.

Day 28: Self-Care Sustainably

Whether it was with the aim of conducting research for this book or because they're just so damn entrancing, I fell down the rabbit hole of ASMR "self-care with me" YouTubers. The pink-washed videos detailing aesthetic and expensive fifteen-step skin care routines, complete with perfectly polished acrylic nails tapping gingerly on each product's packaging. The fizz pops and ice clinks of the "sleepy girl mocktail" hitting a cut-crystal coupe while the sleek, minimalist tub fills with bath bombs and flower petals, topped off with a caddy containing an iPad, Stanley cup full of Ben & Jerry's, and a perfumed candle. Sure, these otherworldly displays can be hypnotic, and to some, they're even aspirational. But these influencer videos are just another tired-ass example of how overconsumption has co-opted the ways in which we can effectively care for and celebrate ourselves.

The concept of self-care first emerged with Socrates, who cautioned that we not seek goods motivated by greed, jealousy, or excessive desires in the process.[1] Later, iconic author and activist Audre Lorde added that self-care is self-preservation and, thus, an act of political warfare.[2] These explanations cast self-care as a lofty pursuit brimming with responsibility. Yet our current self-care culture has deviated from those more purposeful definitions to focus instead on overindulgence and self-coddling. Look, it's nice to get pampered sometimes, but today's marketing communicates that to care for yourself properly, you must engage in performative overconsumption.[3] I mean, are you really giving yourself the TLC you need with that evening jog if you don't follow it up with a massage, cold plunge, LED face mask, and sauna blanket? Sure, you can decompress with your favorite beer and movie, but is that scenario actually calming your nervous system if you're not also wearing temperature-regulating pajamas, burning a seventy-dollar candle, and sipping an organic turmeric latte from a handmade ceramic mug?

When we remove the tacky consumerist window dressing, we find that truly effective self-care actually requires very little and is certainly not predicated on buying a bunch of new stuff. Rather, self-care is practical and holistic. Heck, reading this book and engaging with the Challenge is self-care. The items on your Love List are self-care. Asserting your boundaries with a pushy friend or picking up trash in a local park is self-care. Seeing a therapist, adding vegetables to your diet, drinking more water, and scheduling your medical appointments are self-care.[4] While social media has diminished it to consumerist excess, that's just one approach in a vast universe of options. Whatever pursuits strengthen you and your purpose in this world, well, congratulations—you've just engaged in self-care of the highest order.

So today, I want you, both as a means of celebration for how far you've come during this Challenge and because you're a human being who deserves to unwind and feel good, to self-care sustainably. This first is going to be contingent on what self-care means and what feels satisfying for you. To some, it's the TikTok-touted everything shower and a good read. To others, it might be a midday nap or a yoga class. Whatever it is for you, go about your home wrangling items you already have that can help you have the most restorative time ever, no purchasing necessary.

Action Item 1: Identify time in which you can engage in some self-care that's meaningful and needed for you. And then grab the necessary supplies from stuff you already own to prepare for a successful unwind sesh. Here are a few themed ideas to help you banish stress without buying a damn thing, but definitely consult your Love List for ideas and do whatever makes you feel the most balanced and cared for:

- **Groom and Relax:** You know those beauty samples and forgotten grooming products you found during Day 19's declutter? Corral the ones you've been wanting to try. Run a bath and get some bubbles going with bodywash, shampoo, hand soap, or anything body-safe and sudsy you have. Put on some good music or a gripping true-crime podcast. Lay out your robe, jammies, slippers, old band tee, whatever makes you feel ready to relax. Pour a glass of something yum and lather, rinse, repeat your way to free-sample relaxation nirvana.

- **Dinner and a Movie:** You need not swipe on Tinder to engage in one of life's truly great pastimes—chowing while watching something riveting. So with the skills you honed on Day 22 when you made a meal from ingredients you already had, do just that—and make it extra delish. Use the good olive oil. Throw in the dried shiitakes hiding in the back of your cabinet that you've been saving for a special occasion. This is a special occasion. Plate your meal with care (garnishes and real flatware encouraged), and fire up that movie, show, or sporting event that you've been waiting all week to enjoy.

- **Active Rest:** Go ahead—splurge on your favorite form of movement (remember, the Challenge is totally cool with you spending on an experience like a workout class) or healing modality. Maybe it's a judo lesson or a deep-tissue massage. Then come home to a dreamy get-clean shower and melt into bed.

- **Truly Chill:** Meditation? Yoga? You don't need to go to a spa to get this experience. Dim the lights, roll out a mat if you have one, surround yourself with good-smelling things, tee up a free meditation or class online, and get after it.

- **Stay Cozy:** Have a book or magazine you can't wait to tuck into? Maybe throw in changing into your comfies, the best seat in the house, a cozy blanket, a cup of something warm, and a purring cat? There ya go—truly satisfying self-care.

Day 29: Set Goals Without Stuff

As mentioned, I recently moved. I'd been at my previous apartment for nearly a decade, so while I'm not someone who has a lot of stuff (writing this book would be a weird flex if I were), I did have some basement storage bins of childhood keepsakes I'd been avoiding. And after a week of being annoyed by them piled up in my new living room, I decided to go through and consolidate their contents. First, let me just say that this process took about seven fucking hours, so do with that information what you will when you get the urge to keep all the crap from eras of your life. So there I was, crisscross-applesauce on the wood floor, combing through three decades of untouched cards, letters, photos, and journals. Guys, the journals. Oh, the journals. Oh, little Ashlee and her absolutely mortifying journals, one for each year of my tween-and-beyond life. Those from my preteen days were hilarious, with one bearing this disconcerting inscription on the front page: *This journal belongs to me, Ashlee Piper, and when I reach the age of 16, I wish for it to be buried under the pear tree below my bedroom window.* Like, um, are we okay? Yes. Yeah, I just had quite a flair for drama at a young age. Anyway, one diary in particular stood out—the one from when I was fifteen years old. In addition to being painfully in love with my male best friend who was so obviously not into me, I was obsessed, OBSESSED with getting an apple-green Dodge Neon. Like every fucking page waxed poetic about this mechanical nightmare of a car. And aside from a few entries where I also yearned for a pager (if you know, you know), it was clear that this car, this *thing* was my primary goal in life at the time.

For the better part of two years, I believed strongly that the Dodge Neon was something to ascend to, that this thing defined me and who I wanted to be. Thankfully, when I had saved up enough for a down payment, my parents made the ultimate decision that a used Toyota Corolla was a better choice. So high fives all around for their fully formed prefrontal cortexes. I'm sharing this story not just because I tend toward self-deprecation but also as an example of how our goals can be hijacked by consumerism. Because we are conditioned to tie possessions to our worth, we often associate how we want to improve and who we want to become with material items. Or we use acquiring things as benchmarks of us arriving at our goals. And while some of this is fine, it's also messed with our understanding of true self-improvement and personal growth.

Forgive me for getting deep here, but you're twenty-nine days into the Challenge, so I think we can plumb the depths of your soul for a hot second. Who are you without things? When you strip away the having and the wanting and the surrounding yourself with stuff, what remains? And what do you want to do with that version of you? How do you want to feel? How do you want to move about and interact with the world? See, using stuff as goalposts is lazy personal development. I'm not saying you're lazy, but if we're using possessions to indicate that we've "made it" to ourselves or others, we're not really developing anything, or at least we're not developing anything within our character that's enduring. And this may just be my take, but deep down, I think we know this, and thus reaching these possessions-focused "goals" is ultimately unsatisfying.

Multiple studies support this theory, finding that people who prioritize and even reach their materialistic goals, such as shopping for status or appearance, tend to experience more negative emotions and psychological distress.[1] Just as things are not a way of meaningfully investing in ourselves, materialism does not lend itself to sustainable well-being. In fact, folks who set possessions-related goals are more likely to experience loneliness, eating disorders, depression, and anxiety, because what we really need for self-actualization cannot be bought or found in a store.[2] This doesn't mean you can never aspire to buy something or that goal setting doesn't work (and if you need a refresher, Day 1 is all about the power of writing down your intentions). But some of y'all are really wilding out with bucket lists and vision boards that look like a kid's Christmas letter to Santa. Fine, you want a Birkin bag or a luxury car. What will acquiring those items mean about you? Do they enhance your purpose or contributions in the world? I'm not vilifying stuff—in fact, this isn't really even about the stuff. But just as overconsumption is often a deflection from feeling or to fill emotional voids, the same goes for setting stuff-related goals.

Today, I want you to consider your goals. If you've never done this, there's no time like the present to get started. And if you're a regular goal-setter and -getter, take a look at and reengineer any that could be more feelings-, behaviors-, and accomplishments-focused, rather than revolving around things. For instance, you may have had a goal to buy a new car, but what does having that car represent about you? How will buying the car make you feel? Can you unpack those feelings and find a different way to express the aspiration? Maybe it's less about the act of buying a particular car and more about you finally enjoying some financial security. Perhaps the car is just a symbol of the real achievement of overcoming generational poverty. The things are just totems of the deeper actualization and meaning we truly desire.

I also want you to see if those things-focused goals even still feel good or right-fit to you now that you're nearly done with this Challenge. Do you still really want to buy a bigger house now that you've culled your clutter and stopped buying so much new stuff?

246 Ashlee Piper

Does buying that pair of exclusive new sneakers mean as much to you as it did thirty days ago? If your stuff-focused goals still feel right, well, keep them! If they don't, ask yourself why, and set alternative aspirations that are a better fit for the post-Challenge you. This is also a good opportunity to revisit your Day 1 Visualization to see if what you wrote down nearly thirty days ago has seeded other goals for your future self.

Action Item 1: Review any goals you have, or set out to create goals if you're newer to the practice. If you've never done this before, there are loads of guides online. You can also revisit the prompts from Day 1 to get the aspirational juices flowing.

Action Item 2: Do any of your goals feel overly materialistic or hollow? If so, dig into what having those things actually symbolizes and means for you. Focus on the ways you want to feel and fundamentally change to reengineer more meaningful versions that are less reliant on acquiring stuff.

Action Item 3: Observe how and why your reactions to these goals feel different since you've nearly completed the Challenge. There's probably a juicy reason why some of your old aspirations aren't feeling like the right fit for you now—and it could be because this Challenge has fundamentally changed your relationship to stuff.

Day 30: Calculate and Celebrate

Right now, I'm inclined to blast "End of the Road" by Boyz II Men, because that's what they would do when our middle school socials ended and the gymnasium lights went up. But for you, I will resist this urge because while this is the end of our thirty days together, it doesn't have to be the end of your No New Things ride. And what a ride it's been. In such a short period of time, you've done a whopping amount of work on the outside, as well as on the inside. On the outside, you've decluttered, repaired, and organized your spaces and stuff, built healthier alternative habits to shopping, and begun architecting a rich life that isn't controlled by what you buy. On the inside, you've altered your relationship to overconsumption, understood and managed the deeper reasons behind consumerist impulses, and rewired your brain to explore more ethical and responsible ways of meeting your needs. These are huge, HUGE accomplishments. Even if you only completed a few Challenge days or you are still en route to fulfilling many of the aforementioned milestones, you're doing more to improve your finances, well-being, and environment than most even deign to. It may sound dramatic, but embarking on the last thirty days, especially if you're someone who has spent a lifetime being consumed by consumerism, is a real hero's journey. And it doesn't have to end here.

Before we get into the numbers, let's check out where you

were on Day 1. Take a peek at your Visualization. Were any hopes made manifest by your hard work? Maybe you saved some money or were able to start chipping away at some debt. Perhaps you just wanted to experience some relief from all the marketing messages or social media comparison. Some participants found that not only did they actualize the goals they laid out on Day 1, they knocked them out of the dang park. Like the couple who intended to create a budget, but once they got started, found they were able to set the wheels in motion to start the adoption process. Others discovered that while some hopes didn't materialize, other, potentially better ones surfaced in their place. Like Richard, who hoped to free up some time to get back to his running routine, but found himself gravitating toward investing that time into fun and focused connection with his partner and kids. Jamilah set out to buy less stuff, but a few weeks in realized she had a full-blown shopping addiction. Not only was the pause of the Challenge integral in her having this epiphany, but the money she saved during those few weeks enabled her to afford to start therapy. Maybe you've had realizations of a similar gravitas, or maybe you just finally got around to decluttering your hall closet. Whatever your journey, take some time to reflect on where you started, where you are today, and the arc in between by using the prompts below:

Prompts	Your Answers
How did the Challenge feel for you overall? Did it go smoothly? Why or why not?	

Prompts	Your Answers
Were there days or action items that were especially difficult for you? Which ones and why?	
Were there days or action items that felt especially amazing for you? Which ones and why?	
Did you glean any insights or realizations about your relationship to shopping or stuff that you hadn't realized before? If so, what?	
What aspirations from Day 1's Visualization have been realized over the thirty days?	
What aspirations from Day 1's Visualization have not yet been realized over the thirty days?	
What Love List item became your favorite?	
Did resisting shopping impulses get easier as you moved through the Challenge?	

Once you've engaged in more substantive reflection, it's time to tally that money, honey! Some of you smarties may have a full-blown spreadsheet situation happening, and I fully support that level of thoroughness. If you're more of a pen-to-paper kind of person, use the following totals as your guide:

Calculations	Total
How much did you save from tracking your triggers for Week 4?	$
Total your Trigger Tracking savings since starting the Challenge.	$
How much did you earn from selling items in Week 4?	$
Total your earnings from everything you sold throughout the Challenge.	$
Was there other money you saved or earned (like refunds from returned items)? Total that here.	$
Add your Tracked Trigger savings + any Challenge-related earnings for the full thirty days =	**CHALLENGE TOTAL**

Though money certainly isn't everything, the tallied amounts are often the most exciting and rewarding part for many who do the Challenge, primarily because the numbers don't lie and are usually more staggering than folks initially anticipate when they start No New Things. Like, *How can I be having impulses to spend $6,200 in a single day?* Well, by now, you know, because you've read this book and gone through the motions of understanding your very personal underlying reasons for shopping. And with many folks emerging from the Challenge with hefty numbers, you can feel a real sense of accomplishment. Like, you deflected spending that through reconditioning and hard work.

Now that you've calculated, it's time to move on to the celebrating. This is not limited to your Love List. I want you to celebrate yourself and your incredible journey in a way that feels deeply satisfying for you. While I'm not gonna sit here and say,

"Heck yeah, go on a shopping spree," how you decide to fête yourself doesn't have to be No New Things–compliant. You can go and buy something brand new that you couldn't stop thinking about for the whole thirty days. Pop bottles, go dancing, throw yourself a little (or big) party—whatever, man. What I hear more than I expected from people who've done the Challenge is that, throughout, they were kind of dreaming of what they'd buy when they reached the end. But then Day 30 came and that urge had kind of fizzled out. Now, not everybody felt this way—some people still wild out buying unrequited things, but it's interesting to see how the stuff we crave SO BADLY ends up feeling less exciting once we've tweaked our perspective and habits to get steadier fulfillment from less consumerist places. So whether it's a humble "attaboy" you whisper to yourself as you wake up or a financial free-for-all, do what feels right for you and see if you feel differently about your mode of celebration before and after.

And, no pressure, but now (or even days before) would be a good time to determine whether you want to keep going with or take a break from the Challenge. More often than not, participants are so encouraged by their remarkable progress in such a short time that they're curious about what might happen if they extend No New Things. You already know about my experience. I relished my results so much that my initial one-month target ran on for nearly two whole years. Others decide to take a break, with the intention of doing another monthlong Challenge in the near future. Some folks prefer not to continue (they can't all be superfans) but rather take some lessons and habits with them into their everyday. Whichever camp you fall into, it's my sincerest hope that you got some value from the last thirty days and that your experience has changed your inner and outer existence for the better.

Conclusion: From Lessons to Lifestyle

I always get that little letdown pang when I've completed something awesome. Like the time I binged all the *Hunger Games* books and was so momentarily depressed once I was done that I skipped a girls' night out in favor of sulking in a fleecy blanket burrito. While this book doesn't have nearly as much action, adventure, or sexual tension, if you've done No New Things in any measure, you have just engaged in something pretty involved. And sometimes the end of that journey can feel a little sad. The good news here is that your journey doesn't need to end. You can start all over again from Day 1, or you can just continue with the Challenge tenets as part of your everyday life for as long as you like. Maybe you'd enjoy some company this time around? You can start a local No New Things group or get your friends to join you for round two. And if you're worried a repeat will be boring or old hat, well, fiddlesticks. After doing this for more than a decade, I still have *aha* moments and fine-tune habits with every single Challenge. And No New Things is such an automatic part of how I operate these days that it doesn't even feel like I'm doing anything, let alone a challenge. All this to say, you needn't worry about that end-of-the-road comedown, because your adventure doesn't have to stop today—or ever.

And whether you're continuing on or sprinting to Target to spend all the money you saved, whether you sorta-kinda completed a few days or were an absolute machine rocking the full month to a tee, I want you to reflect on impact for a second. Remember when I mentioned that a few summers ago, around twelve thousand people signed up to do the Challenge? Now, let's say that only half of those folks even deigned to start No New Things, and by the end of the first week, half of those people had dropped off. That leaves us with three thousand bought-in participants who completed a week of the Challenge. And let's say the average participant tracks avoided triggers to the tune of $1,000 a day (which is way less than even my most restrained day of tracking, and I'm arguably a lot more immune to marketing temptations than a Challenge newbie).

Drumroll, please: that's $3 million a day in avoided consumption, and a staggering $21 million in a single week. Just for three thousand people. Yeah, there's a reason beyond my own personal convictions that I'm not getting flown around on corporate press trips. The simple steps I preach in this Challenge are designed to make you financially healthier, happier, and ensure a better planet for all of us, but they sure as shit don't make corporations as rich as they'd like to be. And the thought of you further distancing yourself from the consumerist web they've spent decades creating scares the bejesus out of them. Sure, my rough calculations are oversimplified and lacking nuance, but as you've likely already experienced firsthand, the savings are very real. On an individual level, that's $7,000 a week that someone did not spend, but wanted to. When tempered with even the most conservative stats on how much we act on our impulses, those savings are still in the thousands.

I'm not having delusions of grandeur here. Sure, I created the Challenge, but you're the one who freaking did it. I'm just saying that the financial impact of No New Things for you as an individual is huge. And when you extrapolate that to even small groups of people, that impact has the power to change the whole damn system. Imagine the fat-cat board members shaking in their boots, freaking because now they're gonna have to buy the smaller private jet if one hundred thousand people opt to do the Challenge. That would be almost $3 billion in lost potential sales. Billions of dollars not hanging over people's heads on credit cards, not cluttering up homes, not creating conditions whereby folks had to make a tough choice between paying for health care or putting food on the table. So while I have no intentions of becoming a cult leader or MLM proselytizer, well, ever, I wouldn't be mad if No New Things caught on like a viral video and worked its change-your-life magic on anyone who needed it.

And that's just the financial aspect of the Challenge. When I read the hundreds of testimonials I've received over the years, the stories of lives improved are so moving they almost seem made up. Adopting children and pets and being able to afford fertility treatments. Going back to school or starting therapy. Reversing health conditions because walking outside has replaced scrolling indoors. Spending unfettered quality time with people and on pursuits that matter. Making space for fun and rest that was otherwise crowded by promotions and bills. Acknowledging and processing difficult emotions instead of covering them with a blanket of overconsumption. Finally having the clarity to determine who you are and what contributions you want to make in this world. Real people reaped these benefits.

You've likely experienced some of these results already. And while No New Things was the gentle kick in the tush to get there, I want you to remember that you, my friend, made it happen. You did this. You have shown yourself that you have the power to tell overconsumption to take a hike. You have the agency to put the wheels in motion to make your life better in any ways you choose. And you can keep making it happen for as long as you like. Now's the time where I pass the baton (have I been weeping at the Olympics too much? Yes) to you to take the lessons herein and make them a lifestyle. I'm grateful you went on this journey, and I hope that No New Things expanded your gratitude for the abundance you already have, as well as your faith in yourself.

Notes

Introduction

1.   Decluttr, "Survey Finds 54 Percent of Americans Are Overwhelmed with Clutter and Don't Know What to Do with It," PR Newswire, January 13,2015, https://www.prnewswire.com/news-releases/survey-finds-54-percent-of-americans-are-overwhelmed-with-clutter-and-dont-know-what-to-do-with-it-300019518.html; Sophia Naughton, "Work, Chores, Errands—Oh My! Average Adult Feels Burnt Out 3 Days Each Week," StudyFinds, January 30, 2023, https://studyfinds.org/not-enough-hours-in-the-day; Chris MacDonald, "Drowning in Debt: The Hidden Tsunami Engulfing American Households," Nasdaq, September 28, 2023, https://www.nasdaq.com/articles/drowning-in-debt:-the-hidden-tsunami-engulfing-american-households.

2.   *Our Epidemic of Loneliness and Isolation: The US Surgeon General's Advisory on the Healing Effects of Social Connection and Community* (Washington, DC: Office of the Surgeon General, 2023), https://www.hhs.gov/sites/default/files/surgeon-general-social-connection-advisory.pdf.

3.   Mark Whitehouse, "Number of the Week: Americans Buy More Stuff They Don't Need," *Wall Street Journal*, April 23, 2011, https://www.wsj.com/articles/BL-REB-13793.

4.   Joshua Becker, "21 Surprising Statistics That Reveal How Much Stuff We Actually Own," Becoming Minimalist, https://www.becomingminimalist.com/clutter-stats.

Why Do No New Things?

1.   Newser Editors, "Average Size of US Homes, Decade by Decade," Newser, May 29, 2016, https://www.newser.com/story/225645/average-size-of-us-homes-decade-by-decade.html.

2.   Marni Jameson, "Do You Really Need Self-Storage Space?," *Orlando Sentinel*, February 6, 2016, https://digitaledition.orlandosentinel.com/tribune/article_popover.aspx?guid=5b657e8a-d307-4fd7-9a1e-cbfdf29c41a3.

3.   Anders Wijkman and Janez Potochnik, "A Circular Economy Isn't Enough—We Also Need to Consume Less," New Statesman, June 20, 2023, https://www .newstatesman.com/spotlight/sustainability/energy/2023/06/circular-economy -consume-less-consumption-fashion.

4.   Amelia Josephson, "The Economics of Fast Fashion," SmartAsset, updated September 1, 2023, https://smartasset.com/credit-cards/the-economics-of-fast-fashion.

5.   Decluttr, "Survey Finds 54 Percent of Americans are Overwhelmed with Clutter and Don't Know What to Do with It," PR Newswire, January 13, 2015, https:// www.prnewswire.com/news-releases/survey-finds-54-percent-of-americans-are -overwhelmed-with-clutter-and-dont-know-what-to-do-with-it-300019518.html.

6.   Barbara Brody, "How Clutter Can Affect Your Health," WebMD, reviewed August 28, 2023, https://www.webmd.com/balance/ss/slideshow-clutter-affects-health.

7.   Decluttr, "Survey Finds 54 Percent."

8.   "American Psychological Association Survey Shows Money Stress Weighing on Americans' Health Nationwide," American Psychological Association, February 2015, https://www.apa.org/news/press/releases/2015/02/money-stress.

9.   The Complex Story of American Debt (Philadelphia: Pew Charitable Trusts, 2015), https://www.pewtrusts.org/~/media/assets/2015/07/reach-of-debt-report_artfinal.pdf.

10.   Maurie Backman, "You Don't Need That: Average American Spends Almost $18,000 a Year on Nonessentials," USA Today, May 7, 2019, https://www.usatoday.com /story/money/2019/05/07/americans-spend-thousands-on-nonessentials/39450207/.

11.   Lane Gillespie, "Bankrate's 2024 Annual Emergency Savings Report," Bankrate, June 20, 2024, https://www.bankrate.com/banking/savings/emergency-savings-report /#emergency-savings.

12.   Associated Press, "Study: More Than 25% of Americans Expect to Never Retire," Los Angeles Daily News, April 24, 2024, https://www.dailynews.com/2024/04/24/study -more-than-25-of-americans-expect-to-never-retire.

13.   "Nearly 30% of Americans Prioritize Buying the Latest Tech, Like iPhone 15, Over Paying Bills," Funds Society, September 3, 2024, https://www.fundssociety.com/en /news/markets/nearly-30-of-americans-prioritize-buying-the-latest-tech-like-iphone -15-over-paying-bills.

14.   Lane Gillespie, "Survey: 48% of Social Media Users Have Impulsively Purchased a Product Seen on Social Media," Bankrate, September 18, 2023, https://www.bankrate .com/personal-finance/social-media-survey/#regret.

15.   David Schechter, Haley Rush, and Chance Horner, "As Climate Changes, Climate

Anxiety Rises in Youth," CBS News, March 2, 2023, https://www.cbsnews.com/news /climate-change-anxiety.

16.   Doris Goodwin, "The Way We Won: America's Economic Breakthrough During World War II," *American Prospect*, October 1, 1992, https://prospect.org/health/way -won-america-s-economic-breakthrough-world-war-ii.

17.   "AR5 Synthesis Report: Climate Change 2014," Intergovernmental Panel on Climate Change, https://www.ipcc.ch/report/ar5/syr.

18.   "How Much Do We Need to Consume to Sustain Ourselves?," Enel, October 2022, https://www.enelgreenpower.com/learning-hub/gigawhat/search-articles/articles /2022/10/sustainable-use-natural-resources.

19.   "Will There Be More Plastic Than Fish in the Sea?," WWF, https://www.wwf.org .uk/myfootprint/challenges/will-there-be-more-plastic-fish-sea.

20.   "How Did We Live Before Single-Use Plastic?," GoSili, https://www.gosili.com /blogs/news/life-before-single-use-plastic.

21.   "How Much TV Does the Average American Watch? (2021–2025)," Oberlo, https:// www.oberlo.com/statistics/how-much-tv-does-the-average-american-watch#.

22.   "American Time Use Survey," US Bureau of Labor Statistics, https://www.bls.gov /tus/tables/a6_1115.htm.

23.   Pixie Technology Inc., "Lost and Found: The Average American Spends 2.5 Days Each Year Looking for Lost Items Collectively Costing U.S. Households $2.7 Billion Annually in Replacement Costs," PR Newswire, May 2, 2017, https://www.prnewswire .com/news-releases/lost-and-found-the-average-american-spends-25-days-each-year -looking-for-lost-items-collectively-costing-us-households-27-billion-annually-in -replacement-costs-300449305.html.

24.   Dayana Yochim, "Women Spend 399 Hours a Year Shopping," Motley Fool, updated March 7, 2017, https://www.fool.com/personal-finance/2011/02/28/women -spend-399-hours-a-year-shopping.aspx.

25.   Zachary Sosland, "Americans Report Lack of Time for Cooking, Enjoying Meals," Supermarket Perimeter, December 21, 2023, https://www.supermarketperimeter.com /articles/10631-americans-report-lack-of-time-for-cooking-enjoying-meals.

26.   Amanda Reill, "A Simple Way to Make Better Decisions," *Harvard Business Review*, December 5, 2023, https://hbr.org/2023/12/a-simple-way-to-make-better -decisions.

27.   Stacey Colino, "Decision Fatigue: Why It's So Hard to Make Up Your Mind These Days, and How to Make It Easier," *Washington Post*, September 22, 2021, https://www

.washingtonpost.com/lifestyle/wellness/too-many-choices-decision-fatigue/2021/09/21/2dffce74-1b22-11ec-bcb8-0cb135811007_story.html.

28.   "Buying: The Effect on Self-Worth Feelings and Consumer Well-Being," HEC, February 20, 2019, https://www.hec.edu/en/buying-effect-self-worth-feelings-and-consumer-well-being-0.

29.   "Share of Americans Who Bought Premium or Luxury Items in 2018, by Income," Statista, February 23, 2022, https://www.statista.com/statistics/242827/affluent-americans-who-said-they-prefer-to-buy-designer-or-luxury-brands.

30.   "Ebates Survey: Adults (96%) and Teens (95%) Agree—Retail Therapy Is Good for the Soul," Business Wire, March 15, 2016, https://www.businesswire.com/news/home/20160315005531/en/Ebates-Survey-Adults-96-and-Teens-95-Agree—Retail-Therapy-Is-Good-for-the-Soul.

31.   "Hoarding Is on the Rise: The Causes of Hoarding Disorder," Spaulding Decon, https://www.spauldingdecon.com/blog/hoarding-is-on-the-rise; Grzegorz Adamczyk, "Pathological Buying on the Rise? Compensative and Compulsive Buying in Poland in the Pre- and (Post-)Pandemic Times," *PLoS One* 19, no. 3 (2024): e0298856, https://www.ncbi.nlm.nih.gov/pmc/articles/PMC10956761.

32.   Ericka Podesta McCoy, "More Than 40% of U.S. Adults Cite Apparel Shopping as One of Their Hobbies. Here's a Look at Who They Are, Their Motivations and How Best to Market to Them," Digital Commerce 360, August 30, 2018, https://www.digitalcommerce360.com/2018/08/30/understanding-and-engaging-shoppers-who-view-buying-clothes-as-a-hobby.

33.   Maggie Davis, "69% of Americans Admit to Emotional Spending, Pushing 39% of Them into Debt," Lending Tree, updated September 25, 2023, https://www.lendingtree.com/credit-cards/study/emotional-spending.

34.   Dan Gartlan, "Emotional Advertising: How Brands Use Feelings to Get People to Buy," Stevens & Tate, September 12, 2023, https://stevens-tate.com/articles/emotional-advertising.

From Citizens to Consumers

1.   "Research Starters: Women in World War II," National WWII Museum, https://www.nationalww2museum.org/students-teachers/student-resources/research-starters/research-starters-women-world-war-ii.

2.   "Reflections—Wartime Bond Drives," Army Historical Foundation, https://armyhistory.org/reflections-wartime-bond-drives/; "Victory Garden at the National Museum of American History," Smithsonian Gardens, https://gardens.si.edu/gardens/victory-garden.

3.   Kathryn Horvath, "Getting the Waste out of Fashion Should Be the Next Big Trend," PIRG, February 19, 2024, https://pirg.org/articles/getting-the-waste-out-of-fashion-should-be-the-next-big-trend.

4.   David Pietrusza, "Henry Ford and Alfred P. Sloan: Industrialization and Competition," Bill of Rights Institute, https://billofrightsinstitute.org/essays/henry-ford-and-alfred-p-sloan-industrialization-and-competition.

5.   "The Origin and Myths of Planned Obsolescence," OpenMind, https://www.bbvaopenmind.com/en/technology/innovation/origin-and-myths-of-planned-obsolescence.

6.   World War II & Advertising: Introduction," Duke University Libraries, updated February 24, 2021, https://guides.library.duke.edu/wwii.

7.   John McDonough, ed., *The Advertising Age of Encyclopedia* (New York: Fitzroy, Dearborn, 2003).

8.   "'Continued Employment After the War?': The Women's Bureau Studies Postwar Plans of Women Workers," History Matters, https://historymatters.gmu.edu/d/7027.

9.   "Women Factory Workers of WWII: Going to War," San Diego Air & Space Museum, https://sandiegoairandspace.org/exhibits/online-exhibit-page/women-factory-workers-of-world-war-ii-overview; "'Continued Employment,'" History Matters.

10.   Sarah Pruitt, "The Post World War II Boom: How America Got into Gear," History, updated August 10, 2023, https://www.history.com/news/post-world-war-ii-boom-economy.

11.   "The History of Plastics Part II: 1935 Through 1980," Advanced Plastiform Inc., https://advancedplastiform.com/the-history-of-plastics-part-ii-1935-through-1980.

12.   "Our Planet Is Choking on Plastic," UN Environment Programme, https://www.unep.org/interactives/beat-plastic-pollution; Chris Cillizza, "We Consume up to a Credit Card's Worth of Plastic *Every* Week," CNN, updated November 2, 2022, https://www.cnn.com/2022/10/31/us/microplastic-credit-card-per-week.

13.   "20. Post-War Women," Remedial Herstory Project, November 20, 2022, https://www.remedialherstory.com/20-post-war-women.html.

14.   "CHAPTER 11: Postwar America," US Diplomatic Mission to Germany, https://usa.usembassy.de/etexts/history/ch11.htm.

Marketing Made Me Do It

1.   Wikipedia, s.v. "Torches of Freedom," last modified July 30, 2023, https://en.wikipedia.org/wiki/Torches_of_Freedom; Wikipedia, s.v. "Women and Smoking," last modified July 23, 2024, https://en.wikipedia.org/wiki/Women_and_smoking.

2.   Quentin Fottrell, "When Americans Get Emotional, They Buy Really Sad Things," *New York Post*, updated July 26, 2017, https://nypost.com/2017/03/23/when-americans -get-emotional-they-buy-really-sad-things.

3.   Aimee Picchi, "COVID-19 Is Changing How Americans Spend—Here's What We're Buying," CBS News, April 28, 2020, https://www.cbsnews.com/news/pandemic -buying-coronavirus-things-americans-are-buying.

4.   "Gen Z and Millennials' Financially Irresponsible Era Is Over as Many Adopt 'No-Buy' Financial Trend," Credit Karma, March 14, 2024, https://www.creditkarma.com /about/commentary/gen-z-and-millennials-financially-irresponsible-era-is-over-as-many -adopt-no-buy-financial-trend.

5.   "Do We Buy Cosmetics Because They Are Useful or Because They Make Us Feel Good?," Science Daily, July 22, 2011, https://www.sciencedaily.com/releases/2011 /07/110721095846.htm; Zhihui Cai et al., "Body Image Dissatisfaction and Impulse Buying: A Moderated Mediation Model," *Frontiers in Psychology* 12 (2021): 653559, https://www.frontiersin.org/journals/psychology/articles/10.3389/fpsyg.2021.653559 /full; Rosemary Donahue, "How My Body Dysmorphia Started an Online Shopping Addiction," Fashionista, December 30, 2016, https://fashionista.com/2016/12/body -dysmorphia-online-shopping-addiction-essay.

6.   Rhonda Hadi and Lauren Block, "Warm Hearts and Cool Heads: Uncomfortable Temperature Influences Reliance on Affect in Decision-Making," *Journal of the Association for Consumer Research* 4, no. 2 (2019): 102–14, https://www.journals.uchicago.edu /doi/full/10.1086/701820.

7.   Parija Kavilanz, "The Sneaky, Smart Reasons Malls Have No Windows," CNN, updated June 24, 2024, https://www.cnn.com/2024/06/22/business/malls-lack-windows -curious-consumer.

8.   J. G. Navarro, "Marketing in the United States—Statistics & Facts," Statista, March 12, 2024, https://www.statista.com/topics/8972/marketing-in-the-united-states.

9.   Suzanne Schmitt, "Women in the U.S. Are About to Gain Significant Wealth. Here's What That Means," Fast Company, May 17, 2023, https://www.fastcompany.com /90897283/women-in-the-u-s-are-about-to-gain-significant-wealth-heres-what-that -means; Sandy Carter, "Who Runs the World? Women Control 85% of Purchases, 29% of STEM Roles," *Forbes*, updated March 7, 2024, https://www.forbes.com/sites/digital -assets/2024/03/07/who-runs-the-world-women-control-85-of-purchases-29-of-stem -roles.

10.   Anna Allgaier, "The Purchasing Power of Women," Wise, November 17, 2023, https://wise.com/gb/blog/purchasing-power-women; "78% of Women Identify as

the Primary Household Shopper," *Supermarket News*, April 19, 2023, https://www.supermarketnews.com/news/78-women-identify-primary-household-shopper.

11.   "Purchasing Power of Women," FONA International, December 22, 2014, https://www.mccormickfona.com/articles/2014/12/purchasing-power-of-women.

12.   "Wise Up to Women," Nielsen, March 2020, https://www.nielsen.com/insights/2020/wise-up-to-women.

13.   Rae Nudson, "When Targeted Ads Feel a Little Too Targeted," Vox, April 9, 2020, https://www.vox.com/the-goods/2020/4/9/21204425/targeted-ads-fertility-eating-disorder-coronavirus.

14.   Maggie Mallon, "A New Study Shows Advertisements Are So Sexist, Men Get 7 Times as Many Speaking Roles as Women," *Glamour*, June 23, 2017, https://www.glamour.com/story/geena-davis-institute-study-sexism-advertisements.

15.   Fabrizio Santoniccolo et al., "Gender and Media Representations: A Review of the Literature on Gender Stereotypes, Objectification and Sexualization," *International Journal of Environmental Research and Public Health* 20, no. 10 (2023): 5770, https://www.ncbi.nlm.nih.gov/pmc/articles/PMC10218532; Ella Fisher, "Sneaky Sexism: Why Sexist Advertising Still Exists," Adapt, July 18, 2022, https://www.adaptworldwide.com/insights/2022/sneaky-sexism-why-sexist-advertising-still-exists.

16.   Dante Chinni, "More Women Than Men Have College Degrees. That's Good News for Democrats," NBC News, August 20, 2023, https://www.nbcnews.com/meet-the-press/data-download/women-men-college-degrees-good-news-democrats-rcna100833.

17.   Dakota Kim, "A Constant Barrage: US Companies Target Junk Food Ads to People of Color," *Guardian*, November 11, 2022, https://www.theguardian.com/environment/2022/nov/11/junk-food-marketing-children-of-color; Carson Hardee, "New Study Shows Unhealthy Food Advertising Continues to Disproportionately Target Consumers of Color," UConn Today, November 16, 2022, https://today.uconn.edu/2022/11/new-study-shows-unhealthy-food-advertising-continues-to-disproportionately-target-consumers-of-color; Omni Cassidy et al., "The Impact of Racially-Targeted Food Marketing and Attentional Biases on Consumption in Black Adolescent Females with and Without Obesity: Pilot Data from the Black Adolescent & Entertainment (BAE) Study," *PLoS One* 18, no.1 (2023): e0279871, https://www.ncbi.nlm.nih.gov/pmc/articles/PMC9858861.

18.   Colin Campbell et al., "Diversity Representation in Advertising," *Journal of the Academy of Marketing Science*, December 26, 2023, https://link.springer.com/article

/10.1007/s11747-023-00994-8; Amy Roeder, "Advertising's Toxic Effect on Eating and Body Image," Harvard T. H. Chan School of Public Health, March 18, 2015, https:// www.hsph.harvard.edu/news/features/advertisings-toxic-effect-on-eating-and-body -image; Peter Moore, "Half of Women Have Felt Bad About Their Body After Seeing an Ad," YouGov, September 11, 2015, https://today.yougov.com/society/articles/13264 -body-confidence.

19.   Nadia, "How Many Ads Do We See a Day?," Siteefy, updated August 29, 2024, https://siteefy.com/how-many-ads-do-we-see-a-day.

20.   Douglas Van Praet, "How Your Brain Forces You to Watch Ads," October 30, 2014, https://www.psychologytoday.com/us/blog/unconscious-branding/201410/how -your-brain-forces-you-watch-ads and https://www.mediaed.org/discussion-guides /Killing-Us-Softly-4-Discussion-Guide.pdf.

Consumerism Is Contagious

1.   Juliet Schor, "Learning Diderot's Lesson: Stopping the Upward Creep of Desire," chap. 6 in *The Overspent American: Why We Want What We Don't Need* (New York: HarperCollins, 1999).

2.   Michaeleen Doucleff, "'Anti-Dopamine Parenting' Can Curb a Kid's Craving for Screens or Sweets," NPR, June 12, 2023, https://www.npr.org/sections/health-shots/2023 /06/12/1180867083/tips-to-outsmart-dopamine-unhook-kids-from-screens-sweets.

3.   "This Is Your Brain on Shopping: The Link Between Spending and Our Emotions—with the Help of a Little Science," In the Know, November 20, 2023, https:// www.interac.ca/en/content/life/this-is-your-brain-on-shopping.

4.   "The Truth About Habit Formation: Beyond the 21-Day Myth," Unyte, https:// integratedlistening.com/blog/forming-habits-dont-give-new-years-resolutions-yet; "Exploring the Brain's Relationship to Habits," US National Science Foundation, January 14, 2013, https://new.nsf.gov/news/exploring-brains-relationship-habits.

5.   "Drug Abuse, Dopamine and the Brain's Reward System," Hazelden Betty Ford Foundation, September 1, 2015, https://www.hazeldenbettyford.org/research-studies /addiction-research/drug-abuse-brain.

6.   Amit Lahoti, "Dopamine and Serotonin: Our Own Happy Chemicals," Na- tionwide Children's, February 28, 2023, https://www.nationwidechildrens.org/family -resources-education/700childrens/2023/02/dopamine-and-serotonin.

7.   Shweta Gupta, "Diderot Effect—One Buying Leads to Accumulating and Pur- chasing Many More!!," Medium, September 23, 2023, https://shwetag1907.medium

.com/diderot-effect-one-buying-leads-to-accumulating-and-purchasing-many-more
-2f5de6436234; Wikipedia, s.v. "Diderot Effect," last modified August 27, 2024, https://
en.wikipedia.org/wiki/Diderot_effect.

8.   Jemima Elliott, "Is Donating My Clothes Really Ethical?," Remake, July 14, 2022,
https://remake.world/stories/is-donating-my-clothes-really-ethical.

9.   "What Are the Potential Risks and Challenges of Recommender Systems in
Different Domains and Contexts?," LinkedIn, https://www.linkedin.com/advice/3/what
-potential-risks-challenges-recommender.

10.   Stephan Serrano, "[Guide] Personalized Product Recommendations Tactics for
Profits," Barilliance, June 8, 2023, https://www.barilliance.com/personalized-product
-recommendations-stats; Shopify Staff, "How Ecommerce Product Recommendations
Drive Sales," Shopify, January 5, 2024, https://www.shopify.com/blog/ecommerce
-product-recommendation.

11.   Pulkit Jain, "Recommend Perfect Products with MoEngage's Smart Recommendations," MoEngage, updated August 16, 2024, https://www.moengage.com/blog/smart
-recommendations.

12.   "Annual Reports," Container Store, https://investor.containerstore.com/financial
-reports/annual/default.aspx.

13.   Goran Dautovic, "40 Amazing Customer Loyalty Statistics in 2024," SmallBiz-
Genius, February 6, 2024, https://www.smallbizgenius.net/by-the-numbers/customer
-loyalty-statistics; Arkadiusz Krysik, "Complementary Products: A Way to Increase
Your Online Store Sales You Need to Know," Recostream, September 30, 2021, https://
recostream.com/blog/complementary-products.

14.   Umme Sutarwala, "25 Influencer Marketing Statistics and Their Implications
for Your Brand," Sprinklr, February 9, 2024, https://www.sprinklr.com/blog/influencer
-marketing-statistics.

15.   Bre Goodwin, "Influencers Are Just Gen Z Telemarketers," Flor-Ala, November 17,
2023, https://theflorala.com/15994/opinion/influencers-are-just-gen-z-telemarketers.

16.   "The Teen Brain: 7 Things to Know," National Institute of Mental Health, https://
www.nimh.nih.gov/health/publications/the-teen-brain-7-things-to-know.

17.   Elise Dopson, "30+ Influencer Marketing Statistics You Should Know," Shopify,
November 21, 2023, https://www.shopify.com/blog/influencer-marketing-statistics.

18.   "20 Surprising Influencer Marketing Statistics," Digital Marketing Institute, April
14, 2024, https://digitalmarketinginstitute.com/blog/20-influencer-marketing-statistics
-that-will-surprise-you.

19.   Samira Farivar, "Social Media Influencers Are Causing Anxiety and Depression Among Some of Their Followers," Scroll.in, May 19, 2022, https://scroll.in/article /1024116/social-media-influencers-are-causing-anxiety-and-depression-among-some -of-their-influencers.

How No New Things Works

1.   Jocelyn Solis-Moreira, "How Long Does It Really Take to Form a Habit?," *Scientific American*, January 24, 2024, https://www.scientificamerican.com/article/how-long -does-it-really-take-to-form-a-habit.

2.   "World's Richest 10% Produce Half of Carbon Emissions While Poorest 3.5 Billion Account for Just a Tenth," Oxfam International, December 2, 2015, https://www .oxfam.org/en/press-releases/worlds-richest-10-produce-half-carbon-emissions-while -poorest-35-billion-account.

Week 1: The Foundations

1.   Arlin Cuncic, "An Overview of Broaden and Build Theory," Verywell Mind, December 7, 2023, https://www.verywellmind.com/broaden-and-build-theory-4845903.

Day 1: Visualize Victory

1.   T. Blankert and M. R. Hamstra, "Imagining Success: Multiple Achievement Goals and the Effectiveness of Imagery," Basic and Applied Social Psychology 39, no. 1 (2017): 60–67, https://www.ncbi.nlm.nih.gov/pmc/articles/PMC5351796.

2.   "The Power of Writing Down Your Goals: Evidence from Multiple Studies," OAK Journal, February 8, 2023, https://oakjournal.com/blogs/resources/the-power-of -writing-down-your-goals-evidence-from-multiple-studies.

Day 2: List Your Loves

1.   "Addicted to Spending Money: Understanding Compulsive Shopping," Priory, https://www.priorygroup.com/blog/compulsive-shopping-and-spending-a-sign-of -shopping-addiction.

2.   Stephanie Watson, "Dopamine: The Pathway to Pleasure," Harvard Medical School, April 18, 2024, https://www.health.harvard.edu/mind-and-mood/dopamine -the-pathway-to-pleasure.

3.   Kyla Dewar, "18 Employee Incentive Programs to Engage Your Team," Achievers, August 8, 2024, https://www.achievers.com/blog/employee-incentive-programs.

4.   "Health Benefits of Gratitude," UCLA Health, March 22, 2023, https://www .uclahealth.org/news/article/health-benefits-gratitude; Dana Claudat, "A 5-Step Guide to Cleaning Your Wallet the Feng Shui Way," mindbodygreen, April 2, 2020, https://

www.mindbodygreen.com/articles/how-to-clean-and-organize-your-wallet-according
-to-feng-shui.

5.   "3 Ways Getting Outside into Nature Helps Improve Your Health," UC Davis
Health, May 3, 2023, https://health.ucdavis.edu/blog/cultivating-health/3-ways-getting
-outside-into-nature-helps-improve-your-health/2023/05.

Day 4: Connect with Community

1.   Stephanie Gilbert, "The Importance of Community and Mental Health," NAMI,
November 18, 2019, https://www.nami.org/family-member-caregivers/the-importance
-of-community-and-mental-health.

2.   "The Loneliness Epidemic Persists: A Post-Pandemic Look at the State of Loneliness among U.S. Adults," Cigna, https://newsroom.thecignagroup.com/loneliness
-epidemic-persists-post-pandemic-look.

3.   J. Holt-Lunstad, T. B. Smith, and J. B. Layton, "Social Relationships and Mortality
Risk: A Meta-Analytic Review," *PLoS Medicine* 7, no. 7 (2010): e1000316.

4.   Anita Chaudhuri, "The Buddy Boost: How 'Accountability Partners' Make You
Healthy, Happy and More Successful," *Guardian*, November 27, 2023, https://www
.theguardian.com/lifeandstyle/2023/nov/27/the-buddy-boost-how-accountability
-partners-make-you-healthy-happy-and-more-successful.

5.   Barbara Mantel, "Virtual Body Doubling May Help Your Productivity," Association of Health Care Journalists, June 23, 2023, https://healthjournalism.org/blog/2023
/06/virtual-body-doubling-may-help-your-productivity.

Day 5: Track Your Triggers

1.   Jon Johnson, "What Causes Food Cravings?," Medical News Today, May 16, 2023,
https://www.medicalnewstoday.com/articles/318441.

2.   Amelia Tait, "Buy. Return. Repeat . . . What Really Happens When We Send Back
Unwanted Clothes?," *Guardian*, March 31, 2023, https://www.theguardian.com/global
-development/2023/mar/31/what-happens-when-we-send-back-unwanted-clothes.

3.   Mansoor Ahmed Khan, "15 Important Shopping Cart Abandonment Statistics
for 2024: A Marketer's Point of View," Cloudways, updated June 12, 2024, https://www
.cloudways.com/blog/shopping-cart-abandonment-statistics.

4.   Rhonda Hadi and Lauren Block, "Warm Hearts and Cool Heads: Uncomfortable
Temperature Influences Reliance on Affect in Decision-Making," *Journal of the Association for Consumer Research* 4, no. 2 (2019): 102–14, https://www.journals.uchicago.edu
/doi/full/10.1086/701820.

Day 6: Wrangle Returns

1.   Amelia Tait, "Buy. Return. Repeat . . . What Really Happens When We Send Back Unwanted Clothes?," *Guardian*, March 31, 2023, https://www.theguardian.com/global -development/2023/mar/31/what-happens-when-we-send-back-unwanted-clothes.

2.   Harriet Constable, "Your Brand New Returns End Up in Landfill," BBC Earth, https://www.bbcearth.com/news/your-brand-new-returns-end-up-in-landfill.

3.   John Johnson, "Americans Return a Mind-Boggling Amount of Stuff," Newser, August 19, 2023, https://www.newser.com/story/339035/the-amount-of-stuff-we -return-is-mind-boggling.html.

4.   Tait, "Buy. Return. Repeat."

Day 7: Gather Gift Cards

1.   "Gift Card Statistics," Capital One Shopping, updated May 23, 2024, https:// capitaloneshopping.com/research/gift-card-statistics.

2.   Lane Gillespie, "Survey: 47% of U.S. Adults Have at Least One Unused Gift Card," Bankrate, July 24, 2023, https://www.bankrate.com/personal-finance/unused-gift-cards -survey.

Day 8: Silence Spending

1.   *Email Market, 2019–2023* (Palo Alto, CA: Radicati Group, 2019), https://www .radicati.com/wp/wp-content/uploads/2019/04/Email-Market-2019-2023-Executive -Summary.pdf.

2.   Sara Lebow, "5 Charts Showing the Potential of Text Message (SMS) Market-ing," EMARKETER, January 23, 2024, https://www.emarketer.com/content/5-charts -showing-potential-of-text-message-sms-marketing.

3.   Tanya, "40+ Helpful Push Notification Statistics you Should Know in 2024," Noti-fyVisitors, November 10, 2022, https://www.notifyvisitors.com/blog/push-notification -statistics.

4.   "De-Influenced Anyone? In Some Cases, Social Media Gives Consumers the Shopping Ick," Credit Karma, July 17, 2024, https://www.creditkarma.com/about /commentary/de-influenced-anyone-in-some-cases-social-media-gives-consumers-the -shopping-ick.

5.   Rebecca Driver, "Instagram & the FTC: The Growth of Influencer Marketing & the Government's Ungainly Pursuit," *Journal of Business & Technology Law* 18, no. 2 (2023): 288–307, https://digitalcommons.law.umaryland.edu/jbtl/vol18/iss2/5.

6.   "Influencer or Teacher: Gen Alpha Kids Already Know What They Want to Be

When They Grow Up," *Brussels Times*, November 20, 2022, https://www.brusselstimes .com/322325/influencer-or-teacher-gen-alpha-kids-already-know-what-they-want-to -be-when-they-grow-up.

7.   "How to Stop Junk Mail," Federal Trade Commission, https://consumer.ftc.gov /articles/how-stop-junk-mail.

Day 9: Block the Shop

1.   "56% of Consumers Say Storing Payment Info with Retailers Improves Checkout," PYMNTS, November 22, 2022, https://www.pymnts.com/news/ecommerce/2022/56 -percent-of-consumers-say-storing-payment-info-with-retailers-improves-checkout.

2.   Christine Bergeron, "7 Benefits of Stored Payment Information," Nimble AMS, June 12, 2024, https://www.nimbleams.com/blog/7-benefits-of-stored-payment -information.

3.   *Buy Now, Pay Later: Market Trends and Consumer Impacts* (Washington, DC: Consumer Financial Protection Bureau, 2022), https://s3.amazonaws.com/files .consumerfinance.gov/f/documents/cfpb_buy-now-pay-later-market-trends-consumer -impacts_report_2022-09.pdf.

4.   Ana Teresa Solá, "25% of Consumers Recently Used a Buy Now, Pay Later Loan, Report Finds. What to Know as They Become Popular," CNBC, May 28, 2024, https:// www.cnbc.com/2024/05/28/buy-now-pay-later-loans-are-second-only-to-credit-cards -in-popularity.html.

5.   "Retailers Say BNPL Boosts Sales, Consumers Say It Keeps Them Coming Back," PYMNTS, November 23, 2022, https://www.pymnts.com/buy-now-pay-later/2022 /more-than-half-of-merchants-raise-conversion-brand-awareness-with-bnpl.

6.   Heidi Rivera and Denny Ceizyk, "Survey: 56% of Buy Now, Pay Later Users Have Experienced Issues Like Overspending and Missing Payments," Bankrate, April 11, 2024, https://www.bankrate.com/loans/personal-loans/buy-now-pay-later-survey /#millennials; Jack Pedigo, "Understanding the Risks of Buy Now, Pay Later Apps," CNBC, updated September 20, 2022, https://www.cnbc.com/2022/09/13/understanding -the-risks-of-buy-now-pay-later-apps.html.

Day 10: Slash Subscriptions

1.   Tommy Tindall, "Subscriptions Are Hard to Cancel and Easy to Forget—by Design," NerdWallet, May 7, 2024, https://www.nerdwallet.com/article/finance /subscriptions-are-hard-to-cancel-and-easy-to-forget-by-design.

2.   "The Cost of Unused Subscriptions 2024," Self Financial, https://www.self.inc/ info/cost-of-unused-paid-subscriptions.

3.   Jack Norcross, "New Data Reveals Shocking Amount of Money We Spend on Streaming Services Every Month," WCNC, January 22, 2024, https://www.wcnc.com /article/news/local/connect-the-dots/new-data-reveals-shocking-amount-money -spend-streaming-services-every-month/275-3c4280c8-9a7a-49c0-a012-22a0e07bca8d.

4.   Irina Ivanova, "Your Forgetting to Cancel One of Many Subscriptions Is Big Business: Study Finds up to 200% Sales Boost from Pure Absentmindedness," *Fortune*, August 15, 2023, https://fortune.com/2023/08/15/subscription-economy-forgetfulness -boost-200-study.

Day 11: Delete On-Demand Drains

1.   Sandy Mazza and Brad Schmitt, "Watch Out, Uber Uber Eaters: Online Food Delivery Can Lead to Overspending and Isolation," *Tennessean*, updated June 27, 2019, https://www.tennessean.com/story/money/2019/06/25/online-food-delivery-can-lead -addiction-overspending/1490064001.

Day 12: Understand Upcycling

1.   V. Kumar, K. S. Pavitra, and R. Bhattacharya, "Creative Pursuits for Mental Health and Well-Being," *Indian Journal of Psychiatry* 66, suppl. 2 (2024): S283–S303, https://www.ncbi.nlm.nih.gov/pmc/articles/PMC10911317; A. Chong, S. Tolomeo, Y. Xiong, et al., "Blending Oxytocin and Dopamine with Everyday Creativity," *Scientific Reports* 11, 16185 (2021), https://www.nature.com/articles/s41598-021-95724-x.

2.   Caitlin Pilette, "Creativity and Movement Maintain Synaptic Activity, Improving QOL in Older Adults: A Critical Review," *Expressive Therapies Capstone Theses* 191 (2019), https://digitalcommons.lesley.edu/cgi/viewcontent.cgi?article=1182&context =expressive_theses.

3.   Nina Gbor, "Halloween Waste Is Frightening! How to Have a Sustainable Hallow-een," Eco Style, October 16, 2023, https://www.ecostyles.com.au/blogs/halloween-waste -is-frightening-how-to-have-a-sustainable-halloween; Kelly Sampson, "10 Spooky Facts About Halloween Waste and 5 Ways to Reduce It," Hummingbird International, Octo-ber 21, 2022, https://hummingbirdinternational.net/facts-about-halloween-waste.

Day 13: Slay Secondhand

1.   Olivia B. Waxman, "People Have Been Reusing Clothes Forever but Thrift Shops Are Relatively New. Here's Why," *Time*, August 17, 2018, https://time.com/5364170 /thrift-store-history.

2.   Jennifer Le Zotte, "'Not Charity, but a Chance': Philanthropic Capitalism and the Rise of American Thrift Stores, 1894–1930," *New England Quarterly* 86, no. 2 (2013):

169–95, https://www.jstor.org/stable/43284988?mag=how-thrift-stores-were-born; Waxman, "People Have Been Reusing Clothes."

3.   Clarisa Diaz, "The Secondhand Clothing Market Is Exploding," Quartz, April 10, 2023, https://qz.com/the-secondhand-clothing-market-is-exploding-1850313653.

4.   Debra Kamin, "'Fast Furniture' Is Cheap. And Americans Are Throwing It in the Trash," *New York Times*, October 31, 2022, https://www.nytimes.com/2022/10/31/realestate/fast-furniture-clogged-landfills.html; Kathryn Horvath, "How Many Clothes Are Too Many?," PIRG, May 10, 2024, https://pirg.org/articles/how-many-clothes-are-too-many.

5.   Ellie Hammonds, "Fast Fashion Is the Fuel for the Fire," Climate, March 5, 2024, https://theclimatenews.co.uk/fast-fashion-is-the-fuel-for-the-fire.

6.   Janet Domenitz and Celeste Meiffren-Swango, "Fast Fashion by the Numbers," PIRG, September 20, 2023, https://pirg.org/articles/fast-fashion-by-the-numbers; Nathalie Remy, Eveline Speelman, and Steven Swartz, "Style That's Sustainable: A New Fast-Fashion Formula," McKinsey, October 20, 2016, https://www.mckinsey.com/capabilities/sustainability/our-insights/style-thats-sustainable-a-new-fast-fashion-formula.

Day 14: Ethically Off-Load

1.   Anna De Souza, "This Is What Really Happens to Your Used Clothing Donations," *Reader's Digest*, updated November 28, 2022, https://www.rd.com/article/what-happens-used-clothing-donations.

2.   Oliver Franklin-Wallis, "What Really Happens to the Clothes You Donate," *GQ*, July 20, 2023, https://www.gq.com/story/oliver-franklin-wallis-wasteland-excerpt.

3.   Linton Besser, "Dead White Man's Clothes," ABC News Australia, August 11, 2021, https://www.abc.net.au/news/2021-08-12/fast-fashion-turning-parts-ghana-into-toxic-landfill/100358702; Kenya Wiley, "Donate Clothes? You're Contributing to Africa's 'Mitumba' Problem," *Washington Post*, May 22, 2024, https://www.washingtonpost.com/opinions/2024/05/22/clothes-donations-africa-kenya-waste.

4.   Sarah Johnson, "Castoffs to Catwalk: Fashion Show Shines Light on Vast Chile Clothes Dump Visible from Space," *Guardian*, May 8, 2024, https://www.theguardian.com/global-development/article/2024/may/08/castoffs-to-catwalk-fashion-show-shines-light-on-vast-chile-clothes-dump-visible-from-space; "SkyFi's Satellite Image Confirms Massive Clothes Pile in Chile's Atacama Desert," SkyFi, May 10, 2024, https://skyfi.com/en/blog/skyfis-confirms-massive-clothes-pile-in-chile.

Week 3: Your Space and Stuff

1.　Paul Frysh, "Common Household Hazards," WebMD, reviewed November 30, 2022, https://www.webmd.com/a-to-z-guides/ss/slideshow-common-household -hazards.

Day 15: Unstuff Your Space

1.　Mary MacVean, "For Many People, Gathering Possessions Is Just the Stuff of Life," *Los Angeles Times*, March 20, 2024, https://www.latimes.com/health/la-he-keeping-stuff -20140322-story.html.

2.　Mercari, "Stressed Out by Stuff. Americans Resolve to Tackle Clutter in 2020," PR Newswire, January 6, 2020, https://www.prnewswire.com/news-releases/stressed-out -by-stuff-americans-resolve-to-tackle-clutter-in-2020-300981183.html.

3.　Casey Schow, "Study: Quarantine Made Americans Realize They're Sick of Their Stuff," *Neighbor Blog*, January 29, 2024, https://www.neighbor.com/storage-blog/study -quarantine-americans-stuff.

4.　Asaf Raz, "Rising Star in Real Estate: Self Storage Investing," Agora, February 21, 2024, https://agorareal.com/blog/self-storage-investing.

5.　Kaleigh Moore, "Retailers Selling Non-Essentials See Double & Triple-Digit Increases in Online Sales During COVID-19 Crisis," *Forbes*, April 17, 2020, https://www .forbes.com/sites/kaleighmoore/2020/04/17/retailers-selling-non-essentials-see-double --triple-digit-increases-in-online-sales-during-covid-19-crisis.

Day 16: Polish Your Possessions

1.　Debra Kamin, "'Fast Furniture' Is Cheap. And Americans Are Throwing It in the Trash," *New York Times*, October 31, 2022, https://www.nytimes.com/2022/10/31 /realestate/fast-furniture-clogged-landfills.html.

Day 17: Care for Your Clothes

1.　"What's in Your Closet?," Recycle Smart, https://recyclesmartma.org/2020/12 /whats-in-your-closet-newsletter.

2.　"10 Scary Statistics About Fast Fashion & the Environment," State of Matter, December 11, 2023, https://stateofmatterapparel.com/blogs/som-blog/10-scary-statistics -about-fast-fashion-the-environment.

Day 18: Shop Your Stuff

1.　"Shoppers Still Buying New Clothes Despite Budget Pressures," PYMNTS, March 22, 2024, https://www.pymnts.com/news/retail/2024/shoppers-still-buying-new-clothes -despite-budget-pressures; Elizabeth Reichart and Deborah Drew, "By the Numbers:

The Economic, Social and Environmental Impacts of 'Fast Fashion,'" World Resources Institute, January 10, 2019, https://www.wri.org/insights/numbers-economic-social-and-environmental-impacts-fast-fashion.

Day 19: Groom Your Grooming

1. Rachel Cernansky, "Beauty Has a Waste Problem, and It's Not Packaging," Vogue Business, September 16, 2021, https://www.voguebusiness.com/sustainability/beauty-has-a-waste-problem-and-its-not-packaging.

2. "Beauty Industry Revenue and Usage Statistics 2024," Helplama, updated September 2024, https://helplama.com/beauty-industry-revenue-usage-statistics.

3. "Plastic Waste and Environmental Impact of the Beauty Industry," Zerra & Co., July 9, 2022, https://zerraco.com/blogs/zerra-blog/plastic-waste-and-environmental-impact-of-the-beauty-industry.

4. Laura Yan, "Meet the Beauty Community That Just Wants You to Finish Your Makeup," *Vogue*, April 17, 2021, https://www.vogue.com/article/the-beauty-community-that-just-wants-you-to-finish-your-makeup.

Day 20: Tune Up Your Tech

1. Clara Hernanz Lizarraga, "How Tech Firms Are Resisting the 'Right to Repair,'" Bloomberg, January 19, 2023, https://www.bloomberg.com/news/articles/2023-01-19/why-consumers-are-fighting-tech-firms-for-right-to-repair.

2. John Vidal, "Toxic E-Waste Dumped in Poor Nations, Says United Nations," Our World, December 16, 2013, https://ourworld.unu.edu/en/toxic-e-waste-dumped-in-poor-nations-says-united-nations.

3. "Nearly 30% of Americans Prioritize Buying the Latest Tech, Like iPhone 15, Over Paying Bills," Funds Society, October 12, 2023, https://www.fundssociety.com/en/news/markets/nearly-30-of-americans-prioritize-buying-the-latest-tech-like-iphone-15-over-paying-bills.

4. Alethea L. Blackler, "Life Is Too Short to RTFM: How Users Relate to Documentation and Excess Features in Consumer Products," *Interacting with Computers* 28, no. 1 (2016): 27–46, https://academic.oup.com/iwc/article-abstract/28/1/27/2363584.

Day 21: Rearrange an Area

1. Andie Kanaras, "4 Surprising Mental Benefits of Rearranging Your Furniture, According to Experts," Apartment Therapy, November 11, 2021, https://www.apartmenttherapy.com/mental-benefits-of-rearranging-a-room-37000508.

Day 22: Focus on Food

1.   Bridget Reed Morawski, "The Scope of Food Waste in U.S. Households," one5c, March 14, 2024, https://one5c.com/food-waste-households-136937390.

2.   Natalie Campisi, "Are Your Monthly Grocery Costs Above Average? Here's What Americans Typically Pay," *Forbes*, January 26, 2024, https://www.forbes.com/advisor/personal-finance/grocery-costs-monthly-average.

3.   "Hunger and Food Insecurity," Feeding America, https://www.feedingamerica.org/hunger-in-america/food-insecurity.

4.   "How Overconsumption & Overproduction Cause Food Waste," Skip Shapiro Enterprises, April 23, 2024, https://shapiroe.com/blog/overconsumption-overproduction-food-waste.

5.   "Food Waste in America in 2024," RTS, https://www.rts.com/resources/guides/food-waste-america.

6.   Kathryn Mayer, "These Websites Answer the Age-Old Question: What Can I Make With These Ingredients?," PS, August 15, 2023, https://www.popsugar.com/food/website-that-tells-you-what-to-cook-with-what-you-have-47105294.

7.   Lizeth Aranda, "What Cooking Can Teach You About Innovation and Creativity," Harvard Business Publishing, April 4, 2019, https://www.harvardbusiness.org/what-cooking-can-teach-you-about-innovation-and-creativity.

Day 23: Borrow Before Buying

1.   Sarah Kessler, "The 'Sharing Economy' Is Dead and We Killed It," Fast Company, September 14, 2015, https://www.fastcompany.com/3050775/the-sharing-economy-is-dead-and-we-killed-it.

2.   "The Cost of the First Personal Computer," Inflation Calculator by MES, https://inflationcalculator.mes.fm/money-facts/the-cost-of-the-first-personal-computer.

3.   Juan C. Espinosa, Concha Antón, and Merlin Patricia Grueso Hinestroza, "Helping Others Helps Me: Prosocial Behavior and Satisfaction with Life During the COVID-19 Pandemic," *Frontiers in Psychology* 13 (2022): 762445, https://www.ncbi.nlm.nih.gov/pmc/articles/PMC8828552.

Day 24: Get Good at Gifting

1.   Danielle Inman, "NRF Predicts Healthy Holiday Sales as Consumers Navigate Economic Headwinds," National Retail Federation, November 3, 2022, https://nrf.com/media-center/press-releases/nrf-predicts-healthy-holiday-sales-consumers-navigate-economic.

2.   Richard Laycock, "53% of Americans Admit to Opening Up at Least One Un-wanted Holiday Gift Each Year," Finder, updated December 6, 2023, https://www.finder.com/banking/unwanted-gifts.

Day 25: Pay It Forward

1.   Elizabeth Hopper, "Want to Be Happier? Try Volunteering, Study Says," *Washington Post*, July 29, 2020, https://www.washingtonpost.com/lifestyle/2020/07/29/volunteer-happy-mental-health.

2.   Natalie Silverstein, "Are You Too Busy to Volunteer? Here's Why You Should Make the Time," Katie Couric Media, June 7, 2023, https://katiecouric.com/lifestyle/get-inspired/benefits-of-volunteering-ideas.

3.   Jamie Ducharme, "Volunteering May Boost Kids' Well-Being, Study Says," *Time*, May 30, 2023, https://time.com/6283458/volunteering-good-for-kids-health.

4.   Cecily Townsend, "Health Matters: The Health Benefits of Volunteering," *Independent Record*, July 20, 2024, https://helenair.com/news/local/column/health-matters-column-the-health-benefits-of-volunteering/article_c6be697e-460b-11ef-857b-87518819a8cd.html.

5.   Molly Rose Teuke, "Is 'Busy' the New Status Symbol?," Wisconsin Meetings, September 27, 2023, https://www.wisconsinmeetings.com/2023/09/27/why-busy-is-bad-for-you.

Day 26: Socialize Sans Shopping

1.   John Naughton, "Amazon v the High Street—Which Would You Bet On?," *Guardian*, December 31, 2011, https://www.theguardian.com/technology/2012/jan/01/amazon-versus-the-high-street.

2.   Jordan Cox, "Reconsidering Retail Therapy: Is Shopping a Hobby or a Hidden Habit?," Marshmallow Challenge, June 29, 2024, https://www.marshmallowchallenge.com/blog/reconsidering-retail-therapy-is-shopping-a-hobby-or-a-hidden-habit.

Day 27: Travel Thoughtfully

1.   R. Geoffrey Lacher and Sanjay Nepal, "The Economic Impact of Souvenir Sales in Peripheral Areas: A Case Study from Northern Thailand," *Tourism Recreation Research* 36, no. 1 (2011): 27–37, https://www.researchgate.net/publication/259944817.

Day 28: Self-Care Sustainably

1.   Chris Taylor, "You've Been Getting Self-Care All Wrong. It's a Political Act and Always Has Been," Mashable, September 25, 2019, https://mashable.com/article/self-care-history.

2.   Bryony Porteous-Sebouhian, "Why Acknowledging and Celebrating the Black Feminist Origins of 'Self-Care' Is Essential," Mental Health Today, October 27, 2021, https://www.mentalhealthtoday.co.uk/blog/awareness/why-acknowledging-and -celebrating-the-black-feminist-origins-of-self-care-is-essential.

3.   Laura Knowles and Jorden Cummings, "Influencers' Presentation of Self-Care on YouTube: It's Essential, but Inaccessible," *Journal of Social Media in Society* 13, no. 1 (2024): 53–74.

4.   Nicole McDermott, "Practical Types of Self-Care You Can Do Today," *Forbes*, updated January 26, 2023, https://www.forbes.com/health/mind/mental-self-care.

Day 29: Set Goals Without Stuff

1.   Tim Kasser and Aaron Ahuvia, "Materialistic Values and Well-Being in Business Students," *European Journal of Social Psychology* 32, no. 1 (2002): 137–46, https:// selfdeterminationtheory.org/SDT/documents/2002_KasserAhuvia_EJSP.pdf; Tim Kasser, "Materialistic Values and Goals," *Annual Review of Psychology* 67 (2016): 489– 514, https://www.annualreviews.org/content/journals/10.1146/annurev-psych-122414 -033344.

2.   Natasha Parker, "Values and Goals: Can We Intervene to Reduce Materialism?," CUSP, August 9, 2020, https://cusp.ac.uk/themes/s1/blog-np-goals-for-good.

About the Author

Ashlee Piper is a sustainability expert, commentator, and speaker whose work has been featured on more than three hundred TV segments, including the *Today* show, *Good Morning America*, and CNN, and in *Vogue*, the *New York Times*, the *Washington Post*, the *Atlantic*, and *Newsweek*. Piper's 2018 book, *Give a Sh*t: Do Good. Live Better. Save the Planet.*, has been hailed as a "sustainability bible" by celebrities and reviewers. Piper has spoken at the United Nations and SXSW and has a popular TED Talk. She is also the creator of the #NoNewThings Challenge, for which she received a 2022 Silver Stevie Award for Female Innovator of the Year, and a professor of sustainability marketing. She holds a BA from Brown University and a master's degree from the University of Oxford. She lives in Chicago in a home that's 98 percent secondhand and can often be found singing Seal's "Kiss from a Rose" at any not-so-fine karaoke establishment.